TREASURES
and
TRUTHS

Poetry and Practical
Principles of Proverbs

TREASURES
and
TRUTHS

Poetry and Practical
Principles of Proverbs

W. C. PARKEY

WORD AFLAME PRESS
8855 Dunn Road, Hazelwood, MO 63042
www.pentecostalpublishing.com

Treasures and Truths

by W. C. Parkey

© 2006 Word Aflame Press
Hazelwood, MO 63042

Printed in United States of America

WORD AFLAME PRESS
8855 Dunn Road, Hazelwood, MO 63042
www.pentecostalpublishing.com

Library of Congress Cataloging-in-Publication Data

Parkey, W. C.
Treasures and truths : poetry and practical principles of Proverbs / by W. C. Parkey.
        p. cm.
Includes bibliographical references.
ISBN 13: 978-1-56722-699-7
1. Bible. O.T.—Textbooks. 2. Bible. O.T.—Criticism, interpretation, etc. I. Title.
BS1467.P37 2006
223'.70071—dc22

2006025514

Dedication

To my wife, Betty,

who is the model of a virtuous woman,

as shown in Proverbs 31:10-31.

She has been my constant companion

for the past forty-five years.

She has been the strength and inspiration

that has helped

me to fulfill my ministry.

Treasures and Truths

Poetry and Practical Principles
of Proverbs

(A Thirteen-week Devotional Study of Proverbs)

Table of Contents

	<u>Poem</u>	<u>Devotion</u>

Foreword

The principles of Proverbs are timeless truths that are just as relevant today as the day Solomon dipped his quill in ink and penned these proven axioms of life that are worthy of our constant review and careful consideration. W. C. Parkey has captured the essence of these values in a masterful, poetic expression that reveals its truth in an unmistakable manner, making it easy to grasp and understand. I commend this divine wisdom to everyone who is interested in gaining spiritual excellence by walking in a path of wisdom that leads ever brighter to that perfect day.

Brian Kinsey, pastor
First Pentecostal Church
Pensacola, Florida

Preface

In the summer quarter of 2002, the Word Aflame adult Sunday school curriculum had a series of lessons entitled, "Wisdom from Proverbs and Song of Solomon." As the adult Bible class teacher at my church, I enjoyed teaching the lessons but wanted to find a way to make the proverbs easier to understand.

I thought it would be interesting to paraphrase the Scripture settings for the lessons into rhymed English verse. The class seemed to respond well to the poems, so when the quarter was ended, I continued to write the Book of Proverbs in poetry. Later, I added a devotion to each poetry segment, which became the basis for this book.

Please understand that this book is not a translation, but an exposition, which is the "setting forth of the meaning or purpose (as of a writing)."[1] Because many of the ancient sayings are difficult to understand, I tried to compare several English translations looking for the meaning that seemed the best. I have attempted to convey the general thought of the verses into an approximate statement that is near to the meaning of the original verse, as it might be expressed by the common man of our day.

This book is designed as a quarterly, or thirteen-week, study of the Book of Proverbs. By daily reading one poem and the accompanying devotion, you can complete the book in one quarter, or ninety-one days. Each devotion has a practical application and a prayer.

It is my wish, and the wish of those who assisted me, that you will make your life fuller, your path plainer, and your walk with God closer as you read the poems of Proverbs and the accompanying devotions, prayers, and practical principles. May these timeless truths be a treasure that you will forever hold dear.

W. C. Parkey

Acknowledgments

I wish to thank my children: Beth Dillon, who so graciously consented to edit this book if I would finish it, Barbara Braswell, who acted as her capable assistant, and Bill and Bryan Parkey, who also were involved in the editing process. I also wish to thank my wife for her assistance with this project.

I am grateful to Robert H. Fuller, interim general manager of the Pentecostal Publishing House, and the members of the UPCI Board of Publication, for approving this book for publication.

I am indebted to Richard Davis, Word Aflame editor, and the other members of the UPCI curriculum committee for preparing the *Adult Expository Series*, which presented the lessons on "Wisdom from Proverbs and Song of Solomon" and which inspired the idea and interest for this book.

I would also like to thank Brian Kinsey, pastor of the First Pentecostal Church in Pensacola, Florida, for his kind words of commendation for this book. He uses Proverbs as his daily devotional, teaches it to his adult Sunday school class weekly, and relies on it constantly for his source of wisdom and inspiration. Because of his extensive use of Proverbs, his comments and approval mean much to me.

Week 1

PROVERBS 1

The proverbs of Solomon the son of David, king of Israel; to know wisdom and instruction; to perceive the words of understanding; to receive the instruction of wisdom, justice, and judgment, and equity; to give subtilty to the simple, to the young man knowledge and discretion. A wise man will hear, and will increase learning; and a man of understanding shall attain unto wise counsels: to understand a proverb, and the interpretation; the words of the wise, and their dark sayings.

The fear of the LORD is the beginning of knowledge: but fools despise wisdom and instruction. My son, hear the instruction of thy father, and forsake not the law of thy mother: for they shall be an ornament of grace unto thy head, and chains about thy neck.

My son, if sinners entice thee, consent thou not. If they say, Come with us, let us lay wait for blood, let us lurk privily for the innocent without cause: let us swallow them up alive as the grave; and whole, as those that go down into the pit: we shall find all precious substance, we shall fill our houses with spoil: cast in thy lot among us; let us all have one purse: my son, walk not thou in the way with them; refrain thy foot from their path: for their feet run to evil, and make haste to shed blood. Surely in vain the net is spread in the sight of any bird. And they lay wait for their own blood; they lurk privily for their own lives. So are the ways of every one that is greedy of gain; which taketh away the life of the owners thereof.

Wisdom crieth without; she uttereth her voice in the streets: she crieth in the chief place of concourse, in the openings of the gates: in the city she uttereth her words,

saying, How long, ye simple ones, will ye love simplic-
ity? and the scorners delight in their scorning, and
fools hate knowledge? Turn you at my reproof: behold,
I will pour out my spirit unto you, I will make known
my words unto you.

Because I have called, and ye refused; I have stretched
out my hand, and no man regarded; but ye have set at
nought all my counsel, and would none of my reproof: I
also will laugh at your calamity; I will mock when your
fear cometh; when your fear cometh as desolation, and
your destruction cometh as a whirlwind; when distress
and anguish cometh upon you. Then shall they call upon
me, but I will not answer; they shall seek me early, but
they shall not find me: for that they hated knowledge,
and did not choose the fear of the Lord: *they would*
none of my counsel: they despised all my reproof.
Therefore shall they eat of the fruit of their own way,
and be filled with their own devices. For the turning
away of the simple shall slay them, and the prosper-
ity of fools shall destroy them. But whoso hearkeneth
unto me shall dwell safely, and shall be quiet from fear
of evil.

DAY 1: THE STARTING PLACE (PROVERBS 1:1-7)

The purpose of proverbs by Israel's king
(David's son, Solomon) on most everything:

For training in wisdom and insight to plant,
For true understanding in intelligence.

For giving instruction in that which is just,
In conduct, in duty, in goodness and such.

Understanding for the innocent, for imparting insight—
To the ignorant and simple, of that which is right.

So those who will listen, will learn to advance,
To attain to wise counsel, and gain sound guidance;

To comprehend proverbs, and parables know,
To unravel enigmas, and wisdom to show.

The fear of the Lord is the first place to turn,
But fools despise knowledge and just will not learn!

ON YOUR MARK!

Proverb:

"The fear of the LORD is the beginning of knowledge: but fools despise wisdom and instruction" (Proverbs 1:7).

Precept:

How do you start to learn the wisdom of God? In the schoolroom? In the library? With the dictionary? Exploring the world? The answer to the question is easy! Fear the Lord. You start with your attitude toward God. A proper respect and reverence for Him will prepare you for the lessons that are to follow.

Recently, I met a woman who had been arrested and had spent the night in jail. She told me the incident started when her son was arrested and she became belligerent toward the arresting officer. It ended up with her being arrested and taken to jail as well.

I asked her, "Do you know what you say to a policeman?"

She said, "I guess I don't. What do you say?"

I said, "You say, 'Yes sir!'"

You don't berate, curse, or argue with a policeman. He is in a position of authority. You just say, "Yes sir!"

To revere, respect, and reverence God is one of the first things you should learn in life. When you properly acknowledge God and the position of authority He holds, you are then ready to learn about how you should interact with other people and situations you may encounter.

When do you begin your journey toward understanding and wisdom? A Chinese proverb says, "The longest journey begins with a single step." If you really want your life to be productive and profitable, you can begin *right now*! To begin, align yourself with God and allow Him to mentor and guide you in everything you do. Today is the first day of the rest of your life!

Practice:

Through prayer, daily express your desire to God for His knowledge and understanding. Give Him control of each situation you face. Let Him know that you will honor and respect the teaching of His Word.

Prayer:

Lord, I truly want to honor, reverence, and fear You in the way that I should. I respect Your authority in my life. You know what is best for me.

DAY 2: A PARENTAL WARNING (PROVERBS 1:8-19)

Hear your father's instruction, my son, and obey
The advice of your mother, don't throw it away.

As a jewel of grace, on your head you will hold,
In pride, round your neck like a chain of pure gold.

When the wicked entice you to lead you astray,
Don't listen, my son; don't consent to their way.

"A trap we will lay for an innocent man;
We will wait and his blood we will shed if we can.

"We will swallow him up alive in our trap,
Cast him down to the pit, to the grave, and hell's lap.

"We will blot out his name, in our house put his spoils.
Cast your lot in with us, for one purse be loyal."

My son, never join them; turn your foot from their path,
For their feet run to evil and turn quickly to death.

Surely a net that is spread very plain
To capture a bird is spread but in vain.

Secret snares that you set, other victims to catch,
Will ensnare your own life, your own blood, at the last.

BAD APPLES

Proverb:

"My son, if sinners entice thee, consent thou not" (Proverbs 1:10).

Precept:

It has long been known that a spoiled apple left in the barrel will cause the other apples to spoil as well. So, when an apple begins to spoil, it is wise to separate the bad one from the rest.

People are not apples, but the same principle applies to them. A verse from the Bible speaks of how "evil communications corrupt good manners" (I Corinthians 15:33). However, it is more easily understood when we read the American Standard translation that says, "evil companionships corrupt good morals." This verse clearly indicates that it is best not to join forces with someone who is worldly minded in his concepts, wild in his conduct, and hedonistic in his lifestyle. In other words, stay away from someone who is a "bad apple."

People who choose to live an evil lifestyle should not be despised but rather should be treated with courtesy and respect. However, when you are solicited to have a close relationship, to have a common bank account, to share the same lifestyle, and especially to do things that are immoral or illegal, you must not consent to that solicitation. In fact, you should be very careful to choose companions who are not weak in faith, not engaged in evil, or not addicted to violent or antisocial behavior. You should also avoid anyone who would in any way mar your desire to walk in the ways of God. Your example of choosing good friends and companions may help others who wish to leave their evil lifestyle and choose a better path. You will then be able to lead them to a higher level of righteous behavior.

Practice:

Carefully consider the companions with whom you are presently associating. Are there any who are overtly trying to persuade you to make wrong decisions that would adversely affect your relationship with God? Ask God to help you make a clean break from ungodly friends and to choose new friends who will undergird your desire to be great for Him.

Prayer:

Lord, help me to choose friends who are pleasing to You. Give me friends who will help me make right choices in life. Help me not to continually associate with people who try to influence me to sin. Help me to be a positive influence on the people in my life.

DAY 3: THE VOICE OF WISDOM (PROVERBS 1:20-33)

Wisdom calls us aloud, outside in the streets;
In the open square, her message repeats.

She cries where the crowd has gathered to meet;
She enters the gates of the city and speaks:

"How long will you love your heedless way?
How long will you scorn what I have to say?

"Would you please take heed to the warning I cry?
My words I'll make known, and my Spirit supply.

"But because I have called and you have not listened,
You heeded me not, when with my hand I have beckoned.

"When all of my counsel you have disdained,
My reproof disregarded, and from it abstained.

"I will laugh at you when your plight is severe.
You may seek my face, but there'll be no one near.

"When your terror comes on you like the blast of a storm,
As a whirlwind it strikes with the violence of doom.

"You'll call on me, but I'll not be around.
Though you call on me early, I will not be found.

"When knowledge you have hated, and the Lord refused,
Would have none of His counsel, and despised
    His reproof—

"You shall eat the fruit of that which you embrace
And be filled with your own iniquitous ways.

"By their turning away the simple are slain,
And fools are destroyed by abundance of gain.

"Those who listen to me shall be free of alarm,
Protected from evil, without fear of harm!"

ANSWERING THE CHALLENGE

Proverb:

"Because I have called, and ye refused; I have stretched out my hand, and no man regarded; but ye have set at nought all my counsel, and would none of my reproof: I also will laugh at your calamity; I will mock when your fear cometh" (Proverbs 1:24-26).

Precept:

Life is filled with great opportunities. One of the greatest is the challenge to listen to the voice of wisdom. Many times in Solomon's great Book of Proverbs, wisdom is pictured as a woman who is seeking to gain your attention. She lifts her voice in the streets. She speaks with the voice of experience and promises the presence of God and the opening of doors that are available. With gracious words and entreaties, she asks for a positive response.

Though opportunity will knock at the door, it will not forever continue to wait. John Oxenham said, "To every man there openeth a way, and ways and a way."[2] James Russell Lowell said, "Once to every man and nation comes the moment to decide. In the strife of Truth with falsehood, for the good or evil side."[3] Ultimately, the decision is made, and the fleeting opportunity may be lost forever.

Someone placed a sign on a university message board that said, "Procrastination is my greatest weakness. I will do something about it . . . tomorrow!" But sometimes, if we delay, that tomorrow never comes.

When counsel is unheeded, when reproof is disregarded, when opportunities are refused, then there comes a day of reckoning, a day of regret, and a day of self-recrimination. The best thing to do is to listen to the voice of wisdom. The wise course is to seize the moment and to take advantage of your opportunities. Then you will have no regrets and no sad story of lost privileges and opportunities. What decisions do you need to make for yourself, for your family, and for God? They should be made *sooner, not later,* and *today, not tomorrow.* Listen to the voice of wisdom—now!

Practice:

Make a list of the opportunities that have been presented to you—on the job, at home, at church, in relationships. Write the things that might challenge each opportunity. Ask God to help you seize the moment and wisely respond to each opportunity given.

Prayer:

Lord, give me the wisdom to take advantage of every opportunity that You bring my way. Help me not to procrastinate, but to quickly obey Your voice as You give me direction.

PROVERBS 2

My son, if thou wilt receive my words, and hide my commandments with thee; so that thou incline thine ear unto wisdom, and apply thine heart to understanding; yea, if thou criest after knowledge, and liftest up thy voice for understanding; if thou seekest her as silver, and searchest for her as for hid treasures; then shalt thou understand the fear of the LORD, and find the knowledge of God. For the LORD giveth wisdom: out of his mouth cometh knowledge and understanding. He layeth up sound wisdom for the righteous: he is a buckler to them that walk uprightly. He keepeth the paths of judgment, and preserveth the way of his saints. Then shalt thou understand righteousness, and judgment, and equity; yea, every good path.

When wisdom entereth into thine heart, and knowledge is pleasant unto thy soul; discretion shall preserve thee, understanding shall keep thee: to deliver thee from the way of the evil man, from the man that speaketh froward things; who leave the paths of uprightness, to walk in the ways of darkness; who rejoice to do evil, and delight in the frowardness of the wicked; whose ways are crooked, and they froward in their paths: to deliver thee from the strange woman, even from the stranger which flattereth with her words; which forsaketh the guide of her youth, and forgetteth the covenant of her God. For her house inclineth unto death, and her paths unto the dead. None that go unto her return again, neither take they hold of the paths of life. That thou mayest walk in the way of good men, and keep the paths of the righteous. For the upright shall dwell in the land, and the perfect shall remain in it. But the wicked shall be cut off from the earth, and the transgressors shall be rooted out of it.

DAY 4: THE PATHWAY OF LIFE (PROVERBS 2:1-10)

My son, take to heart all the words that I say;
Treasure up my commandments, in every way.

Turn your ear to my wisdom (I speak unto you),
And to clear understanding, turn your mind and heart, too.

If you call for intelligence, and for knowledge cry aloud,
Seek insight as treasure and as silver searched out,

Godly fear you'll receive, and true reverence find
For our God's knowledge of every kind.

It is He who gives wisdom, and out of His mouth,
Cometh wisdom and knowledge, insight and truth.

He stores up salvation for the truly upright;
He's a shield and a buckler when it comes to a fight.

He's a guardian of justice; His saints He'll protect—
Those who righteousness follow and evil reject.

Then you'll understand justice, right living, and duty,
Pursuing the path of perfection and beauty.

When wisdom is welcomed into your heart,
God's knowledge will please you, and joy will impart.

TREASURE HUNT

Proverb:
    "If thou seekest her as silver, and searchest for her as for
hid treasures; then shalt thou understand the fear of the LORD"
(Proverbs 2:4-5).

Precept:
    In January 1848, James Marshall found gold at John
Sutter's mill on the American River. His discovery began one of
the greatest gold rushes in American history, as men got the
gold fever and went west to dig for gold. When word of the gold
strike became public, it started a pandemonium as everyone
began to dream about the possibility of becoming fabulously
rich. One of my ancestors, a married man with five children, left
his family to join the gold rush. Some forty years later, he was in
Globe, Arizona, still searching for the elusive treasure of gold.
    The search for godly wisdom must be accomplished with
the same dedication and fervor. No, we should not leave our
families or do other unwise things that some men did in 1849,
but we must have the same dedication, the same tenacity, and
the same hunger that causes us to search out the things of God.
    When men were going by the thousands to the gold mines,
many were deceived by the various, and often ludicrous, get-
rich-quick schemes of hucksters, such as buying a salve that
supposedly produced money if they rubbed it on their body and
rolled around on the ground. They experienced humiliation and
despair when they realized they had been duped and would
have to gruelingly forge on, just like everyone else. To try to
gain wisdom, knowledge, and truth by any "get rich quick" sort
of way is just as senseless. Wisdom cannot be acquired by day-

dreaming or simply wishing. You must seek for it as men seek for treasure.

The story is told of a man who lived in Africa who wanted to become rich. He left his mud hut and went to search for diamonds. The person who moved into his deserted hut noticed a glimmer in a stone, which caught his eye. He extracted the stone and discovered that it was a diamond—what the former resident had left to find. Our search for wisdom must be accompanied by dedication, energy, and perseverance. You can find it, if you seek for it as men seek for silver, gold, and precious stones.

Practice:

You do not have to be a global traveler to find wisdom. You can begin your search at home. Realize the importance of finding the answers to life's questions in the Word of God. Remember that fearing God is the beginning. Purpose to search for knowledge, as men seek for silver and gold.

Prayer:

Lord, help me to understand that there are hidden treasures in Your Word. Help me not to be discouraged or distracted easily when I read passages of Scripture. Help me to find a nugget of wisdom each day that will give direction for my life.

DAY 5: THE BLESSING OF WISDOM (PROVERBS 2:11-19)

Discretion and counsel in safety will keep you.
Understanding and prudence will guard and protect you.

They will keep your way safe from that which does ill,
From perversity of men who speak with self-will,

From those who waver from paths that are right
And wander to walk in the shadows of night.

Who revel in wickedness, rejoice in their wrong;
Admiration they have for the dissolute throng.

Their devious paths will turn you away
From the road that leads straight to the light of the day.

You'll be saved from strange women, the wife of another,
The seductress with smooth words to utter and flatter.

Who leaves her companion, the guide of her youth,
Forsaking her covenant with the great God of truth.

Her house leads to death; none who go there return
Nor recover their steps, for life's pathway they spurn.

AT THE CROSSROADS

Proverb:
"None that go unto her return again, neither take they hold of the paths of life" (Proverbs 2:19).

Precept:
In the second chapter of Proverbs, much is said about paths. These are some that are mentioned: (verse 9) the "good path," (verse 13) the "paths of uprightness," (verse 15) the "froward [devious] paths," (verse 18) the "paths unto the dead," (verse 19) "the paths of life," and (verse 20) "the paths of the righteous."

When you come to the crossroads of life, there are many paths from which to choose. It is as though you come to a place where a myriad of roads intersect: an interstate highway, a local thoroughfare, a circuitous road that leads away from the main road, a road to a cemetery, or a road to a gated community reserved for only those who have a pass. You have to make a choice as to which road or path you will take.

When you make wrong choices, they sometimes lead to the cemetery or to a meandering trail that stops at a dead-end street. Some people will choose paths for their lives that lead to a place of privilege and honor. Others will choose a devious route that leads to shame and dishonor. Immorality and perversion will always lead you away from the paths of life.

The best road to travel is the way of right living. Not only will it bring you happiness and fulfillment in this life, but it will also ultimately lead to a life of righteousness and peace with God. The path of life has not only the promise of the life that now is, but also of that which is to come. When you are standing at a cross-roads, always consider which road is best for you and your family, but keep foremost in mind the road that leads to life eternal.

Practice:

What life decisions are you facing today? Do you want to change jobs? Get married? Leave your spouse? As you consider the choices before you, prayerfully consider where each choice may take you. Ask God to help you choose the right path—a path that leads to life and not destruction.

Prayer:

Lord, I want to choose the right path for myself and for my family. Show me clearly the consequence of each path that is before me. Help me take the path that You show me, even if it is not the one that I would choose.

DAY 6: HEROES (PROVERBS 2:20-22)

But you shall be found in the path of good men,
With justice and righteousness walking therein.

For the upright, the blameless, the just shall survive,
With the wicked cut off, no longer alive!

GOOD MEN

Proverb:

"That thou mayest walk in the way of good men" (Proverbs 2:20).

Precept:

Good men are hard to find! Man is a strange creature. The Bible says in Ecclesiastes 7:29, "God hath made man upright; but they have sought out many inventions." In other words, men may start out right but will often go looking for trouble. It is not in man to guide his footsteps. Isaiah 53:6 says, "All we like sheep have gone astray; we have turned every one to his own way." And,

"There is none righteous, no, not one" (Romans 3:10). It would be easy to write off the possibilities of finding a good man.

However, man is made in the image of God. And God is good. "Truly God is good to Israel, even to such as are of a clean heart" (Psalm 73:1). And God likes to do good things for His people. "Every good gift and every perfect gift is from above, and cometh down from the Father of lights, with whom is no variableness, neither shadow of turning" (James 1:17). There are good men who are inspired by the love of God, the love of their wife, and the love of their children. Therefore, friends can be faithful. People can be good citizens. In the time of danger, men rise to the defense of their country. Great men arise to benefit all humanity.

The motto of the U.S. Army is "A Few Good Men!" A familiar text in Scripture says, "I sought for a man, that should make up the hedge, and stand in the gap" (Ezekiel 22:30). Sam Walter Foss wrote, "Bring me men to match my mountains, Bring me men to match my plains, Men with empires in their purpose, And new eras in their brains."[4]

God is still looking for good men. The world needs good men. Our country needs good citizens and good leaders. Wives need good husbands, and children need good fathers. Men and women need good men of courage and strength who will set an example before them. Are you someone who is walking in the path of good and godly men? Let today's proverb inspire you to walk in the way of good men.

Practice:

Who is the best man you know? What qualities do you admire in him? Choose that man, or someone like him, to become your mentor. Let him inspire you to be the kind of man you want to be and that God desires you to be.

Prayer:

Lord, thank You for the good and godly men You have placed in my life. Help me to follow in the path that they have left for me by their footprints. Help me to live the kind of life that would set a good example for someone else.

PROVERBS 3

My son, forget not my law; but let thine heart keep my commandments: for length of days, and long life, and peace, shall they add to thee. Let not mercy and truth forsake thee: bind them about thy neck; write them upon the table of thine heart: so shalt thou find favour and good understanding in the sight of God and man. Trust in the LORD with all thine heart; and lean not unto thine own understanding. In all thy ways acknowledge him, and he shall direct thy paths.

Be not wise in thine own eyes: fear the LORD, and depart from evil. It shall be health to thy navel, and marrow to thy bones. Honour the LORD with thy substance, and with the firstfruits of all thine increase: so shall thy barns be filled with plenty, and thy presses shall burst out with new wine. My son, despise not the chastening of the LORD; neither be weary of his correction: for whom the LORD loveth he correcteth; even as a father the son in whom he delighteth.

Happy is the man that findeth wisdom, and the man that getteth understanding. For the merchandise of it is better than the merchandise of silver, and the gain thereof than fine gold. She is more precious than rubies: and all the things thou canst desire are not to be compared unto her. Length of days is in her right hand; and in her left hand riches and honour. Her ways are ways of pleasantness, and all her paths are peace. She is a tree of life to them that lay hold upon her: and happy is every one that retaineth her. The LORD by wisdom hath founded the earth; by understanding hath he established the heavens. By his knowledge the depths are broken up, and the clouds drop down the dew.

My son, let not them depart from thine eyes: keep sound wisdom and discretion: so shall they be life unto thy soul, and grace to thy neck. Then shalt thou walk in thy way safely, and thy foot shall not stumble. When thou liest down, thou shalt not be afraid: yea, thou shalt lie down, and thy sleep shall be sweet. Be not afraid of sudden fear, neither of the desolation of the wicked,

when it cometh. For the LORD shall be thy confidence,
and shall keep thy foot from being taken.

Withhold not good from them to whom it is due, when
it is in the power of thine hand to do it. Say not unto thy
neighbour, Go, and come again, and to morrow I will
give; when thou hast it by thee. Devise not evil against
thy neighbour, seeing he dwelleth securely by thee. Strive
not with a man without cause, if he have done thee no
harm. Envy thou not the oppressor, and choose none of
his ways. For the froward is abomination to the LORD: but
his secret is with the righteous. The curse of the LORD is
in the house of the wicked: but he blesseth the habitation
of the just. Surely he scorneth the scorners: but he giveth
grace unto the lowly. The wise shall inherit glory: but
shame shall be the promotion of fools.

DAY 7: ATTITUDE TOWARD THE LORD
(PROVERBS 3:1-12)

Son, forget not my teaching and the rules that I say,
But keep my commandments, and my precepts obey.

Length of days and long life will they add unto you,
While peace and abundance will be yours, too.

Let not mercy, fidelity, and truth you forsake,
But bind them forever, like a chain round your neck.

You will have high esteem in God's sight, and then,
You'll be provident with good in the sight of all men.

Put your trust in the Lord, with all of your heart,
And make not your own understanding a part.

Acknowledge the Lord in the way that you tread,
And He shall direct in your pathway ahead.

Don't be wise in your own eyes, but give God your fear.
Depart from all evil and never go near.

You'll find health for your body, for your bones a cure.
It will bring a refreshment and keep you secure.

With your substance give honor to God, if you would,
And give Him the firstfruits of your increase in goods.

Then your barns will be filled with plenty, I know,
And with new wine your vats will soon overflow.

My son, the chastening of God don't despise,
Nor detest His correction, for He is all wise.

For whom the Lord loves, He corrects as He will.
Like a father, his son he reproves, but loves still.

SOUND ADVICE

Proverb:

"Trust in the LORD with all thine heart; and lean not unto thine own understanding" (Proverbs 3:5).

Precept:

In spite of the fact that America is supposed to be a Christian nation, it is becoming more difficult to say anything positive about Christianity or even to talk about God in a public venue. Yet many of the founders of our nation had religious connections and were not ashamed to openly proclaim their faith in God. Their faith is seen in the fact that every coin minted in the United States bears the words "Liberty" and "In God We Trust." The Declaration of Independence speaks forcefully that "all men are created equal and that they are endowed by their Creator with certain unalienable rights."[5] A Supreme Court Decision made in 1892 states: "Our civilization and our institutions are emphatically Christian. This is a religious people." It concludes: "This is a Christian nation."[6]

The admonition to "trust in the LORD" is sound advice and worthy of acceptance. We should acknowledge Him in all our ways. We should believe in Him, depend on Him, and call on Him with all our hearts. We are also advised to lean not to our own understanding. We should develop the virtue of self-reliance in all that we are able to do. However, we should not become arrogant in believing that we can get along without God's assistance and approval.

At the Constitutional Convention where our "more perfect union" was created, there was a discussion of whether prayers should be made at the convention. Benjamin Franklin, one of our country's foremost statesman and brightest minds, spoke and said, "In the beginning of the contest with Britain . . . we had daily prayer in this room for the divine protection. Our prayers, Sir, were heard—and they were gloriously answered. Do we imagine we no longer need its assistance? I have lived, Sir, a long time, and the longer I live, the more convincing proofs I see of this truth, that God governs in the affairs of men. And if a sparrow cannot fall to the ground without His notice, is it probable that an empire can rise without His aid?"[7]

Let us heed the sound advice and acknowledge God—for ourselves, for our family, and for our country. If we will not lean to our own understanding, He will direct our paths. In God we trust!

Practice:

Are you guilty of trying to take care of everything in your own strength and power? Instead of trying to figure it out on your own, trust God to work it out.

Prayer:

Lord, help me to trust You in every area of my life. Help me not to try to make things happen through my own human ability but to trust You to provide for every situation and to work it out according to Your will.

Week 2

DAY 8: THE VALUE OF WISDOM (PROVERBS 3:13-24)

Happy is the man who true wisdom can gain,
Or the one who has prudence and understanding obtains.

For her profit is better than silver can do,
And better than gold is her own revenue.

She's more precious than rubies and other things rare,
But none you desire with her could compare.

Length of days, we may find, in her right hand she holds,
In her left she has honor and riches untold.

Her ways are all pleasant, and her paths are all peace.
Those who grasp her, fastly hold her, like a tree in the seas.

The Almighty by wisdom made the earth with great skill.
By understanding He established the heavens to fill.

By knowledge, the deeps opened up and brought forth.
The clouds dropped down moisture upon the whole earth.

My son, these things should not slip from your sight.
Keep sound wisdom and discretion, and retain what is right.

They will ever be with you, as life to your soul,
As a precious adornment, like a necklace is worn.

So that you may travel in security and in peace,
That your foot may not stumble where-e'er your path leads.

You may lie down at night, and will not be in fear,
But sleep sweetly in peace, knowing wisdom is near!

In Good Hands

Proverb:

"When thou liest down, thou shalt not be afraid: yea, thou shalt lie down, and thy sleep shall be sweet" (Proverbs 3:24).

Precept:

The world is not a safe place. Jacob, an Old Testament patriarch, said, "Few and evil have the days of the years of my life been" (Genesis 47:9). However, we should not be pessimistic—always expecting the worst to happen. Neither should we be so optimistic that we cannot see the threat of danger. We should be realists—comfortable and confident in life yet always on guard against any kind of harm to ourselves or our loved ones.

For many, the above-mentioned state of mind is difficult to achieve. Often our worries overwhelm us. Sometimes we feel threatened and insecure. But in order to face what each day may bring, we cannot allow ourselves to be depressed or consumed with anxiety; instead, we must place our lives, and those of our loved ones, in God's hands. When we do this, we can rest assured that we are in good hands.

We do not have to be afraid during the day, because we know that God is watching over us. We can pray for divine protection from God and His angels. We can seek His direction and guidance in whatever we do. We can keep a prayerful attitude at all times. We can cast our cares on Him, knowing that He cares for us (I Peter 5:7). We can then sleep peacefully at night without worry or fear, because God gives His beloved sleep (Psalm 127:2).

Several years ago, a friend of mine went to a church service and heard a great sermon on God's protection. That evening, after he returned home, he went from room to room praying the protection of the blood of Jesus Christ over his home and his family. Much later that night, a man in a stolen vehicle sped recklessly through the city, pursued by the police. In his effort to escape, he turned down a certain street but lost control of his vehicle and plowed into the nearest house, which just happened to be the house of my friend. The vehicle crashed through the walls of the house and landed in the nursery, where the bumper came to rest against his baby's crib. When they rescued the baby, he was still asleep, even though he was only inches from destruction.

The safest place to be is in God's care and protection. Why not try making God your confidence? You will be in good hands!

Practice:

On different slips of paper, write the things about which you are worried. Take each need and present it to God in prayer, then tear it up and throw it away. This is a way to symbolize giving your problems to God, then letting go of them. Whenever you feel fretful or anxious, remind yourself that you have given the problem to God and He is well able to take care of it. Put your confidence in God.

Prayer:

Lord, help me not to constantly live in fear of what each day will bring or how every situation will turn out. Help me to be confident in Your ability to take care of me, my family, and the needs that we have.

DAY 9: ATTITUDE TOWARD FELLOW MEN (PROVERBS 3:25-32)

You should never be afraid when sudden terror to you comes,
Or when wicked men cause trouble that will bring them to
　　their ruin.

For the Lord shall be your confidence. He is over all your way.
He will keep your foot from shaking. He'll support you
　　every day.

When you know that someone's needing something only
　　you can do,
Don't withhold the good you're keeping, if you're able to
　　see it through.

Don't excuse yourself by saying, "Sometime soon I'll make
    it right."
Give your neighbor what is owed him. Not tomorrow,
    but tonight!

Don't plan evil toward your neighbor, who has put his
    trust in you.
Don't have trouble with another, when there's nothing
    he can do!

Have no envy for oppressors, and refuse their way
    to choose.
The wicked are disgusting, but the righteous will know
    God's views.

THE GUY NEXT DOOR

Proverb:

"Withhold not good from them to whom it is due, when it
is in the power of thine hand to do it. . . . Devise not evil against
thy neighbour, seeing he dwelleth securely by thee" (Proverbs
3:27, 29).

Precept:

How do you and your neighbor get along? I once read a
story about a woman who had some trouble with her neighbor.
She and the other woman became so estranged that they did not
even speak. The first woman needed someone to talk to, so she
joined a pen-pal club. She used the name "White Swan" and
began to share her "neighbor" trouble with her new anonymous
friend. Her pen pal wrote back and explained that she understood completely the kind of "neighbor" trouble she was having,
as she herself was so mad at her neighbor that she would not
even speak to her.

The years went by, and one day "White Swan" heard the
news that her detested neighbor had passed away. She decided
that to honor the family, she would go over to express her con-
dolences. For obvious reasons, they were not very friendly and
just let her sit in the living room while they talked with the others who were present. She finally picked up a notebook from a

side table. When she opened it, she found that it was filled with letters from "White Swan." She discovered at that moment that the person she knew to be such an understanding friend was actually the neighbor to whom she would not even speak.

In answer to the question, "Who is my neighbor?" Jesus explained in the story of the Good Samaritan (Luke 10:29-37) that your neighbor is not just the guy who lives next door but anyone who is in need that you can help. The world is in need of good neighbors. You should be friends with those who live next door. However, you may also be able to befriend or help someone else who lives across town. Do not withhold your ability to help from anyone who really needs you. Don't be a "White Swan" who cannot get along with your neighbor, but be a good Samaritan and reach out to someone in need.

Practice:

Have you taken time to get acquainted with your neighbors? If not, make it a point to spend time talking with them outside or invite them to dinner. Try to be aware of significant things that are happening in their lives—sicknesses, deaths, births, divorce—and respond appropriately. Everyone needs a good neighbor.

Prayer:

Lord, help me to show Your love to those who are in need. Help me to be a good neighbor—not just to the people who live around me but to anyone You bring my way who has a need that I can meet.

DAY 10: GOD'S WAY OF WORKING (PROVERBS 3:33-35)

He curses the house of the wicked,
But He blesses the house of the just.

He heaps scorn on the head of the scorner;
To the lowly, He giveth His grace.

The wise shall inherit all glory;
The promotion of fools shall be shame.

[The Lord is the King of the ages,
And glory be unto His name!]

WHAT WILL YOU INHERIT?

Proverb:

"The wise shall inherit glory: but shame shall be the promotion of fools" (Proverbs 3:35).

Precept:

Paul wrote that "every one of us shall give account of himself to God" (Romans 14:12). A day is coming when every man will be rewarded according to his deeds. The scales of God are just and contain no false weights. A certain reward is reserved for every man that is appropriate for the decisions he has made. The wise will inherit glory, but fools will be rewarded with shame.

The apostle Peter spoke of "an inheritance incorruptible, and undefiled, and that fadeth not away, reserved in heaven for you" (I Peter 1:4). What a beautiful promise given to those who are wise unto salvation! Peter emphasized the enduring nature of the eternal reward that comes from God alone. Your reward for living a godly life will not consist of a substance that can be tarnished by the elements of this life, but "ye shall receive a crown of glory that fadeth not away" (I Peter 5:4).

The sad fate of the fool is not the absence of reward but rather the presence of shame. Living for oneself and rejecting the wisdom of God guarantee the disapproval of the Master. Jesus told a parable in Matthew 25 about three men who were each given a different number of talents. Two men took their talents and multiplied them for the master's use. The man who had been given one talent took his talent and buried it in the earth. The two men who had multiplied their talents were commended by the master. However, the one who squandered his opportunity became the focus of the master's wrath. The master took away his talent, condemned him for his slothfulness, and cast him out of his presence into everlasting darkness.

Life is filled with many uncertainties, but one thing that is certain is our eternal reward. Our inheritance is not left to chance, but it is determined by the choices of our life. "The wise shall inherit glory: but shame shall be the promotion of fools" (Proverbs 3:35). What will you inherit?

Practice:

Let your every word and action glorify the Lord. Use the talents with which God has blessed you to, in turn, bless your church and community.

Prayer:

Lord, I want to reap a reward for the good that I have sown while here on earth. Help me to use the talents that You have given me so that I can inherit eternal life.

Proverbs 4

Hear, ye children, the instruction of a father, and attend to know understanding. For I give you good doctrine, forsake ye not my law. For I was my father's son, tender and only beloved in the sight of my mother. He taught me also, and said unto me, Let thine heart retain my words: keep my commandments, and live. Get wisdom, get understanding: forget it not; neither decline from the words of my mouth. Forsake her not, and she shall preserve thee: love her, and she shall keep thee. Wisdom is the principal thing; therefore get wisdom: and with all thy getting get understanding. Exalt her, and she shall promote thee: she shall bring thee to honour, when thou dost embrace her. She shall give to thine head an ornament of grace: a crown of glory shall she deliver to thee. Hear, O my son, and receive my sayings; and the years of thy life shall be many. I have taught thee in the way of wisdom; I have led thee in right paths. When thou goest, thy steps shall not be straitened; and when thou runnest, thou shalt not stumble. Take fast hold of instruction; let her not go: keep her; for she is thy life.

Enter not into the path of the wicked, and go not in the way of evil men. Avoid it, pass not by it, turn from it, and pass away. For they sleep not, except they have done mischief; and their sleep is taken away, unless they cause some to fall. For they eat the bread of wickedness, and drink the wine of violence. But the path of the just is as the shining light, that shineth more and more unto the perfect day. The way of the wicked is as darkness: they know not at what they stumble.

My son, attend to my words; incline thine ear unto my sayings. Let them not depart from thine eyes; keep them in the midst of thine heart. For they are life unto those that find them, and health to all their flesh. Keep thy heart with all diligence; for out of it are the issues of life. Put away from thee a froward mouth, and perverse lips put far from thee. Let thine eyes look right on, and let thine eyelids look straight before thee. Ponder the path of thy feet, and let all thy ways be established. Turn not to the right hand nor to the left: remove thy foot from evil.

DAY 11: THE SUPREME GUIDE OF MEN (PROVERBS 4:1-9)

Oh my children, hear your father's wise instruction and
    you'll know.
Be attentive, learn this lesson, and you will
    understanding show.

For I give you perfect doctrine; my advice do not forsake.
Learn by precept and example; it is offered, now partake.

I am thankful for my father, and I'm proud that I'm his son.
I was special to my mother, in her eyes, the only one.

My own parents were my teachers, and they gave me
    words to keep.
"Let your heart hold fast our sayings; let their meaning
    sink down deep.

"Obtain wisdom, understanding—whatever else you have
   to learn.
Don't forget it. Don't forsake it. From our words do
   not return.

"She will keep you. She will guide you. If you love her, it
   will pay.
She'll defend you. She'll protect you, be your safeguard all
   the way.

"Above all else please get wisdom, for it is the
   principal thing.
And make sure with all thy getting, understanding it
   will bring.

"If you wish to have promotion, exalt wisdom, you will see;
Just embrace her, she'll bring honor, and you will
   promoted be.

"Don't leave wisdom; she'll preserve you. A crown of
   glory she'll bestow.
A crown of grace and crown of pleasure, wisdom's gift
   will be also."

My Dad Said

Proverb:

"For I was my father's son, tender and only beloved in the
sight of my mother. He taught me also, and said unto me, Let
thine heart retain my words: keep my commandments, and live"
(Proverbs 4:3-4).

Precept:

Everyone has a biological father, but not everyone is fortunate enough to have a real dad, one who has the heart of a father
and who is present in the home. Divorce has separated many
children from their fathers. Children born of illegitimate relationships also often grow up with no father present in the home.
Death, disease, accidents, and violence have caused others to
grow up without a father. These are those who are less fortunate.

However, if you have had a father—one who gave you sincere advice and unconditional love—you are very fortunate. I am blessed to be one of the fortunate ones. My own father was the best man I ever knew. Not only did he love me, but he also instructed me. He showed me by his conduct what a Christian should be. He told me wise words that I will never forget. And though he did not leave me a great legacy of earthly goods, he left me a faith that is more precious than gold.

The apostle Paul said you have many instructors, but only one father. (See I Corinthians 4:5.) He was speaking of a spiritual relationship that anyone can have with a man who is his father in the gospel. If you are in need of a father figure in your life, find a man of God and let him be a father to you. There may be a minister in your life, or another godly man, who cares for you and your soul, who would love to be a father to you if you would let him. Let him teach you the ways of God. Let him instruct you in the commandments of His Word. Follow his godly leadership, and pattern yourself after his example.

If you have not known the tender love of an earthly father, please do not allow the cycle to continue and withhold this privilege from your own children. Be the kind of father to them that you never had. Be involved with your children and help to mold their lives. Speak words of wisdom and encouragement to them. Teach, by both word and example, godly principles that will guide them.

Practice:

Do you remember specific things that your dad said? Are they things that uplift and encourage you, or are they things that make you angry and frustrated? Determine to speak positively and kindly to your children. Purpose to instruct them in the ways of righteousness.

Prayer:

Lord, help me to teach my children the things that are necessary to live a victorious Christian life. Help me show them by words and by my actions how a Christian is supposed to live.

DAY 12: THE GOOD AND EVIL WAY (PROVERBS 4:10-19)

My son, if you hear and my sayings believe,
Many years of long life you'll be sure to receive.

I have taught you the path of wisdom to know,
And I led you straightforward in the way you should go.

The way that you walk should not be impeded.
When you run, you won't stumble; you'll not be defeated.

Hold firm to instruction; experience will show
That instruction is life, so do not let her go.

The path of the wicked to you is forbidden;
The way of the wicked from you must be hidden.

Avoid it, never follow it, shun it, and stay clear.
Just keep a safe distance; don't even go near.

Until the wicked do mischief, they cannot find sleep,
And they toss and they turn till they make someone weep.

For to them working wickedness is like eating bread,
And for them doing violence goes like wine to their head.

For the path of the just is as the light of the way,
And it shines ever brighter unto a more perfect day.

When the wicked walk their pathway, it's like groping for
the light;
They don't know on what they stumble, as they fumble in
the night.

STEP BY STEP

Proverb:
"The path of the just is as the shining light, that shineth more and more unto the perfect day" (Proverbs 4:18).

Precept:

Great things are not usually accomplished overnight. They are done as someone continually progresses, little by little, toward his goal. Likewise, God accomplishes His work in us by revealing His will like a light that shines upon our pathway, illuminating each step. Jesus said, "I thank thee, O Father . . . because thou hast hid these things from the wise and prudent, and hast revealed them unto babes" (Matthew 11:25). The great God of the universe, who conceals the future until it unfolds to us, lets us progress gradually unto His perfect will.

In this process, we begin walking with God by faith. As we take each step that is revealed, we go from faith to faith and from strength to strength. With each step, we become stronger. We grow in grace and favor with God. We grow in knowledge, wisdom, and spiritual stature. We go beyond the first principles of the doctrine of Christ, and we go on to perfection.

Someone told the story of a man who had an operation on his blinded eyes. After the operation, his family asked, "Will he be able to see, Doctor?" The doctor replied, "He can already see. But if we immediately expose his eyes to all of the light, he would be blinded again." The doctor continued, "We will keep the heavy bandages on while his eyes heal, and then we will remove them, one by one. As his eyes grow accustomed to the light, he will gradually see more and more until he is no longer blinded by the light."

In the same way, God reveals His will to us. As our eyes become accustomed to the light, He reveals more light for us to follow. Rome was not built in a day, and neither are the great truths of God's Word all learned at one time. Precept must be upon precept, and line upon line; here a little and there a little. (See Isaiah 28:10.)

When I was a child, our home had no electricity, so I read by the light of a kerosene lamp. Later, we had an "Aladdin lamp," a much greater source of light. When I was seventeen, an electric company brought electricity into our home. Our first lights were just bulbs hanging down from the ceiling on a cord, but what an improvement!

Now that we have the advantage of sophisticated modern lighting, I would not want to go back and be forced to use kerosene lamps. When God reveals truth to us, we should not choose to remain in ignorance. We should go from revelation to revelation and from victory to victory. We should continue to progress and mature in God, step by step, as long as we live.

Practice:

Do not be one who wavers from position to position or as someone who is ever learning, but never able to come to the knowledge of the truth. You should be open and eager to accept truth as it is presented to you from the Word of God. Be thankful for every new revelation of truth that God illuminates for you.

Prayer:

Lord, let Your Word be a lamp into my feet. Help me to follow in the light that You have revealed to me.

DAY 13: WISE WORDS (PROVERBS 4:20-27)

Would you give your close attention to the words that I
   have said?
Please incline your ear unto them lest you choose the
   wrong instead.

Do not let their fountains fail thee nor from your
   eyes depart.
Be not wanting in retention; keep them safe within
   your heart.

They are life to those who find them; health to all your
   flesh they'll bring.
They'll put grace upon your shoulders, cause a cure
   for everything.

Keep your heart with utmost diligence, for from it life's
   issues flow,
So that you may live and prosper, everywhere that you
   may go.

Cleanse your mouth of every evil; watch your lips in what
    they say.
Perverse words and crooked speeches, you must put them
    all away.

Keep on looking straight before you; let your eyes before
    you gaze.
Seek for justice, truth, and mercy, facing forward all
    your days.

You must ponder the direction of the path your feet
    will take,
That your ways may be established and firm footsteps you
    will make.

Never swerve from the right pathway; never take a
    foolish step.
Keep your feet away from evil, on the right or on the left.

PLOWING A STRAIGHT FURROW

Proverb:

"Ponder the path of thy feet, and let all thy ways be established. Turn not to the right hand nor to the left: remove thy foot from evil" (Proverbs 4:26-27).

Precept:

Some things are simple. An old preacher told me, "Don't be like a goose. It can be walking one direction but with its head turned and looking behind it." The preacher said, "Keep your nose and your toes in the same direction!"

I was raised on a farm, although my parents quit raising crops before I was old enough to participate in the process. But this one thing I did learn: If you are plowing a furrow in the field, do not look to the right or left; keep your eyes on the end of the row and plow that direction. By doing so, the row that you plow will be straight.

Farmers used to pride themselves on how straight a row they could plow. People also used to pride themselves on how close to God they could walk. Unfortunately, the world has many amusements and attractions that distract people from their walk with God. However, we should still strive to seek first the kingdom of God and His righteousness. (See Matthew 6:33.)

God delivered Lot, his wife, and his family from Sodom. The one thing that was stressed as they left the city was "Do not look back!" (See Genesis 19:17.) Lot's wife had daughters in the city. Her heart was divided by the choice of leaving some of her children behind and going out with the ones who were escaping. How sad that Lot's wife turned back and became a pillar of salt. The Bible gives us the solemn warning: "Remember Lot's wife" (Luke 17:32).

The Israelite nation escaped from Egypt's bondage. With Moses as their leader, they crossed the Red Sea in a miracle of deliverance. They drank water from the rock and ate manna sent from heaven. All of their enemies were defeated. But, according to the Bible, they turned back to Egypt "in their hearts." Even as they were walking toward deliverance, they were looking back toward bondage. Ultimately, they all died in the wilderness, with the exception of Joshua and Caleb.

Your direction is very important, no matter how slowly you are moving. But your attention is also important! You need not only to be traveling toward heaven with your body, but your heart, mind, and soul need to be centered in that direction as well. Do not make the mistake of looking back toward the world of sin from which Christ has delivered you. "But our citizenship is in heaven. And we eagerly await our Savior from there, the Lord Jesus Christ" (Philippians 3:20, NIV). Christ will appear the second time unto "them that look for him" (Hebrews 9:28).

Do not be a goose. Keep your nose and your toes in the same direction!

Practice:

Stop for a moment and consider the direction you are headed. Are you putting God first in every area of your life? Are you doing the right things outwardly but inwardly desiring the things of the world? If so, ask God to help you to desire to do the things that are pleasing to Him.

Prayer:

Lord, please establish my ways. Help me to keep my eyes on You.

PROVERBS 5

My son, attend unto my wisdom, and bow thine ear to my understanding: that thou mayest regard discretion, and that thy lips may keep knowledge. For the lips of a strange woman drop as an honeycomb, and her mouth is smoother than oil: but her end is bitter as wormwood, sharp as a twoedged sword. Her feet go down to death; her steps take hold on hell. Lest thou shouldest ponder the path of life, her ways are moveable, that thou canst not know them. Hear me now therefore, O ye children, and depart not from the words of my mouth. Remove thy way far from her, and come not nigh the door of her house: lest thou give thine honour unto others, and thy years unto the cruel: lest strangers be filled with thy wealth; and thy labours be in the house of a stranger; and thou mourn at the last, when thy flesh and thy body are consumed, and say, How have I hated instruction, and my heart despised reproof; and have not obeyed the voice of my teachers, nor inclined mine ear to them that instructed me! I was almost in all evil in the midst of the congregation and assembly.

Drink waters out of thine own cistern, and running waters out of thine own well. Let thy fountains be dispersed abroad, and rivers of waters in the streets. Let them be only thine own, and not strangers' with thee. Let thy fountain be blessed: and rejoice with the wife of thy youth. Let her be as the loving hind and pleasant roe; let her breasts satisfy thee at all times; and be thou ravished always with her love. And why wilt thou, my son, be ravished with a strange woman, and embrace the bosom of a stranger? For the ways of man are before the eyes of the LORD, and he pondereth all his goings. His own iniquities shall take the wicked himself, and he shall be holden with the cords of his sins. He shall die without instruction; and in the greatness of his folly he shall go astray.

DAY 14: THE WRONG WOMAN (PROVERBS 5:1-14)

Hear the wisdom of your father, as he plainly to you shows.
Oh, my children, give attention, for he understanding knows.

Good advice I give unto you, so my teaching don't forsake,
That you may regard discretion, and your lips true
    knowledge keep.

Let me tell you of a woman, with her evil, strange device,
As she speaks with words of honey, smoothly trying
    to entice.

But her end is very bitter, like a noxious, poison drink.
Like a two-edged sword she'll pierce you, devouring
    in a blink.

And her feet will lead you farther than you ever meant to go.
Those who fool around with folly end with death and
    hell below.

She'll prevent your mind from pondering paths of life, lest
    you escape.
She's unstable, so she leads you like a blind man in
    her wake.

Hear me, therefore, oh ye children. Don't depart from
    what I say.
Get as far from her as possible; from her dwelling
    stay away.

Lest your honor, which you value, should to other persons go.
And your years of life be cruel, without mercy here below.

Lest a stranger should inherit all the wealth that you
    have made,
And the stranger's house be furnished with the things for
    which you've paid.

And your life be filled with mourning, with no remedy
    in sight.
When your flesh and body perish, you will question what
    is right:

"Tell me why I would not listen, when my teachers taught
    the truth?
Would not listen to instruction, and my heart would
    spurn reproof?

"Almost everything that's evil has brought ruin unto me,
Brought me into condemnation, from the
    whole community."

HANKY-PANKY

Proverb:

"For the lips of a strange woman drop as an honeycomb,
and her mouth is smother than oil" (Proverbs 5:3).

Precept:

Let us face it; the sex drive is one of the most powerful
influences in the life of a man or woman! In many of the biblical passages, often the figure of sexual temptation and immoral
behavior is that of a woman. She is pictured as the temptress,
the one who initiates intimate contact, and the one to be
blamed. Many of the proverbs are written to a young man.
Naturally, a father would point out the dangers of someone
who would try to seduce his son!

However, we live in a different age, where women are com-
monly exposed to the same vulnerability as men with regard to
temptation and unfaithfulness. A man can be tempted by a
woman, but a woman can also be tempted by a man. So the
warnings about avoiding a seducer can apply to both.

Both a temptress and a tempter are sweet. Their words are

gracious, like the honey dripping from the honeycomb. Most affairs start with a conversation. Many men with faithful wives are tempted by a sweet-talking woman. She is not surrounded by household duties and seemingly has lots of time for intimate conversations with her selected victim. As he compares her with his wife, his wife comes out second best. But the Bible admonishes that if you like honey, or sweetness, you had best get it out of your own jar. Do not be fooled by a sweet-talking woman.

A woman can also be tempted by a sweet-talking man. She does not know that these kinds of men talk that way to every woman—except to their wives! They usually have a way of putting their wives down. Beware of men who know how to sweet-talk a woman. Do not let sweet words and smooth operators seduce you into getting involved in an affair.

It is not strange that the "lips" and the "mouth" are emphasized in this warning. The first step in seduction is conversation, and the next step is a kiss. Beware of conversation that is designed to "sweet talk" you into an intimate relationship. Watch out for smooth operators who try to manipulate you into a compromising activity. Bail out of the situation before it ever gets to a kiss. You will be glad that you have learned how to identify the "strange woman" or the "strange man" who has marked you for the next conquest. Give the credit to the warning you heard from "the wise man."

Practice:

Whether you are single or married, male or female, you should be on guard against someone of the opposite sex who would try to seduce you. Do not allow yourself to be enticed into an illicit relationship by his or her smooth words. Ask God to help you to keep yourself pure and to resist any temptation that may come your way. Seek God for wisdom to quickly discern a person's true motive and character.

Prayer:

Lord, I want to honor You in everything that I do and in every relationship in my life.

Week 3

Day 15: The Right Woman (Proverbs 5:15-20)

So drink water from no other but the cistern that you own.
Drink no more from running water, than the well that's
yours alone.

Should your offspring be dispersed as water in the street?
Should you invite every stranger to pollute your
private stream?

Make your treasures your own pleasures and enjoy them
as you want,
For the strangers have no portion in your
private covenant.

Let your married fount be blessed, as it is in very truth,
And find comfort and contentment with the wife who's
yours since youth.

As a loving deer and faithful wife, of beauty and of charm,
Let her form and figure satisfy, and every need perform.

And, my son, why should you hunger for the love of
someone's mate?
Why accept the warm embraces of adultery, which you hate?

A Private Pool

Proverb:
 "Drink waters out of thine own cistern, and running waters
out of thine own well" (Proverbs 5:15).

Precept:

Marriage is the first institution God made. He planned the church before the foundation of the world, and He made marriage as a type of the relationship that He has with His church. The "first Adam" was a figure of Him that was to come—Jesus Christ! Thus, Jesus Christ is called the "Second Adam." When God said that a man shall leave his father and mother, and cleave to his wife (Matthew 19:5), He was also speaking of the church and how it should relate to Christ.

God's ideal for marriage is that it should consist of one man and one woman who are faithful to one another unto death. However, as with many other things God made, man has distorted the ideal that God intended. Because civilization before the Flood had become evil and every imagination was continually evil, God started over after the Flood with Noah and his wife, and his sons, and their wives. (See Genesis 6.) Once again, it was one man and one woman in marriage. Throughout the Old Testament, there were horrible examples of polygamy, concubinage, prostitution, and incest, but Jesus said, "From the beginning it was not so" (Matthew 19:8).

Every couple should regard marriage according to the ideal that Jesus envisioned from the beginning. In Proverbs 5:15, marriage is compared to a cistern. In Bible times, a cistern was a reservoir that collected the water that flowed off the roof of a home. It was for the householder and his family alone. In this same verse, marriage is also compared to a flowing well on your property that belongs to you exclusively. The instruction is to drink from your own well, implying that we should not drink from polluted public places, which would bring contamination into our lives.

Our loyalty to marriage is justified by many biblical slogans: "It is not good that the man should be alone" (Genesis 2:18). "Whoso findeth a wife findeth a good thing" (Proverbs 18:22). "Art thou bound to a wife? seek not to be loosed" (I Corinthians 7:27). "Marriage is honourable in all, and the bed undefiled" (Hebrews 13:4). "Live joyfully with the wife whom thou lovest all the days of the life of thy vanity" (Ecclesiastes 9:9). "To avoid fornication, let every man have his own wife, and let every woman have her own husband"(I Corinthians 7:2). "For the Lord . . . saith that he hateth putting away" (Malachi 2:16).

In an age in which marriage and the family are under attack from the forces of hell, it is wonderful to drink water from your own cistern and your own flowing well. What a blessing to have a wife or husband who is faithful!

Practice:

As a married person, vow to be faithful to your husband or wife. Determine not to look outside your marriage for the emotional or physical satisfaction that you need. If you are single, choose to honor the marriage vows of others. Do not do anything that would cause someone else to break his or her marriage covenant.

Prayer:

Lord, I thank You for the covenant of marriage that You have designed. Help me to honor my marriage vows and those of others.

Day 16: The Trap (Proverbs 5:21-23)

With the Lord, our ways are open and are disclosed to
    His eyes,
And He ponders all our goings, should our path be
    wrong or wise.

Those who favor lust and license shall be taken unaware,
And will find they are entrapped in the mesh of their
    sin's snare.

They shall die from lack of discipline, at
    overwhelming cost.
Through the greatness of their folly, they'll be ruined and
    they'll be lost!

Tangled Up

Proverb:

"His own iniquities shall take the wicked himself, and he shall be holden with the cords of his sin" (Proverbs 5:22).

Precept:

As a teenage boy, I was asked to take a colt to a farm pond to get a drink. He had a rope around his neck and he was thirsty, so he went along with me readily. After getting a drink, he became anxious to get back to his mother, for he was not yet weaned. He began to run around me, and before I knew it, he had wrapped the rope around my feet and I could not get loose. He gave a big heave, and I fell down and he began dragging me toward his mother. Fortunately, someone else was near, and he caught the rope and stopped the colt before he dragged me to death. I thought I was leading the colt, but he ended up dragging me!

Sin is like that. As you begin to dally with various types of disobedience, sin begins to wrap its rope around you until you are so entangled that with a great lurch, sin knocks you off your feet. The sins that you thought you could control are now controlling you! Profanity is just a curse word or two, and then it becomes a habit. Drink, drugs, or other vices may just be an experiment, but then the habit forms. Suddenly you are not controlling them, but they are controlling you. Immorality may start with a one-night stand. However, if you get under its power, it can become the ruler of your life. That is why the apostle Paul said to "flee fornication" (I Corinthians 6:18).

Paul also said, "To whom ye yield yourselves servants to obey, his servants ye are" (Romans 6:16). Discipline is imperative if you are to retain control of your life and not allow sin to rule. Paul said in I Corinthians 9:27, "I keep under my body, and bring it into subjection: lest that by any means, when I have preached to others, I myself should be a castaway."

Sometimes we are so tempted by sin that we cannot break its hold on us. That is when we seek the power of the Holy Spirit to help us overcome our temptations. God has promised that if we are tempted, He will not allow us to be tempted more than we can bear but will with the temptation make a way for our escape. (See I Corinthians 10:13.)

The writer of Hebrews compared the Christian life with a race, perhaps an Olympic race, and he said, "Let us lay aside every weight, and the sin which doth so easily beset us, and let us run with patience the race that is set before us" (Hebrews 12:1). Certainly we should avoid sin at any cost and not let it entangle us in its cords. We should also avoid other things that may not necessarily be sin but that have the capacity to weigh us down and impede our progress with God. Paul said, "All things are lawful unto me, but all things are not expedient: all things are lawful for me, but I will not be brought under the power of any" (I Corinthians 6:12).

"No man that warreth entangleth himself with the affairs of this life; that he may please him who hath chosen him to be a soldier" (II Timothy 2:4). Make sure that the things with which you are involving yourself do not have sinful cords that will ultimately bring you under their power.

Practice:

Take a moment to evaluate your life. Are you doing anything questionable that you think is harmless but that may have the power to overcome you? Repent. Ask God to forgive you for your carelessness. Untangle yourself from anything sinful.

Prayer:

Lord, please help me to search my life for anything that would entangle me in sin. I do not want anything to hinder my relationship with You.

PROVERBS 6

My son, if thou be surety for thy friend, if thou hast stricken thy hand with a stranger, thou art snared with the words of thy mouth, thou art taken with the words of thy mouth. Do this now, my son, and deliver thyself, when thou art come into the hand of thy friend; go, humble thyself, and make sure thy friend. Give not sleep to thine eyes, nor slumber to thine eyelids. Deliver thyself as a roe from the hand of the hunter, and as a bird from the hand of the fowler.

Go to the ant, thou sluggard; consider her ways, and be wise: which having no guide, overseer, or ruler, provideth her meat in the summer, and gathereth her food in the harvest. How long wilt thou sleep, O sluggard? when wilt thou arise out of thy sleep? Yet a little

*sleep, a little slumber, a little folding of the hands to
sleep: so shall thy poverty come as one that travelleth,
and thy want as an armed man.*

*A naughty person, a wicked man, walketh with a
froward mouth. He winketh with his eyes, he speaketh
with his feet, he teacheth with his fingers; frowardness
is in his heart, he deviseth mischief continually; he
soweth discord. Therefore shall his calamity come suddenly; suddenly shall he be broken without remedy.
These six things doth the LORD hate: yea, seven are an
abomination unto him: a proud look, a lying tongue,
and hands that shed innocent blood, an heart that
deviseth wicked imaginations, feet that be swift in running to mischief, a false witness that speaketh lies, and
he that soweth discord among brethren.*

*My son, keep thy father's commandment, and forsake
not the law of thy mother: bind them continually upon
thine heart, and tie them about thy neck. When thou
goest, it shall lead thee; when thou sleepest, it shall keep
thee; and when thou awakest, it shall talk with thee. For
the commandment is a lamp; and the law is light; and
reproofs of instruction are the way of life: to keep thee
from the evil woman, from the flattery of the tongue of a
strange woman. Lust not after her beauty in thine heart;
neither let her take thee with her eyelids. For by means of
a whorish woman a man is brought to a piece of bread:
and the adulteress will hunt for the precious life. Can a
man take fire in his bosom, and his clothes not be burned?
Can one go upon hot coals, and his feet not be burned? So
he that goeth in to his neighbour's wife; whosoever
toucheth her shall not be innocent. Men do not despise a
thief, if he steal to satisfy his soul when he is hungry; but
if he be found, he shall restore sevenfold; he shall give all
the substance of his house. But whoso committeth adultery
with a woman lacketh understanding: he that doeth it
destroyeth his own soul. A wound and dishonour shall he
get; and his reproach shall not be wiped away. For jealousy is the rage of a man: therefore he will not spare in
the day of vengeance. He will not regard any ransom;
neither will he rest content, though thou givest many gifts.*

DAY 17: STEERING CLEAR (PROVERBS 6:1-5)

My son, let me give you a word of advice—
If you have made bond for a friend—to be nice.

You've been snared by the utterance you've made to
your friend;
Caught by the words of your mouth you have been.

To set yourself free this very hour,
From the trap that has placed you in your
neighbor's power:

Go quickly to your neighbor as straight as you can.
Give no sleep to your eyes, but follow this plan.

Humble thyself, and your friend beseech now,
To pay his debt, and release from the vow.

Deliver yourself, like a deer from the hunter,
Or as a bird who flies free, from the hand of the fowler.

DON'T LOSE YOUR SHIRT

Proverb:
"My son, if thou be surety for thy friend, if thou hast
stricken thy hand with a stranger, thou art snared with the
words of thy mouth, thou art taken with the words of thy
mouth" (Proverbs 6:1-2).

Precept:
A common remark about someone who has lost big in a
gamble, a scam, or a wild business scheme is that "he lost his
shirt," meaning, he may have lost everything he owned, perhaps,
even his shirt! The Bible has good advice for every area of life,
and especially concerning money matters. It advises against
surety, "making yourself financially liable for a stranger or even
for a friend." In other words, do not lose your shirt!

One of my ancestors was not quite so lucky. As the son of
a white man and an Indian woman, he grew up with exposure

to both cultures. Although he lived as a white man, because he was highly respected by his Indian tribe, he was given a 640-acre tract of ground by a river when the Indians sold their land in Tennessee. There he established a stand (an early form of motel) for travelers on the Natchez Trace, providing food and sleeping accommodations. He also operated a ferryboat business on the Buffalo River, as well as a forge and a blacksmith shop where he fixed hoes, wagon wheels, and other items for the travelers. His land contained iron ore that would later be the basis for a company that employed two hundred people. But one day some friends persuaded him to co-sign a note so they could borrow money to start a business. When they were unable to repay their loan, the courts determined that he was responsible for the debt and that his land would be taken for the payment. He lost his shirt! He lost his section of land, his ferryboat business, his forge, and his stand on the Natchez Trace. He had no choice but to go to live among the Indians.

The world is full of scams and schemes. If you have money or property, someone is going to try to get you to put everything at risk to sign their note or put your money in their scheme. They will tell you that your money will multiply many times if you invest in whatever it is they are trying to sell you. Do not listen! If you have already been asked to sign a note, please do not do it. If you have already signed, then seek to be released from your obligation as quickly as you can. Be alert to anything that would cause you to lose everything you own. If you have money to place in secure investments, that is your business. But you would be wise not to be surety for someone else. Do not lose your shirt!

Practice:

Follow the wise advice of this proverb and do not sign a note for another person. Even though a person is a friend or a family member, you still should not make yourself responsible for his or her debt.

Prayer:

Lord, give me wisdom. Help me to make wise choices and to be able to stand firm in my decisions even when others may try to convince me otherwise.

DAY 18: SONG OF THE SLEEPER (PROVERBS 6:6-11)

Go learn from the ant, you sluggardly man.
Consider her ways, and be wise if you can.

Which having no ruler, overseer, or guide,
In the summer of harvest, her food will provide.

How long will you sleep, oh, you lazy buffoon?
Will you waken yourself and arise very soon?

Just a little more slumber, a dream, just one more,
Adjust your position, sleep on as before;

Till your poverty, as vagabond thieves, shall appear,
Or your hunger, like robbers with guns, shall draw near.

STRUGGLE FOR SURVIVAL

Proverb:
"How long wilt thou sleep, O sluggard? when wilt thou arise out of thy sleep?" (Proverbs 6:9).

Precept:
After Adam had disobeyed in the garden, God said, "In the sweat of thy face shalt thou eat bread, till thou return unto the ground" (Genesis 3:19). Adam's punishment for his disobedience was that he would be able to till the soil and produce a living, but he was going to have to work for it. Though some men receive inheritances that free them from the obligation of work, most men must be employed in some useful occupation in order to exist on the earth.

How sad then that some men do not realize their responsibilities and approach life with a lazy, shiftless, inactive, good-for-nothing attitude—which accurately defines the word "sluggard." Such men had rather sleep than work, rather sleep than eat. Instead of being stirred into activity by their needs, their response is just to go to bed!

In the agricultural days in which this proverb was written, the sluggard would not plant a crop. Therefore, he did not have to worry about harvesting it. He was left in the winter without food, without shelter, and without clothes. He would have to look for a place to sleep and beg or steal a piece of bread to eat.

The early church tried a great experiment in its infancy. Many Christians gave everything they had to the church in Jerusalem. They were expecting the Lord to return quickly to the earth, so they spent their time in praying and going from house to house, which was a very worthwhile endeavor. However, the church at Jerusalem began to suffer financially. When all the money they had received was spent and there were no other funds, they had to receive help from other churches in other places.

The apostle Paul was one who was involved in gathering goods and taking them to the church in Jerusalem. However, Paul eventually realized that the noble experiment at Jerusalem had failed. He decreed that if any man would not work, neither should he eat. (See II Thessalonians 3:10.) He instructed the church not to take responsibility for women who were not "widows indeed" (I Timothy 5:3). He even taught that if any provide not for his own household, he should be treated as an unbeliever. (See I Timothy 5:8.)

The Bible admonishes men to work while it is day, for the night cometh when no man can work. (See John 9:4.) The poet, Samuel Coleridge, said, "Oh sleep! It is a gentle thing, beloved from pole to pole!"[8] Everyone needs sleep as a time to rest and refresh the body. But we should not sleep when it is time to work.

Practice:

Make the necessary adjustments to your schedule so that you can get a good night of rest. This will enable you to awaken refreshed and ready to face the day ahead. Set goals of things that you wish to accomplish, and rejoice in your accomplishments at the end of the day.

Prayer:

Lord, thank You for sleep and the refreshing that it gives to my mind and body. Give me the energy that I need to "work while it is day."

DAY 19: SONG OF THE SCOUNDREL (PROVERBS 6:12-15)

A wicked man is worthless, and he has an evil walk.
He's a scoundrel, he's a villain, and he deals in
   crooked talk.

With winking eyes, shuffling feet, and fingers he can use,
He masterminds malicious schemes that perpetrate
   his ruse.

His heart is filled with perversity, and plotting evil plans.
He is continually making mischief, sowing discord where
   he can.

His doom shall come quite suddenly, as calamity awaits.
He'll be broken without remedy, and ruin is his fate!

GOOD-FOR-NOTHING

Proverb:
"A naughty person, a wicked man, walketh with a froward mouth. He winketh with his eyes, he speaketh with his feet, he teacheth with his fingers; frowardness is in his heart, he deviseth mischief continually; he soweth discord. Therefore shall his calamity come suddenly; suddenly shall he be broken without remedy" (Proverbs 6:12-15).

Precept:
Having been in ministry for over fifty years, I have been called upon many times to officiate at the funeral service for a departed loved one. It is natural that on such a public occasion a man's friends and relations would want him to be shown in the best light. In my opinion, a funeral is not a time to place judgment on an individual. It is best to let God be the judge of those who have passed on, for what is publicly said about them has no bearing on their final destination.

At times I have felt sorry for those who, having nothing to say about a man's religious experience, look for something that can be said that will show the deceased as having had some good virtues. Once I was asked if I would mind saying that the deceased person was a good whistler. I replied that I had no objection to mentioning that fact.

Unfortunately, some funeral speakers have very few requirements that they expect anyone to satisfy. They can take a person whose life has absolutely no commendable virtues, and by the time they are finished with the eulogy, they have painted him or her as an angel or a newly-departed saint. The story is told of a minister who did such a masterful job of changing the deceased's character during the funeral sermon that the wife of the departed husband told her son to go look in the casket to see if it was really his daddy inside. She did not recognize the person the preacher was describing as the husband she had known.

Once, I attended a funeral for a town barber in which the preacher yielded to the pressure of trying to rewrite history in order to please the relatives. He said, "Now, this man was a barber, and we all know that a barber has to deal with all kinds of people. If he hadn't loved people, he wouldn't have been a barber. Since he loved people, we know that he must have loved God." The preacher, trying hard to change the record for the departed barber, continued, "And we know that this man had a Bible. If he had a Bible, we know that he must have read it!" With these two distorted facts he proceeded to make a case that the man was gloriously saved and was at that moment entering the pearly gates!

How sad that some people leave no record of goodness or of any inclination toward God. They never prayed, gave an offering, helped the unfortunate, attended a church service, or had an encounter with God. Instead, the memory they leave behind is of selfish obstinance, antisocial behavior, public and private blasphemies, disorderly behavior, despicable habits, ruined relationships, and broken promises and vows.

Do not be such a good-for-nothing that the only kind thing someone can find to say is, "He knew how to whistle!" Let your life be filled with concern for others, righteous behavior, strong relationships with friends and family, and most of all, a genuine faith in God.

Practice:
Evaluate your life at this moment. What would others say about you? Are there areas in your life that you would change if

you knew that your life here on earth was almost over? Determine that you will do something today that will bring you closer to God and help to make you the kind of person He wants you to be.

Prayer:
Lord, I want my life to be a reflection of You. Help me in my relationships with those around me. Help me to be filled with Your Spirit and to show the fruit of that Spirit in my life.

DAY 20: SEVEN DEADLY SINS (PROVERBS 6:16-19)

There are six deadly sins that the Almighty hates;
Seven are loathsome to Him (as Proverbs relates).

Haughty eyes, and a tongue filled with lies that it's said,
Guilty hands that are stained with pure blood that
they've shed;

A heart filled with wickedness, that plots evil schemes,
And feet that run quickly to evil (it seems);

A false witness who fabricates lies with his word,
One who sows discord among brothers beloved.

DEADLY POISON

Proverb:
"These six things doth the LORD hate: yea, seven are an abomination unto him" (Proverbs 6:16).

Precept:
I do not like snakes! Others may keep a snake for a pet, but I will not. There are three main reasons for my dislike of snakes: (1) It was a snake that tempted Eve. (2) Some snakes are poisonous, and I do not know the difference. (3) I just don't like snakes. I do not want to be bitten by a snake of any kind—even a harmless garter snake—but I absolutely do not want to be bitten by a rattlesnake, a copperhead, or a water moccasin. They are deadly.

Some people divide sins into big and small categories, with some being worse than others. To them, there is nothing wrong with telling a harmless white lie, as it falls into the small sin category. However, the Scripture is clear in that "he that is guilty of the least is guilty of the whole" (James 2:10). What is wrong is wrong, and what is right is right. Nevertheless, there are some sins that are deadly, sins that God especially hates.

The writer of Proverbs told us plainly about the sins that God hates. They are an abomination unto Him; in other words, He is so repulsed by them that it makes Him sick. Committing one of these sins is the equivalent to being bitten by a poisonous snake.

1. A Proud Look. God hates pride. Pride goes before destruction and a haughty spirit before a fall. Learn to be humble. Do not wait for God to humble you. The Bible teaches us to humble ourselves. God will not despise a broken and a contrite heart, but He hates a proud look.

2. A Lying Tongue. God is a God of truth, and He hates lying! We should speak truth, the whole truth, and nothing but the truth. Psalm 120:2 says, "Deliver my soul, O LORD, from lying lips, and from a deceitful tongue." Ephesians 4:25 gives us this instruction: "Wherefore putting away lying, speak every man truth with his neighbour."

3. Hands That Are Swift to Shed Innocent Blood. You may not be guilty of literally killing someone, but have you ever misjudged someone? Have you ever accused someone of being wrong, only to discover that they were innocent? God is always on the side of the innocent. That is why God tells us not to judge anything before its time (I Corinthians 4:5) and that it is folly to answer a matter before you fully hear it (Proverbs 18:13). Always judge a man as innocent until he is proven guilty.

4. A Heart That Deviseth Wicked Imaginations. Sin always starts in the heart. God has given us spiritual weapons that enable us to "cast down imaginations, and every high thing that exalteth itself against the knowledge of God, and [to bring] into captivity every thought to the obedience of Christ" (II Corinthians 10:4-5). We must control our heart, our mind, and our thoughts to prevent sinful imaginations from becoming reality.

5. Feet That Be Swift in Running to Mischief. Some people are quick to get involved in wrongdoing. They do not think twice

about doing something illegal or immoral. But they need to think twice, because God detests their actions. Instead of running toward sin, they need to run from it. The Bible instructs us: Flee fornication (I Corinthians 6:18); flee youthful lusts, flee from idolatry (I Corinthians 10:14); and flee from strife, evil surmisings, and the love of money (I Timothy 6:4-11).

6. A False Witness That Speaketh Lies. It is bad enough to lie, but your iniquity is compounded when you give false evidence against a man who is accused. You are not only lying, but you are committing a crime called perjury, or giving false testimony. And God hates it.

7. He That Soweth Discord among Brethren. God loves unity among brethren (Psalm 133). He hates for someone to be the cause of disunity. Some people delight in sowing discord. They love a dispute, a division, or a fight (I Corinthians 1:10). But God loves peace, tranquility, and unity!

The Garden of Eden was paradise until the serpent tempted Eve to sin. The world was a garden until sin entered. All sin is wrong, but the sins God hates are like the presence of a poisonous snake. Avoid them like the plague! Hate the things that God hates, and love the things that He loves. Keep the serpent out of your garden.

Practice:

Practice the fruit of the Spirit in your life. Increase the amount of love, joy, peace, longsuffering, patience, gentleness, goodness, and self-control in your daily life. This will help you to flee from the sins that would poison your life.

Prayer:

Lord, I want to look at things through Your eyes and be an instrument of Your righteousness. Help me to guard my heart against pride, lies, mischief, and evil imaginations.

DAY 21: WARNINGS AGAINST ADULTERY (PROVERBS 6:20-35)

My son, keep your father's commandment always,
And forsake not the law of your mother, I say.

Bind them forever on your heart, let them stay;
Tie them securely so they won't get away.

Their teachings will lead you and shine light on your life;
As you sleep, they will keep you safe from all strife.

When you wake, they will tell you just what to do.
[So listen, and hear what they say unto you!]

The commandments are a lamp and the law a shining light.
The reproofs are guides for the way of life.

So stay clear of a married woman; watch and don't be
        led astray
By her flattery, her beauty, or her eyes that turn your way.

You may consort with a harlot, pay her price, a piece
        of bread.
This one's seeking, not your money, but your precious
        life instead!

Can a man a fire kindle on his breast and not be charred?
Can he walk on coals of fire but not be blistered nor
        be scarred?

So who goes in to a neighbor's wife shall unpunished
        not remain.
He must surely pay the price, if he e'er returns again.

Men do not despise a thief if he's hungry and he steals.
Yet, if he is apprehended, all his house he'll have to yield.

But adultery with a woman is committed by a fool.
He destroys himself who does it, for he's broken life's
        great rule.

For dishonor's wounds he'll carry, until his own life's
        dying day,
And the disgrace that's his portion will not ever
        pass away!

So vindictive is a husband's wrath, there's no pity
that remains.
He is swallowed up in sorrow, in great anger and
great pain.

He will not regard a ransom, neither will he rest content;
Though he's offered many presents, he'll have nothing
but contempt.

LEAVE THE LIGHT ON!

Proverb:
"For the commandment is a lamp; and the law is light; and reproofs of instruction are the way of life" (Proverbs 6:23).

Precept:
A popular slogan used by a well-known motel chain is "We'll leave the light on for you!"[9] They want you to know that no matter what time of day or night or what circumstances you face, they are awaiting and anticipating your arrival. Likewise, Proverbs 6:23 reminds us of the fact that God's commandments are like a lamp, and His law is like a light giving instruction that will bring us safely to the house of God.

As a boy, I often walked several miles to church. The walk to church was not that bad, but returning those several miles in the dark was a challenge to my young mind because I would hear the howling of animals and imagine them to be close by. I had to walk over seven hills to get to my home. But when I topped the last hill, I could see the lamp shining through the kitchen window. It was a source of great gladness and relief as I headed toward home with the light showing me the way.

"The entrance of God's word giveth light." (See Psalm 119:130.) The Word of God is like a beacon to a weary mariner that signals his journey is almost over and he will soon reach the safe haven of home port. It is also a welcoming light to someone who is trying to find his way home.

Some close friends of mine were a very faithful couple who raised their children in the fear and admonition of the Lord. Sadly, when their son turned eighteen, he slipped through his bedroom window during the night and left home. His parents were shocked and dismayed the following morning when they found him missing, along with a note explaining his decision to denounce his godly upbringing and pursue his own path. Although they were heartsick, they decided to leave the window unlocked and the light on in his room, in hopes that he would return.

Several years later, the young man came to a camp meeting and stood outside, listening as the sermon was preached. As the preacher appealed to those who had wandered away from God, the young man was persuaded to go to the altar, where he rededicated his life to God. Although he did not crawl back through the bedroom window, the light of the Word showed him the pathway home.

Psalm 119:105 says, "Thy word is a lamp unto my feet, and a light unto my path." It is important that we leave the light on—for ourselves and for others who may be lost in darkness and trying to find their way home.

Practice:

As you read God's Word, allow His "light" to shine on your heart and to show you areas that you need to improve. Shine the light of God to those around you. Be sensitive to God's leading. You may be the one whom God uses to light the path for a lost soul trying to find its way home.

Prayer:

Lord, as I read Your Word, help me to allow Your light to penetrate any darkness in my life, and use me to show Your light to those around me.

Week 4

PROVERBS 7

*My son, keep my words, and lay up my command-
ments with thee. Keep my commandments, and live;
and my law as the apple of thine eye. Bind them upon
thy fingers, write them upon the table of thine heart.
Say unto wisdom, Thou art my sister; and call understanding thy kinswoman: that they may keep thee from
the strange woman, from the stranger which flattereth
with her words.*

*For at the window of my house I looked through my
casement, and beheld among the simple ones, I discerned
among the youths, a young man void of understanding,
passing through the street near her corner; and he went
the way to her house, in the twilight, in the evening, in
the black and dark night: and, behold, there met him
a woman with the attire of an harlot, and subtil of
heart. (She is loud and stubborn; her feet abide not in
her house: now is she without, now in the streets, and
lieth in wait at every corner.) So she caught him, and
kissed him, and with an impudent face said unto him,
I have peace offerings with me; this day have I payed
my vows. Therefore came I forth to meet thee, diligently to seek thy face, and I have found thee. I have
decked my bed with coverings of tapestry, with carved
works, with fine linen of Egypt. I have perfumed my
bed with myrrh, aloes, and cinnamon. Come, let us
take our fill of love until the morning: let us solace
ourselves with loves. For the goodman is not at home,
he is gone a long journey: he hath taken a bag of money
with him, and will come home at the day appointed.
With her much fair speech she caused him to yield,
with the flattering of her lips she forced him. He goeth*

*after her straightway, as an ox goeth to the slaughter,
or as a fool to the correction of the stocks; till a dart
strike through his liver; as a bird hasteth to the snare,
and knoweth not that it is for his life.*

*Hearken unto me now therefore, O ye children, and
attend to the words of my mouth. Let not thine heart
decline to her ways, go not astray in her paths. For she
hath cast down many wounded: yea, many strong men
have been slain by her. Her house is the way to hell,
going down to the chambers of death.*

DAY 22: WATCH OUT! (PROVERBS 7:1-4)

My son, keep my words and store them as treasure
[In spite of temptations by women of pleasure].

If you keep my commands you will live and not die,
So keep my directions as the apple of your eye.

Like a seal on your fingers do not let them depart;
Remember to write them on the door of your heart.

You should say unto wisdom, "You're a sister so dear!"
And unto understanding, "You're my kinsman, it's clear!"

THE APPLE OF YOUR EYE

Proverb:
"Keep my commandments, and live; and my law as the
apple of thine eye" (Proverbs 7:2).

Precept:
The term "apple of your eye" originally had to do with the
round pupil in the center of your eye. However, it has come to
mean that which you prize—the person or thing that you care
for the most. Scripture recommends that we regard God, His
teaching, and His commandments as the apple of our eye—the
things we value greater than anything else in life.

How much do you revere the commandments of God? Are

they just good philosophies that are helpful if you wish to use them? Are they rules and principles that will help you have a richer and fuller life, if you heed their teachings? Or are they essential ingredients without which you would be sadly deficient in your earthly life, and are they absolutely necessary for you to inherit the promises of the life to come?

In the wisdom of the writer of Proverbs, in the teachings of other portions of Scripture, and in the strong opinion of this writer, the commandments of God must be valued above everything else. The teachings of Scripture are essential ingredients to live an overcoming Christian life, and they are absolutely necessary for any one of us to inherit the promises of eternal life.

In the beginning, God made one man and woman whom He instructed to multiply and replenish the earth. He also gave them oversight of the beautiful Garden of Eden. He left only one prohibition to them (as far as the Word of God reveals), which was that they should not eat of the tree of the knowledge of good and evil. (See Genesis 2:17.) When Adam and Eve disobeyed God's commandment, death came on the entire world and creation was drastically altered. Man's life was affected for centuries to come. If God responded in such a manner when there were only two people on the earth, how careful we should be to treasure and obey His commandments today!

When Noah and his wife and family were saved by grace in order to perpetuate the human race, Noah was careful to build the ark of their salvation exactly as God had said. "Thus did Noah; according to all that God commanded him, so did he" (Genesis 6:22). When God instructed Moses to build a tabernacle, He said, "According to all that I shew thee, after the pattern of the tabernacle, and the pattern of all the instruments thereof, even so shall ye make it" (Exodus 25:9).

Although we are not commanded to tend a garden, as Adam; or to build an ark for the saving of our household, as Noah; or to build a tabernacle, as Moses; the principle is the same. We should examine the Bible line upon line and precept upon precept. (See Isaiah 28:13.) We should "study to shew [ourselves] approved unto God . . . rightly dividing the word of truth" (II Timothy 2:15). Jesus said, "Search the scriptures; for in them ye think ye have eternal life: and they are they which testify of me" (John 5:39).

If God required Adam to keep His commandments, if He required Noah to build the ark as he was instructed, if He required Moses to make everything according to the pattern He had shown him, then it is logical to believe that God wants us to treat His laws, His words, and His commandments as "the apple of our eye"!

Practice:

Treasure the law of the Lord. Reading your Bible, memorizing Scripture, taking notes during sermons, and praying and singing the Word are all ways that we can prize and value the commandments of the Lord. "Thy word have I hid in mine heart, that I might not sin against thee" (Psalm 119:11).

Prayer:

Lord, help me to treasure Your Word. Let me love Your law and meditate upon the godly and righteous principles it contains. Help me to honor Your Word by my obedience to it each day.

DAY 23: THE STRANGE WOMAN (PROVERBS 7:5-27)

To keep you from the woman who is strange in His sight,
Who shows up with flattery to allure in the night.

For at my casement window, I looked out to see
A picture of folly, as sure as could be.

I beheld from my casement a young man in his prime;
He was absent of wisdom, out for a "good time."

Passing the corner of the strange woman's street,
And taking the road to her house, to meet

With this woman, he met, out of everyone's sight,
In the twilight of evening, in the black of the night.

Sure enough, she met him, with purpose concealed.
She was dressed like a harlot, and her heart was as well.

She was fickle, she was worldly, she was stubborn
    and wrong,
And her heart could not rest in her own house for long.

She was out in the streets, now in the town square.
She was lurking in ambush; where he looked,
    she was there.

When she saw him she gave him a kiss and invited
With an impudent face as she wooed and enticed.

"A great feast I have made as I finished my vow;
Since the table is laid, won't you go with me now?

"I've been looking for you, as I searched to and fro,
And now that I've found you, I can't let you go.

"I have furnished my bed with tapestry that's rare,
With linens from Egypt and carved works everywhere.

"There's expensive perfume of life's very best,
Myrrh, aloes, cinnamon, and all of the rest.

"Come, let us take our fill of love till the day.
Let us eat, let us drink of our love every way.

"I am married, it's no matter, my husband is gone
On a faraway journey, so we're safe, we're alone.

"He has taken a large bag of money to spend,
And he won't arrive home till the holiday's end."

So she wooed him, she begged him, she urged, and she won,
With her smooth speech and lips till the foul deed was done.

Like an ox that is led to the slaughter he came,
Like a fool who is put in the stocks for his shame.

Like a bird unsuspecting flies straight to a snare,
Never seeing the signs of the danger that's there.

And now, all my children, you must listen to me!
Attend to the words of my mouth and you'll see,

Your heart must not be enticed by her talk
Or be tempted to follow the path that she walks.

She has cast down her wounded and slain her strong men.
[We must see that this never happens again!]

The strange woman's house is a place, I can tell,
That will lead to the chambers of death and of hell.

OUT OF THE NIGHT

Proverb:

"Passing through the street near her corner; and he went the way to her house, in the twilight, in the evening, in the black and dark night" (Proverbs 7:8-9).

Precept:

What is really going on here? A young man, with no discernment, has gone out into the streets to look for a good time. He is not a wicked person, but he has a wrong set of values and is looking for a certain kind of woman who will satisfy his desires. Unfortunately, there are immoral women (and men) who are willing to flaunt their sexual favors to anyone they can seduce. This particular night, this young man is deceived by one such a woman.

She is married, but her husband is gone on a business trip. She can't stand to stay at home, so she has dressed herself as a prostitute and is working the streets as she looks for a victim. She tries one street corner and then another. She is loud, crude, and impudent. When she sees the young man, she catches him and kisses him. With flattery, she entices him to come to her home where she has a beautiful room, nice smelling ointments, and a soft bed. The young man yields to her charms and finds himself following her home like an ox being led to the slaughter.

Although the young man thinks he is just out for a good time, he does not realize that the path down which this woman is leading him heads straight to death and hell. She cares nothing for him but will cast him aside after she has had her fill. What seemed so alluring in the shadows and darkness of night will have little appeal in the harsh light of morning.

Jesus taught that evil men hate the light. The light exposes the hideousness of their deeds. John 3:19-21 says, "And this is the condemnation, that light is come into the world, and men loved darkness rather than light, because their deeds were evil. For every one that doeth evil hateth the light, neither cometh to the light, lest his deeds should be reproved. But he that doeth truth cometh to the light, that his deeds may be made manifest, that they are wrought in God."

Although we live in a wicked world where every kind of evil imaginable is available, we should not be entrapped by those who love darkness. We should come out of the night into His marvelous light.

Practice:

Do not let yourself be deceived by the darkness that surrounds us. Keep a true perspective of the actions and attitudes that prevail in our world today. Recognize those that take you into the dark places. Determine that you will follow the light of God into abundant life.

Prayer:

Lord, please keep me from straying into the darkness. Help me to stay in the light of Your goodness and truth.

PROVERBS 8

Doth not wisdom cry? and understanding put forth her voice? She standeth in the top of high places, by the way in the places of the paths. She crieth at the gates, at the entry of the city, at the coming in at the doors. Unto you, O men, I call; and my voice is to the sons of man. O ye simple, understand wisdom: and, ye fools, be ye of an understanding heart. Hear; for I will speak of excellent things; and the opening of my lips shall be right things. For my mouth shall speak truth; and wickedness is an abomination to my lips. All the words of my mouth are in righteousness; there is nothing froward or perverse in them. They are all plain to him that understandeth, and right to them that find knowledge. Receive my instruction, and not silver; and knowledge rather than choice gold. For wisdom is better than rubies; and all the things that may be desired are not to be compared to it.

I wisdom dwell with prudence, and find out knowledge of witty inventions. The fear of the LORD *is to hate evil: pride, and arrogancy, and the evil way, and the froward mouth, do I hate. Counsel is mine, and sound wisdom: I am understanding; I have strength. By me kings reign, and princes decree justice. By me princes rule, and nobles, even all the judges of the earth. I love them that love me; and those that seek me early shall find me. Riches and honour are with me; yea, durable riches and righteousness. My fruit is better than gold, yea, than fine gold; and my revenue than choice silver. I lead in the way of righteousness, in the midst of the paths of judgment: that I may cause those that love me to inherit substance; and I will fill their treasures.*

The LORD *possessed me in the beginning of his way, before his works of old. I was set up from everlasting, from the beginning, or ever the earth was. When there were no depths, I was brought forth; when there were no fountains abounding with water. Before the mountains were settled, before the hills was I brought forth: while as yet he had not made the earth, nor the fields, nor the highest part of the dust of the world. When he prepared the heavens, I was there: when he set a compass upon the face of the depth: when he established the clouds above: when he strengthened the fountains of the deep: when he gave to the sea his decree, that the waters should not pass his commandment: when he appointed the foundations of the earth: then I was by him, as one brought up with him: and I was daily his delight, rejoicing always before him; rejoicing in the habitable part of his earth; and my delights were with the sons of men.*

Now therefore hearken unto me, O ye children: for

blessed are they that keep my ways. Hear instruction,
and be wise, and refuse it not. Blessed is the man that
heareth me, watching daily at my gates, waiting at the
posts of my doors. For whoso findeth me findeth life,
and shall obtain favour of the LORD. But he that sinneth
against me wrongeth his own soul: all they that hate me
love death.

DAY 24: WISDOM'S OFFER (PROVERBS 8:1-10)

Is it Wisdom's voice that I hear crying out?
Understanding speaking to us with a shout?

On top of the heights, beside the way,
Where the crossroads meet, Wisdom stays.

She cries out at the gates, takes her stand in the streets;
At the entrance of the town, she loudly speaks:

"To you, oh men, my voice cries to you all.
To the sons of men, I'm making my call.

"To the simple and thoughtless, lacking discretion,
To the selfish fools, please pay attention.

"I've a message to give, honesty and insight;
With my lips I'll disclose all the things that are right.

"For my mouth shall speak nothing but truth to the Lord.
Lying lips are a disgrace to God and His Word.

"All the words of my mouth are sincere and upright;
There is nothing deceitful, nothing crooked in sight.

"It is wisdom, plain and simple, for those who will learn;
It is right for those who will knowledge discern.

"Choose instruction instead of silver so pure,
And wisdom in place of fine gold that endures."

SPEAKING OUT

Proverb:

"Doth not wisdom cry? and understanding put forth her voice?" (Proverbs 8:1).

Precept:

Edmond Burke said, "All that is necessary for the triumph of evil is for good men to do nothing."[10] It is a time for men and women of wisdom to speak out for the things that need to be said.

In the Book of Proverbs, wisdom is personified as a woman. She cries, or lifts up her voice, in the high places. She speaks in the city gate; she speaks at the crossroads. Sometimes when you see all the wrong that is done, all the injustices that exist, and the evil that is triumphing, you think, Why doesn't somebody say something? Martin Niemoeller, a pastor in Hitler's Germany, said, "They came first for the Communists, and I didn't speak up. . . . Then they came for the Jews, and I didn't speak up. . . . Then they came for the trade unionists, and I didn't speak up. . . . Then they came for the Catholics, and I didn't speak up. . . . Then they came for me."[11]

Hans Christian Andersen's story, "The Emperor's New Clothes," supports the premise that those who are wise should speak up. In this story, the emperor was noted for his love of new clothes. When swindlers came to town, they persuaded him that they could weave a beautiful fabric of brilliant colors that had the power to become invisible to someone who was unfit for his or her office or position. They proceeded to fit the emperor, then went through the motions of weaving the beautiful, magical cloth. The emperor sent different people to check on the progress of the new cloth, but no one would admit that they could not see anything, for fear of being labeled as stupid and unfit for their position. When the emperor finally came out wearing his supposed "new clothes," everyone exclaimed about them, except for a small child who exclaimed, "But he hasn't got anything on!" One person began to whisper to another, until the whole town proclaimed the truth that the emperor was not wearing any clothes.[12]

The Bible tells the story of two kings who were discussing

going into battle against a common enemy. (See II Kings 22.) One king called in his prophets, who all began to foretell a great victory. The other king asked specifically for a prophet of Jehovah to come so they could ask his advice. While the other prophets continued to predict success, Micaiah told the king that he was being misled by the other prophets and that the battle would end not in victory but in defeat. Although he had to speak out against the majority, Micaiah told the truth. Everything came to pass just as he had prophesied.

In a world where the majority is speaking out against morality and everything godly, it is time for someone to speak out about injustice and wrong, sin and unrighteousness, and the need for repentance, faith, and revival. I am reminded of a line I had to use while learning to type in high school that read, "Now is the time for all good men to come to the aid of their country." It is time for good men and woman to come to the aid of their church, their city, their state, and their country by speaking out about Christ and the gospel and about the coming of our Lord.

Practice:

Take a stand for what is right in your city, state, and nation. Stay informed of upcoming decisions that will affect Christians and act accordingly. In the electronic age in which we live, it is very easy to keep abreast of the latest happenings and to let your voice be heard by signing petitions or sending email to your congressmen and senators. Do not stand by and do nothing. Speak out, and let your voice be heard.

Prayer:

Lord, I want truth and righteousness to prevail. Help me to do my part to further the cause of Christ and to stand for what is right.

DAY 25: THE BENEFITS OF WISDOM (PROVERBS 8:11-21)

To know wisdom is better than jewels so rare,
And no choice possession can with her compare.

I, Wisdom, inhabit the place prudence lives;
There I find out the knowledge intelligence gives.

The fear of the Lord makes all evil despised,
All arrogance, hypocrisy, perversity, and pride.

Sound wisdom, wise counsel, and fortitude are mine.
I have strength, I have insight, I have prudence besides.

It is through me rulers govern the people and state,
Lawgivers render justice and decide on men's fate.

All the princes and nobles are made rulers by me,
And the judges of the earth will make their decrees.

To all who love me, I will return their love freely.
Seek me early; you will find me if you seek me diligently.

You'll find riches and honor and glory that's secure,
Position, good fortune, great possessions that endure.

My fruit is something better than gold, the choicest kind,
And my revenue much surpasses the best silver you
        can find.

I do rightly and fairly; all I want is righteousness.
The path of justice is where you are blessed.

Those who love me, I will bless them, with great riches I'll fill,
Give treasures aplenty to them in my will.

EARLY-BIRD SPECIAL

Proverb:
    "I love them that love me; and those that seek me early
shall find me" (Proverbs 8:17).

Precept:
    Everybody knows that the early bird gets the worm.
Department stores have utilized this theory with their "early-

bird specials." They put specific items on sale from 6 AM until NOON. Only those who make it to the store within that time frame can purchase the advertised item for the sale price. Sleepyheads will miss out on all the bargains.

Although God is not a department store that operates only during certain hours, He does have his own early-bird special. His Word promises that those who seek Him early shall find Him. Early is not necessarily a specific time, but it is the act of seeking God first at the beginning of your day, whatever time your day begins. Matthew 6:33 instructs us, "Seek ye first the kingdom of God, and his righteousness; and all these things shall be added unto you." Jeremiah 29:13 says, "And ye shall seek me, and find me, when ye shall search for me with all your heart." If you seek Him, you will find Him. And that is quite a bargain!

Practice:

Set a specific time at the beginning of your day to seek God. If you can, try to get up very early one morning just for the specific purpose of spending time with God. There is something very special about being alone with God in the early morning hours.

Prayer:

Lord, help me to seek first the kingdom of God every day and in all that I do. I want You to have first priority in my life. I do not want to miss out on anything special that You may want to do for me or through me during the course of my day. Thank You for helping me to seek You early, that I may find You! In Jesus' name. Amen.

DAY 26: A PERSON NAMED WISDOM (PROVERBS 8:22-36)

The Lord possessed me (before He began
His Creation of old) as the first of His plan.

Established from eternity, ere the earth did appear,
When it was created, I was already here.

Before there were great depths of water, I was there,
Before all earth's fountains sprang up in the air.

Before mountains were pushing their way to the sky,
Before all the hilltops were made, I was nigh!

When the new world and its land and fields were all bare,
Ere a clod of the earth lifted up, I was there!

I was with God when He made all the heavens appear;
When He fixed the foundations of earth, I was near.

When He made firm the skies in the heavens so high
And established the deep foundations besides,

When He settled the level of the oceans He made
So the waters would not pass the decree that He laid,

I stood close beside Him as a helper always;
He delighted in me as a friend, day by day.

When Creation was done, I rejoiced at the sight,
And the men whom God made were His greatest delight.

Therefore, hearken to me, oh ye children of mine,
For you are blessed if you do not reject what is thine.

Be wise, and listen to what I say;
You are happy if you will my words obey.

For blessed is he with a listening ear,
Who at the gate is watching for me to appear.

He who finds wisdom, finds life and is wise,
And receives the favor of God as a prize.

He who loses on wisdom has his own self to hate,
For to fail to find wisdom is a fatal mistake.

WHO IS WISDOM?

Proverb:

"I was set up from everlasting. . . . When there were no depths, I was brought forth. . . . When he prepared the heavens, I was there" (Proverbs 8:23, 24, 27).

Precept:

Who is the mysterious person who goes by the name "wisdom"? To understand this passage you must realize that the figure of speech, personification, is being used. Personification is giving human traits (qualities, feelings, action, or characteristics) to non-living objects (things, colors, qualities, or ideas). In this proverb, wisdom is the virtue that is given a feminine personification.

You cannot separate a man from his word. You can speak of a man's word, a man's wisdom, or a man's face, but you are actually talking about the man himself. Likewise, you cannot separate God from His Word or His wisdom.

John 1:1-3 states, "In the beginning was the Word, and the Word was with God, and the Word was God. The same was in the beginning with God. All things were made by him; and without him was not any thing made that was made."

Genesis 1:1-3 states, "In the beginning God created the heaven and the earth. And the earth was without form, and void; and darkness was upon the face of the deep. And the Spirit of God moved upon the face of the waters. And God said, Let there be light: and there was light."

When God spoke, it was His Word, and when God created, it was His wisdom. Wisdom was set up from everlasting (Proverbs 8:23). Wisdom was brought forth when there were no depths (Proverbs 8:24). When the heavens were prepared by God, wisdom was there (Proverbs 8:27). It was not someone else—a creature other than God—it was God!

That is why the beginning of wisdom is to fear God. That is why to have wisdom is to know God. Who is wisdom? Wisdom is God's personification!

Practice:

Is there an area of your life in which you lack wisdom to deal with it appropriately? Have you checked to see what God's

Word says about it? Use a concordance to find verses of
Scripture that deal with that particular topic. Pray as you read
those verses that God's wisdom may be revealed to you.

Prayer:
Lord, I want to know You. Help me to hear Your voice as it
speaks Your wisdom to me. Let Your Word give needed guidance for my situation or area of struggle.

PROVERBS 9

*Wisdom hath builded her house, she hath hewn out
her seven pillars: she hath killed her beasts; she hath
mingled her wine; she hath also furnished her table. She
hath sent forth her maidens: she crieth upon the highest
places of the city, Whoso is simple, let him turn in hither:
as for him that wanteth understanding, she saith to him,
Come, eat of my bread, and drink of the wine which I
have mingled. Forsake the foolish, and live; and go in the
way of understanding. He that reproveth a scorner getteth to himself shame: and he that rebuketh a wicked
man getteth himself a blot. Reprove not a scorner, lest he
hate thee: rebuke a wise man, and he will love thee. Give
instruction to a wise man, and he will be yet wiser: teach
a just man, and he will increase in learning. The fear of
the LORD is the beginning of wisdom: and the knowledge
of the holy is understanding. For by me thy days shall be
multiplied, and the years of thy life shall be increased. If
thou be wise, thou shalt be wise for thyself: but if thou
scornest, thou alone shalt bear it.*

*A foolish woman is clamorous: she is simple, and
knoweth nothing. For she sitteth at the door of her
house, on a seat in the high places of the city, to call passengers who go right on their ways: Whoso is simple, let
him turn in hither: and as for him that wanteth understanding, she saith to him, Stolen waters are sweet, and
bread eaten in secret is pleasant. But he knoweth not
that the dead are there; and that her guests are in the
depths of hell.*

DAY 27: THE HOUSE OF WISDOM (PROVERBS 9:1-5)

This is the house that wisdom made,
With seven pillars all arrayed,

Mixed her wine and killed the beasts,
And set the table for the feast.

On the streets her maidens cry
Out to every passerby:

"Let the simple turn this way,
To the senseless hear me say:

"'Come and eat of what I've fixed;
Drink the wine that I have mixed.'"

RSVP

Proverb:

"Wisdom hath builded her house, she hath hewn out her seven pillars. . . . She saith . . . Come, eat of my bread, and drink of the wine which I have mingled" (Proverbs 9:1, 4, 5).

Precept:

It is customary to send out invitations for a special occasion that you may be hosting and to request an RSVP. The term "RSVP" comes from the French expression *répondez s'il vous plait*, meaning "please respond."[13]

In this Proverb, Wisdom is having a party. She is inviting her guests. Her building is finished and preparations are being made for those who will come. Her first invitation is to the simple, or those who are ignorant of the conventions. They are welcome to attend. Her object is to teach the uninformed of the ways of wisdom.

There is no shame in not knowing, if you have not had the opportunity to learn. There is a great difference in being uninformed and being deliberately foolish. Some of the greatest and most successful men on earth are men who did not have a formal education.

I remember a man who was born in the French part of Louisiana. He did not know very much, and his English was heavily accented. But he had a desire to learn. After he received the Holy Ghost, he determined to master his lack of education. In the same area, there was a lovely, Spirit-filled lady who was a well-educated schoolteacher. She was respected for her learning and her gracious manner.

When the man without an education and the educated woman decided to marry, there were those who had doubts about the relationship. Some ministerial leaders called the lady to discuss her marriage plans. They warned her about the dangers of such a fine person as herself marrying someone of such limited education. They advised her to break off the courtship and cancel the marriage plans.

However, the lady saw potential in the man she had agreed to marry. She had a genuine love for him and expectations for his improvement and his future. In spite of the warnings she had received, she married the young man, who became a minister. As a teacher, she used her education and teaching skills to help him overcome his educational deficiency and to reach his ambitions. He was a voracious reader, and he sought every opportunity to broaden his experience and knowledge. He became a successful pastor and an outstanding evangelist, preaching camps and conventions far and wide. Those who heard him never forgot the sermons he preached. He became a district and national leader of men and ministers and lived a life of honor and wisdom. He had answered the invitation and accepted the opportunity to enter the house of wisdom.

What will your answer be? Will you respond to Wisdom's invitation? Do you wish to trade your inadequacies for better understanding, more knowledge, and greater wisdom? Fear God, for this is the beginning of wisdom. Profit from instruction, reproof, and correction. Read voraciously, listen intently, and pray consistently. You will find yourself in the house of seven pillars, feasting at the table of wisdom and knowledge.

Practice:

Learning does not have to take place in a classroom environment but can happen in a variety of ways. You can learn by reading books or listening to audio books as you travel. You may learn by example, by letting someone else show you or tell you how it is done, or by experiencing it for yourself. The key is to always be looking for opportunities to learn. Have an open mind and apply yourself to learning new skills, languages, crafts, or subjects. Most importantly, continue to seek after wisdom and knowledge that come only from God.

Prayer:

Lord, I desire to have wisdom. Open my understanding of You. Help me to find the time and the ways to increase my knowledge.

DAY 28: WISDOM'S PLEA (PROVERBS 9:6-12)

If folly you forsake, you will certainly live;
Understanding and prudence to you I will give.

When scoffers you reprove, for yourself you get blame,
And rebuke of the wicked will bring you the same.

Reprove not an arrogant man or he'll hate you;
Rebuking a wise man will cause him to love you.

If a man of good sense you will teach something more,
He'll gain knowledge and wisdom he was missing before.

The beginning of wisdom's to give the Lord fear,
For the knowledge of God brings the holy One near.

For by me all your days will be multiplied, it's true,
So that many more years shall be added to you.

If true wisdom you gain, you're the one who can shout.
If you scorn and reject, you're the one who's left out.

UNINVITED GUESTS

Proverb:

"He that reproveth a scorner getteth to himself shame: and he that rebuketh a wicked man getteth himself a blot" (Proverbs 9:7).

Precept:

If you are having a feast, do not invite a scorner. He will ridicule you, accuse you, and revile you. There is no use in inviting such a person to the house of wisdom.

It has been said that ridicule is the weapon of fools. If a man does not have the basis for an argument, he will use ridicule against you. The word for "scorner" in this passage means "make a face at"! A scorner will try to refute your sane and sensible arguments with mockery in order to discredit you.

While living in the dorm during my college years, I often talked to people about God and the Bible. One particular fellow liked to come to my room to talk about verses of Scripture with me, although he usually asked questions in a ridiculing way. Once he asked, "Are you one of those people who jabber in tongues?" He knew full well that I did believe in and had experienced the infilling of the Holy Ghost with the evidence of other tongues. Most of the time, his questions led to arguments, as he would try to dispute my beliefs. And if he could not, he would then begin to attack with ridicule and mockery.

One day while discussing a particular doctrinal subject, the debate became rather loud. After a few minutes, there was a knock on my door. It was the dorm supervisor's wife. She immediately asked, "Bill, what religion are you?" As I explained to her my religious beliefs, she began to weep. She then said, "I am a backslider from your faith. I am married to an atheist. Would you pray for me and my husband?"

The scorner was unaffected by the religious discussion, but this woman was drawn to the truth and expressed her desire for herself and her family to be saved. It is my good pleasure to recount that both she and her husband were converted and lived godly lives in their church in the South. Their son, who is the namesake of his father, is presently a foreign missionary of many years. Both of his sons (the dorm supervisor's grandsons) are also ministers.

To correct a mocker invites insult. But one who is wise will gladly receive instruction.

Practice:

Do not waste your time arguing or debating with those who scorn your walk with God and ridicule what you believe. Your argument will not convince them to change their position but will only leave you frustrated and discouraged. Jesus taught this principle in Matthew 7:6 when He said, "Give not that which is holy unto the dogs, neither cast ye your pearls before swine, lest they trample them under their feet, and turn again and rend you." He admonished that you should "bless them that curse you, and pray for them which despitefully use you" (Luke 6:28).

Prayer:

Lord, I want to be a soulwinner and tell others about You. As I approach people, give me wisdom to know who is open to receive or who is scornful and full of unbelief. Help me to learn that it is not profitable to engage in an argument to establish a doctrinal position and that I should use wisdom to deflect a confrontation. Lead me to people who are hungry to hear about You.

Week 5

Day 29: The Foolish Woman (Proverbs 9:13-18)

A woman who's foolish is fickle and vain;
She needs someone to keep her from bringing more shame.

She sits on a seat at the door in her gown,
In a visible place in the sight of the town,

And calls out to them who pass by on their way,
"I've a message for you, and here's what I say:

"Whosoever is simple, just turn right in here."
If you lack understanding, she speaks to your ear:

"Stolen water is sweet; I've a message to share,
That bread eaten in secret is more pleasant—if you dare."

But you never would know, and the dead cannot tell
That her guests all are ghosts and they're already in hell.

No Thanks!

Proverb:
"A foolish woman is clamorous: she is simple, and knoweth nothing. For she sitteth at the door of her house, on a seat in the high places of the city, to call passengers who go right on their ways" (Proverbs 9:13-15).

Precept:
Wisdom is not the only one who is sending out invitations for people to come to her house. There is also a foolish, simple, clamorous, ignorant woman who is sitting at her door, calling for people to stop at her place for a while. This is the house of Folly.

Just as wisdom is personified as a woman, so folly is personified as a woman who is the embodiment of evil. In this passage, she is giving an invitation to the passersby to enter her house and stay awhile.

Waiting inside is a rendezvous with a scandalous person for a sinister purpose. Folly offers "stolen waters" that are sweet and "bread eaten in secret" that she advertises as "pleasant." Why is it that the forbidden is so attractive to some people? They flaunt the law, mock at conviction, and assert that they are not subject to the moral and social restraints of others. These are the people who seek to partake in something forbidden, something secret, or something scandalous.

However, our reply to the solicitation to participate in promiscuous activities, lewd and immoral behavior, or secretive indecencies is to quickly and firmly reply, "No thanks! I am not interested in a dalliance with a promiscuous person. I am not interested in wasting my money, endangering my health, and injuring my character by succumbing to such enticements."

The writer of Proverbs revealed the unspoken dangers that await someone who is enticed by this woman named Folly: "But he knoweth not that the dead are there; and that her guests are in the depths of hell" (Proverbs 9:18). In answer to the many temptations of this world that would offer stolen waters and secret sins, just remember the end result that leads to death and hell, and say, "No thanks!"

Practice:

The easiest way to insure that you will be able to say no is to plan ahead and to make guidelines that you will abide by. Thinking about dangers and temptations before you are faced with them will give you the courage to say no.

Prayer:

Lord, help me to resist temptation. Give me the courage to say no when I find myself faced with a situation that threatens to take me down the path of folly. Guard my heart and my mind, I pray.

PROVERBS 10

The proverbs of Solomon. A wise son maketh a glad father: but a foolish son is the heaviness of his mother. Treasures of wickedness profit nothing: but righteousness delivereth from death. The LORD will not suffer the soul of the righteous to famish: but he casteth away the substance of the wicked. He becometh poor that dealeth with a slack hand: but the hand of the diligent maketh rich. He that gathereth in summer is a wise son: but he that sleepeth in harvest is a son that causeth shame.

Blessings are upon the head of the just: but violence covereth the mouth of the wicked. The memory of the just is blessed: but the name of the wicked shall rot. The wise in heart will receive commandments: but a prating fool shall fall. He that walketh uprightly walketh surely: but he that perverteth his ways shall be known. He that winketh with the eye causeth sorrow: but a prating fool shall fall. The mouth of a righteous man is a well of life: but violence covereth the mouth of the wicked. Hatred stirreth up strifes: but love covereth all sins.

In the lips of him that hath understanding wisdom is found: but a rod is for the back of him that is void of understanding. Wise men lay up knowledge: but the mouth of the foolish is near destruction. The rich man's wealth is his strong city: the destruction of the poor is their poverty. The labour of the righteous tendeth to life: the fruit of the wicked to sin. He is in the way of life that keepeth instruction: but he that refuseth reproof erreth. He that hideth hatred with lying lips, and he that uttereth a slander, is a fool. In the multitude of words there wanteth not sin: but he that refraineth his lips is wise. The tongue of the just is as choice silver: the heart of the wicked is little worth. The lips of the righteous feed many: but fools die for want of wisdom. The blessing of the LORD, it maketh rich, and he addeth no sorrow with it. It is as sport to a fool to do mischief: but a man of understanding hath wisdom. The fear of the wicked, it shall come upon him: but the desire of the righteous shall be granted. As the whirlwind passeth, so is the wicked no more: but the righteous is an everlasting foundation. As vinegar to the teeth, and as smoke to the eyes, so is the sluggard to them that send him.

The fear of the LORD prolongeth days: but the years of the wicked shall be shortened. The hope of the righteous shall be gladness: but the expectation of the wicked shall perish. The way of the LORD is strength to the upright: but destruction shall be to the workers of iniquity. The righteous shall never be removed: but the wicked shall not inhabit the earth. The mouth of the just bringeth forth wisdom: but the froward tongue shall be cut out. The lips of the righteous know what is acceptable: but the mouth of the wicked speaketh frowardness.

DAY 30: NUGGETS OF KNOWLEDGE (PROVERBS 10:1-9)

A father is glad if his son becomes wise;
A fool will bring weeping to his mother's eyes.

Ill-gotten treasure brings no profit, I know;
Righteousness delivers from death here below.

The Lord will not suffer the righteous to starve.
The desire of the wicked He'll not let them have.

You're bound to be poor if your hand becomes slack,
But the hand of the diligent is sure not to lack.

He who gathers in summer is a wise son, indeed.
He who sleeps during harvest causes shame, you will see.

A blessing will cover the head of the pure;
Disaster will darken the wicked one's door.

The memories of righteous men live on in favor.
The name of the wicked shall be cursed forever.

A man who is wise can an ordinance obey.
A fool and his chatter shall be soon cast away.

He who walks uprightly walks a path that's secure;
Walking paths that are crooked will fare badly, I'm sure.

BLESSED MEMORIES

Proverb:

"The memory of the just is blessed: but the name of the wicked shall rot" (Proverbs 10:7).

Precept:

Precious memories—everyone should have some. Memories of people who were good and just. Memories of people who have made a lasting impression on your life, such as a mother who was a model of care and concern. Or a father who looked after your physical, financial, and spiritual needs. Or a pastor or a pastor's wife who took time to listen to your problems and who was genuinely concerned for you and your future. I have many such memories.

I remember my grandpa, who gave me a nickel on my sixth birthday, some sixty-nine years ago. I remember my primary Sunday school teacher. I remember the testimonies of elderly saints when I was a boy. I remember a youth leader who gave me his ties to wear when he was finished with them. I remember my pastor, who died at an early age. He baptized me and was a shining example to me. I remember my praying mother and my godly father. I remember the evangelist and his wife who let me go with them to revivals and sing and play the piano for their meetings. They called me their "gospel worker." I remember a young man who had only one lung, but he would try to sing with that one lung. As he attempted to sing in spite of his difficulty, it made me want to sing all the harder.

The memories of the just are blessed, but the memories of the wicked are rather to be forgotten. Very few people want to name their children after Judas Iscariot, Benedict Arnold, or Adolph Hitler. Such names bring an unpleasant sensation of past misdeeds, injustices, and cruelties. How sad it is that some people leave no pleasant memories for their loved ones to recall. Their passing leaves no fragrance of their lives. There is just an empty place where a person used to be. The only thing left is the sadness of a wasted life or the missed opportunity.

Psalm 116:15 says, "Precious in the sight of the LORD is the death of his saints." Even God notes the passing and the memory of the just. Job, a man who was perfect and upright, who feared God and shunned evil, spoke of his desire for God to appoint him a set time and remember him. (See Job 14:13.) Malachi 3:16 tells us that God has a book of memories: "Then they that feared the LORD spake often one to another: and the LORD hearkened, and heard it, and a book of remembrance was written before him for them that feared the LORD, and that thought upon his name."

Live your life in such a way that your actions, words, and deeds are worthy of being recorded in God's book of remembrance. Give your children and grandchildren precious memories to hold dear, long after you are gone, of your love for God, for life, and for each of them. Be just, so that even the memory of you will be blessed.

Practice:

Think of the memories you have of people who influenced your life for the good. What characteristics made them the people they are or were? What strengths did they possess that you would like to have in your own life? Work on adding these strengths and characteristics to your life. You will insure that the memories you leave behind will be good and pleasant.

Prayer:

Lord, I want the memories that others have of me to be pleasant and to bring honor and not shame. Help me to live a life that is dedicated to goodness and truth.

DAY 31: CONTRASTS (PROVERBS 10:10-17)

To wink at a fault causes sorrow and woe;
An open rebuke will bring peace here I know.

The mouth of the righteous is a life-giving well;
The mouth of the wicked with violence will spill.

Hate stirs up strife and starts it again,
But love covers over our every sin.

His lips of understanding no wisdom shall lack,
But vanity's void brings a rod to your back.

The men who are wise will speak of construction,
But fools with their mouths are near to destruction.

The rich man's wealth is like a city with walls;
The poor man's want is the reason he falls.

The labor of righteousness tendeth to life;
The fruit of the wicked is much sin and strife.

The words of instruction will show you the way;
Refusing to listen will send you astray.

COVER UP

Proverb:
"Hatred stirreth up strifes: but love covereth all sins"
(Proverbs 10:12).

Precept:
As a student in the 1940s, typing on a manual typewriter, I
quickly learned I should not make mistakes. The only way to
correct a mistake was to use a rubber eraser that would scuff
the paper, making it look smudged. But sometimes mistakes
happened anyway.

In the 1950s, a single mother, Bette Nesmith Graham,
working as a secretary to provide for herself and her son, also
needed a better way to correct typing errors. Realizing that
artists paint over their mistakes on canvas, she wondered why
she could not just paint over her typing mistakes. She used her
kitchen blender to mix up a batch of tempera water-based
paint colored to match the stationary she used. She then put

the substance in a bottle and took it to work to paint over her mistakes. Soon the other secretaries wanted some of this new correcting liquid. So she poured it in bottles and labeled it "Mistake Out." Her "mistake out" later became known as Liquid Paper, and by the 1970s her company was producing over 25 million bottles a year.[14] It takes lots of white liquid to cover up lots of mistakes.

Thankfully, someone invented a solution for covering over typing mistakes, but how do you cover up the personal mistakes of yourself and others? The Good Book gives us the answer. The ingredient needed to cover our sins is love. First of all, God's love covers our sins. John 3:16 says, "For God so loved the world, that he gave his only begotten Son, that whosoever believeth in him should not perish, but have everlasting life." Jesus Christ willingly took upon Himself the sins of the world at Calvary. Because He gave His life as a sacrifice, our sins are covered by His blood. (See I Peter 2:24.) God's sacrificial love is the "mistake out" that we need. "Though your sins be as scarlet, they shall be as white as snow; though they be red like crimson, they shall be as wool" (Isaiah 1:18).

God's love covered our sins when we were undeserving and had no hope of salvation. His sacrificial love for us, in spite of our shortcomings, is the example that shows us how we should treat others when they have made mistakes. We should not delight in exposing the misfortunes and failures of others. We should not gleefully recount their weaknesses and vulnerabilities. If we truly love them, we will cover their mistakes. This does not mean that we condone their sin but that, after the mistake has been made, we will continue to treat them with respect and keep the embarrassing information to ourselves instead of revealing it to others.

If someone has wronged you, hatred is not the answer. Love is! Why don't you let love be your "mistake out" for the sins of others? Love them as Christ loved you.

Practice:
Say "I love you" often. Show love by serving, helping, and encouraging your family, friends, and others with whom you come in contact on a daily basis. Love those who may act unlovable. Christ hates sin but loves the sinner, and He is our

example. "By this shall all men know that ye are my disciples, if ye have love one to another" (John 13:35).

Prayer:

Lord, help me to love others with a love like Yours. Help me to look beyond their faults and their failures. Help me to treat them as I would wish to be treated.

DAY 32: CONVERSATIONS (PROVERBS 10:18-21)

No matter how hatred is hidden with lies,
It's a fool, who to slander a character tries.

Talking too much may cause you to sin,
But watching your words is a much wiser plan.

As precious as silver, the tongue of the just;
The heart of the wicked is worthless as dust.

The lips of the righteous cause many to thrive;
For their lack of true wisdom, the foolish will die.

I DIDN'T LISTEN

Proverb:

"The lips of the righteous feed many: but fools die for want of wisdom" (Proverbs 10:21).

Precept:

God gives us many sources of godly wisdom to help us make wise choices in our lives. He gives us parents, pastors, teachers, friends, elders, and many others to help us navigate through life's twists and turns. The words of the righteous are sustenance to the soul as food is to the body. We can be strengthened and sustained if we learn to feed on the words of the upright. However, a fool will despise the banqueting table of godly counsel and will perish as a result of his own neglect.

One of America's favorite pastimes is eating. It seems like every time I turn around someone is building a new restaurant in our small town. We all know the path that leads to the refrigerator and the kitchen table. However, do we know how to seek out the lips of the righteous when we need godly counsel? Do we beat a path to our elder's door when we are starving for spiritual impartation? Do we feed upon things that provide nourishment and sustenance for our soul? What value do we place on the counsel of the godly?

Only a fool would reject the counsel of a godly parent or pastor in order to pursue his or her own agenda. I was so proud the first time my father let me drive his car without him being present. He pointed out that it was a used car and it should not be driven at an excessive speed because the motor would not be able to tolerate it. Naturally, I drove it at a high rate, and the engine blew a rod. I was disappointed and humiliated that I had not listened to my father's good advice.

We are surrounded by godly men and women whose advice will help us make the right decisions. However, it is up to us to pursue and obey the counsel that is given. A blessing will come to all who are fed by the lips of the righteous, but the foolish will reject the advice of others and will perish in their own conceit.

Practice:

Do you seek godly counsel for your decisions? Do you pray for God's leading as you navigate through life? Many pitfalls can be avoided if we will heed godly advice. Learn to ask for godly advice, hear it, and heed it.

Prayer:

Lord, I do not want to make decisions that ignore godly counsel and lead me in paths that are a danger to my spiritual well-being. Thank You for my pastor, parents, and other godly men and women in my life who give me godly counsel. Help me to heed their advice.

DAY 33: THE RIGHTEOUS (PROVERBS 10:22-32)

The Lord maketh rich with His blessing, so much,
And it never brings sorrow, or trouble, or such.

As a sport or a joke is the mischief of fools,
But wisdom will cause you to live by the rules.

The fear of the wicked shall soon hold him fast;
The desires of the righteous are granted at last.

As the whirlwind that passes, the wicked will be gone,
But the foundation of the righteous will go on and on.

As eyes filled with smoke and as vinegar to the teeth,
Is a sluggard who is employed as a messenger to speak.

The reverent fear of the Lord will prolong your days,
But the years of the wicked will vanish away.

The hope of the righteous is gladness and trust;
The fate of the wicked is ashes and dust.

The Lord is a stronghold for the upright in heart;
Destruction is the downfall for the evil man's part.

The righteous will never be removed from their place,
And the wicked won't abide on the earth in their days.

The talk of the righteous many good things brings forth;
The false tongue of the wicked is removed from his mouth.

The lips of the just know just how to please;
The mouth of the wicked knows how to deceive.

No Strings Attached

Proverb:
"The blessing of the LORD, it maketh rich, and he addeth no sorrow with it" (Proverbs 10:22).

Precept:
God's gifts do not come to those who grovel. God does not hold His blessings behind His back until we beg Him enough to release them into our life. On the contrary, God is highly motivated

to pour out His blessings upon those who love Him. Jesus asked the question, "If ye then, being evil, know how to give good gifts unto your children, how much more shall your Father which is in heaven give good things to them that ask him?" (Matthew 7:11).

Most parents are naturally and lovingly motivated to provide good things for their children. When a gift is given in love, it is not given with strings attached. The gift giver only expects the recipient to receive the gift with a spirit of thanksgiving. No loving parent would hold a birthday gift ransom while requiring a little child to work, beg, or struggle as a prerequisite for receiving the gift. In like manner, our heavenly Father blesses without adding sorrow.

True riches can only be measured by the abundance of God's blessings. God delights in pouring out His blessings upon His people. James said, "Every good gift and every perfect gift is from above, and cometh down from the Father of lights, with whom is no variableness, neither shadow of turning" (James 1:17). Truly, God is the source of everything that is good in our life.

God does not want His children to stress, sorrow, or struggle over His blessings. The anxiety of receiving comes with our perceived need to somehow earn the gift that He desires to give to us. However, we could never earn or deserve the blessings of God. Paul wrote, "For by grace are ye saved through faith; and that not of yourselves: it is the gift of God: not of works, lest any man should boast" (Ephesians 2:8-9). Therefore, let us learn to receive the gifts of God with a song and not with sorrow, with grace and not with a groan.

Practice:

Acknowledge the gifts of God that He extends to you each day. When you receive a financial increase, a job promotion, or an unexpected blessing, give thanks to God. Find His blessings in the small things that surround you each day: hugs, smiles, letters, gifts, health, strength, forgiveness. His abundant blessings are all around you. Receive them with thankfulness.

Prayer:

Lord, for every blessing that You have given to me and my family, I give You thanks. I praise You because You are good and Your mercy endureth forever.

PROVERBS 11

A false balance is abomination to the LORD: but a just weight is his delight. When pride cometh, then cometh shame: but with the lowly is wisdom. The integrity of the upright shall guide them: but the perverseness of transgressors shall destroy them. Riches profit not in the day of wrath: but righteousness delivereth from death. The righteousness of the perfect shall direct his way: but the wicked shall fall by his own wickedness. The righteousness of the upright shall deliver them: but transgressors shall be taken in their own naughtiness. When a wicked man dieth, his expectation shall perish: and the hope of unjust men perisheth. The righteous is delivered out of trouble, and the wicked cometh in his stead. An hypocrite with his mouth destroyeth his neighbour: but through knowledge shall the just be delivered.

When it goeth well with the righteous, the city rejoiceth: and when the wicked perish, there is shouting. By the blessing of the upright the city is exalted: but it is overthrown by the mouth of the wicked. He that is void of wisdom despiseth his neighbour: but a man of understanding holdeth his peace. A talebearer revealeth secrets: but he that is of a faithful spirit concealeth the matter. Where no counsel is, the people fall: but in the multitude of counsellers there is safety. He that is surety for a stranger shall smart for it: and he that hateth suretiship is sure. A gracious woman retaineth honour: and strong men retain riches. The merciful man doeth good to his own soul: but he that is cruel troubleth his own flesh. The wicked worketh a deceitful work: but to him that soweth righteousness shall be a sure reward. As righteousness tendeth to life: so he that pursueth evil pursueth it to his own death. They that are of a froward heart are abomination to the LORD: but such as are upright in their way are his delight. Though hand join in hand, the wicked shall not be unpunished: but the seed of the righteous shall be delivered. As a jewel of gold in a swine's snout, so is a fair woman which is without discretion. The desire of the righteous is only good: but the expectation of the wicked is wrath. There is that scattereth, and yet increaseth; and there is that withholdeth more than is meet, but it tendeth to poverty. The liberal soul shall be made fat: and he that watereth shall be watered also himself. He that withholdeth corn, the people shall curse him: but blessing shall be upon the head of him that selleth it. He that diligently seeketh good procureth favour: but he that seeketh mischief, it shall come unto him. He that trusteth in his riches shall fall: but the righteous shall flourish as a branch. He that troubleth his own house shall inherit the wind: and the fool shall be servant to the wise of heart. The fruit of the righteous is a tree of life; and he that winneth souls is wise. Behold, the righteous shall be recompensed in the earth: much more the wicked and the sinner.

DAY 34: A GOOD CHRISTIAN IS A GOOD CITIZEN (PROVERBS 11:1-11)

God hates when you cheat and lie on your sales;
You'll be short when your life has been weighed on
    His scales!

Don't be too proud; it will bring you to shame.
If you can, make humility part of your name.

A good man's integrity makes "Do Right" his master;
The wicked's perverseness will lead to disaster.

Your riches won't profit in the day of God's wrath,
But righteousness always delivers from death!

When you do the right thing, that's the way to be blessed;
The wicked shall fall by his own wickedness.

The upright shall live when their good works are known;
The wicked shall die when their bad deeds are shown.

The death of the wicked means his hopes are gone,
But the hopes of the righteous shall live on and on.

The good man escapes from life's troubles, quite safe,
But if you look, you'll find wicked men in his place.

Through slander, the hypocrite tries to destroy;
Through knowledge, the just his escape can enjoy.

When the good people win, the whole town will turn out;
With the wicked defeated, there's reason to shout.

A city will rise when the good run the town;
When the wicked take over, it's on the way down!

A TIME TO CELEBRATE

Proverb:
   "When it goeth well with the righteous, the city rejoiceth: and when the wicked perish, there is shouting" (Proverbs 11:10).

Precept:
   A sense of justice permeates most everyone's attitude and thinking. In every culture and society group, there is a consensus that the righteous (person doing right) should be blessed and the evildoer should be punished. Therefore, laws and governments are created to ensure that justice prevails. Does it always happen? Unfortunately not! However, as a society we still strive to preserve the ideal that the best man should win— and when he does, there is cause for rejoicing.
   Cities celebrate with those who have achieved greatness through sacrifice, discipline, and hard work. Newspapers herald the achievements of great people. Special proclamations are made to express the goodwill of the community toward those who actively work for good causes. Conversely, cities rejoice when the wicked man receives his just dessert. While the wicked flee and escape the recompense of their reward, anxiety and fear abound. When they are caught and punished for their evil deeds, the city rejoices.
   Several years ago, a young man drove a yellow Ryder rental truck to the Alfred P. Murrah building in Oklahoma City. Soon after he got out of the truck and walked away, a bomb inside the truck went off. The blast shattered one-third

of the seven-story federal building to bits, wounded over five hundred people, and left 168 people dead, including men, women and children. It was a horrific scene, with horrific consequences. The city and its people were forever changed by the unprecedented and unwarranted act of homegrown terrorism. Although it could not assuage the grief or bring back those who were taken, Timothy McVeigh's execution was a significant occasion to those who survived the horror of that day.[15]

I was a boy of ten when our country was drawn into World War II by the Japanese attack on Pearl Harbor. I can still remember the community prayer meetings asking God to preserve our nation, protect our troops, and deliver the world from the unrighteous enemy who fought against us. When the war ended and Germany and Japan were subdued, the whole world erupted in celebration and rejoicing. In London, England, over a million people gathered in the streets to celebrate victory in Europe. In the United States, there was rejoicing from east to the west and from north to the south, because good had triumphed over evil.

Practice:

In every city and town there are good people who do good things for others. Take note of the good things people do in the area in which you live. Rejoice with them in their success. Rejoice when good triumphs over evil.

Prayer:

Lord, I thank You for the people, churches, and other organizations in my city who are concerned about doing good for others. Even though they may not know You in fullness of truth, I thank You for godly people who are compassionate and will stand for righteousness.

Day 35: Men and Their Deeds (Proverbs 11:12-22)

A man with no sense will his neighbor despise;
Wise men hold their peace and learn how to survive.

A talebearer tells everyone whom he can;
A secret is safe with a trustworthy man.

Without any counsel the people will fall,
But plenty of counsel gives safety to all.

If you're surety for strangers, you'll suffer and pay;
To abhor such a surety's a much surer way.

A woman is gracious who still keeps her class;
A rich man is glad to hang on to his cash.

A merciful man helps his own soul as well;
A man who is cruel causes woe to himself.

The bad deeds of the wicked are filled with deceit;
The reward of the righteous is sure and it's sweet.

Every road leads to life, if you're not going wrong.
Chasing evil will lead you to death, yes, your own!

It's an insult to God to be crooked at heart;
It's a pleasure to Him when men chose the right part.

The wicked will pay, though they walk hand in hand;
The results of the righteous will go as God planned.

A jewel of gold in the snout of a swine
Is like a fair girl who acts indiscreetly at times.

SOMETHING STINKS

Proverb:
"As a jewel of gold in a swine's snout, so is a fair woman which is without discretion" (Proverbs 11:22).

Precept:
The house was a beautiful house, in a beautiful neighborhood, inhabited by beautiful people, but the owner of the house looked at me and said, "Something stinks!" I was there for a

visit, and we were having a great time until the obnoxious odor wafted through the room. The owner of the house searched everywhere, trying to find the elusive smell that was invading his personal space. How amazing it was that in such beautiful surroundings, the environment was so quickly tainted by an unidentified odor. Finally, he discovered a parcel of meat that had been removed from the upright freezer and placed on top. There it had sat, unseen by the household until it began emitting the terrible odor.

A jewel is counted precious because of the rarity of the gem and the beauty that it brings to the eye of the beholder. However, there is not a jewel on earth whose beauty would not be tainted by its insertion into the nose of a stinking pig. You might recognize that the jewel is precious, beautiful, and even priceless, but you would quickly conclude that "something stinks!" Could you even enjoy the beauty of the jewel in the presence of a stinking, snorting, slimy pig?

A beautiful woman without discretion is like that pig with a jewel placed in its nose. The natural beauty that God gives a woman can be nullified by her loose tongue and her lack of wisdom. On the outside, she may present the image of beauty and class, but if her spirit is sour, those around her will say, "Something stinks!"

Do not let your beauty be discounted by ugly words and poor choices, but rather let it be accentuated by your discretion and diplomacy. Jesus said, "Let your light so shine before men, that they may see your good works, and glorify your Father which is in heaven" (Matthew 5:16).

Practice:

Do you stink? Do you have a negative attitude or an ungrateful spirit? Do you encourage those around you with your words and actions or do you drag them down with your foul spirit? Fill your life with fragrance by spending time with the Rose of Sharon and the Lily of the Valley. Let your life offer a sweet aroma to those around you. "Now thanks be unto God, which always causeth us to triumph in Christ, and maketh manifest the savour of his knowledge by us in every place. For we are unto God a sweet savour of Christ, in them that are saved, and in them that perish" (II Corinthians 2:14-15).

Prayer:

Lord, help me to realize when there is something that just does not smell right in my life. Please cleanse me from the stench of sin and selfishness. Refresh me with the fragrance of Your Spirit. Let my life be a sweet-smelling savor unto You and everyone around me.

Week 6

DAY 36: RICHES AND REWARDS
(PROVERBS 11:23-31)

The righteous desire is for nothing but good,
But the wicked fears wrath for his sin, as he should!

You can give to the Lord and have money to spend,
Or just hoard all you have, lose it all in the end.

So be lavish with God and receive a reward.
Be a blessing yourself; you'll be blessed by the Lord!

The people despise one who hoards needed grain,
But blessings will come if he sells for his gain.

If you seek after good, then good will prevail;
If you're looking for evil, it will come, without fail.

He who trusts in his riches, disappointed will be,
But the righteous shall flourish like the branch of a tree.

He who troubles his house shall inherit the wind,
And the fool shall be servant unto the wise man.

The fruit of the righteous is a tree of life,
And he who winneth souls is wise.

If the just man is rewarded for the record he's made,
How much more will the wicked and sinners be paid?

THE GIVING PARADOX

Proverb:

"There is that scattereth, and yet increaseth; and there is that withholdeth more than is meet, but it tendeth to poverty" (Proverbs 11:24).

Precept:

Another translation of this verse reads, "One man gives freely, yet gains even more; another withholds unduly, but comes to poverty" (Proverbs 11:24, NIV). It is not what you hold on to that counts; it is what you give away! God's giving paradox is this: the more you give, the more you get. Are you running low on funds, friends, or food? Learn to give, and watch God supply your every need.

The story of the widow at Zarephath beautifully illustrates this principle. (See I Kings 17:9-16.) This lady had only enough supplies to make one last meal for her son and herself, and then they expected to die. However, the prophet Elijah appeared and asked her to make a cake for him first. He promised that if she would give the first cake to him, God would replenish the flour and oil, and she and her son would be provided for. Instead of hoarding her meager rations, she did just as the man of God said. Miraculously, the flour in the barrel and the oil in the cruse were continuously sustained during the famine in their land. The widow emptied her pantry to make a meal for the man of God, and that meal was multiplied many times over.

In a church I once pastored was a compassionate man, a precious saint. He was always helping someone in need: the poor, the widows, and the disabled. Although he wasn't wealthy and had a large family himself, there was always room for his children's friends at their family table. He worked as a produce manager in a grocery store, and when lettuce or other vegetables were wilted or bruised, he would remove them from the bins. Instead of throwing them away, as may have been expected, he would save them to give away to the needy people he knew.

An elderly neighbor, whom he often helped, became bedfast and was placed in a nursing home. She had no children, so he continued to visit her and be her friend. One day she said to him, "I don't want to stay here any longer. I would like for you and your wife to take care of me. I'll buy a house big enough for you and your family. If you will care for me until I die, the house will become yours." The man was stunned as he had thought she was very poor, when, in fact, she was a wealthy woman. She did buy a brand-new, large, beautiful home in a nicer area of town into which he and his family moved. They cared for the widow until her death, and the house did become theirs. He learned the secret of the giving paradox: "Give, and it shall be given unto you; good measure, pressed down, and shaken together, and running over, shall men give into your bosom. For with the same measure that ye mete withal it shall be measured to you again" (Luke 6:38).

Practice:

Go out of your way today to give of yourself and help someone else. Bless a family or a church with your monetary gift. Time is a precious gift that you can give to your family, your church, and your community. Use your talents such as painting, cooking, or business knowledge to bless someone. Give and it shall be given unto you.

Prayer:

Lord, I want to be used by You to give of myself to those around me. Thank You for the talents and the gifts that You have given to me. Help me to use those gifts to be a blessing to someone else today.

PROVERBS 12

Whoso loveth instruction loveth knowledge: but he that hateth reproof is brutish. A good man obtaineth favour of the LORD: but a man of wicked devices will he condemn. A man shall not be established by wickedness: but the root of the righteous shall not be moved. A virtuous woman is a crown to her husband: but she that maketh ashamed is as rottenness in his bones. The thoughts of the righteous are right: but the counsels of the wicked are deceit. The words of the wicked are to lie in wait for blood: but the mouth of the upright shall deliver them. The wicked are overthrown, and are not: but the house of the righteous shall stand. A man shall be commended according to his wisdom: but he that is of a perverse heart shall be despised. He that is despised, and hath a servant, is better than he that honoureth himself, and lacketh bread. A righteous man regardeth the life of his beast: but the tender mercies of the wicked are cruel. He that tilleth his land shall be satisfied with bread: but he that followeth vain persons is void of understanding. The wicked desireth the net of evil men: but the root of the righteous yieldeth fruit. The wicked is snared by the transgression of his lips: but the just shall come out of trouble. A man shall be satisfied with good by the fruit of his mouth: and the recompence of a man's hands shall be rendered unto him. The way of a fool is right in his own eyes: but he that hearkeneth unto counsel is wise. A fool's wrath is presently known: but a prudent man covereth shame. He that speaketh truth sheweth forth righteousness: but a false witness deceit. There is that speaketh like the piercings of a sword: but the tongue of the wise is health. The lip of truth shall be established for ever: but a lying tongue is but for a moment. Deceit is in the heart of them that imagine evil: but to the counsellers of peace is joy. There shall no evil happen to the just: but the wicked shall be filled with mischief. Lying lips are abomination to the LORD: *but they that deal truly are his delight. A prudent man concealeth knowledge: but the heart of fools proclaimeth foolishness. The hand of the diligent shall bear rule: but the slothful shall be under tribute. Heaviness in the heart of man maketh it stoop: but a good word maketh it glad. The righteous is more excellent than his neighbour: but the way of the wicked seduceth them. The slothful man roasteth not that which he took in hunting: but the substance of a diligent man is precious. In the way of righteousness is life; and in the pathway thereof there is no death.*

DAY 37: WORDS THAT BLAST AND BLESS (PROVERBS 12:1-10)

Love correction, love knowledge, love to be shown the rule;
If a man hates correction, he's revealed as a fool.

A good man, whom the Lord loves, obtains favor from Him;
Those with wicked intentions, the Lord will condemn.

Wicked men cannot prosper nor be established always,
But the root of the righteous is put there to stay.

A crown to her husband is a wife causing pride;
With a wife who is shameless, he feels rotten inside.

The thoughts of the righteous are honorable and true;
The wicked's thoughts are deceitful and treacherous, too.

The words of the wicked tell of blood they will shed,
But the mouth of the upright will deliver instead.

The wicked are overthrown and not seen again,
But the house of the righteous will firmly stand.

A man shall be commended if he wisdom can show;
The persons of perversity are despised where they go.

It is better to be lowly, to have work and be fed,
Than to be self-exalted and be looking for bread.

The righteous are kind to a dumb brute in need,
But the cruel have no mercy for a man or his steed.

EVEN THE HORSE WILL KNOW

Proverb:
   "A righteous man regardeth the life of his beast: but the tender mercies of the wicked are cruel" (Proverbs 12:10).

Precept:

My first memory is of a time when I was three years old. My family had gone to a tent revival. I remember lying outside the tent in the "bundle wagon" (a wagon with sideboards arranged to carry bundles of wheat to the combine) while my parents went to the service. My father was filled with the Holy Ghost that night, and when he came back to the wagon, my brother said that he was so different that the horses didn't even know him! I guess even horses will recognize the difference in the way they are treated by a man who has just been converted, or by an unsaved man who does not know the love of God.

The writer of Proverbs said that even the "tender mercies of the wicked are cruel." In other words, even if he tries to be congenial, he is still so filled with wickedness that he cannot stop being a rascal. On the other hand, the just man is so kind that he is even concerned about the welfare of his animals. What a difference!

Living for God makes you a better person, a better husband or wife, a better neighbor, and a better friend. How many sinners have gotten up from an altar of repentance to discover that the sun was brighter, the grass was greener, their wives were prettier, and their children were more precious than ever before? Living for God changes your perspective for the better.

At their best, the good deeds of the wicked are just a cruel mockery of all that is righteous. Without proper motivation, the tender mercies of the wicked are simply a way to further their own evil agenda. Any semblance of kindness from the wicked is just a web to entrap the innocent in order to satisfy his cruel desires.

True compassion can only flow from the heart of righteousness. We should seek not only to do good deeds but to do them with a righteous heart. The psalmist asked the question, "Who shall ascend into the hill of the LORD? or who shall stand in his holy place?" (Psalm 24:3). The answer: "He that hath clean hands, and a pure heart; who hath not lifted up his soul unto vanity, nor sworn deceitfully" (Psalm 24:4). When your heart is transformed, everyone feels the ripple effect of God's love flowing through you. Your family, your friends, your co-workers, and even the horse will know that God dwells in you.

Practice:

Allow the Holy Spirit to change you into His likeness. Let the love of God shine forth in you as you smile at your neighbor, give an encouraging word to a friend, show respect to your elders, love your family, and even treat animals with kindness.

Prayer:

Lord, let my deeds today reflect Your goodness. Let me make a difference in the lives of those with whom I come in contact today. May their day, and mine, be brightened by the touch of Your hand.

DAY 38: PRINCIPLES (PROVERBS 12:11-20)

He who labors on his land will have plenty of bread;
He who vanity follows has no sense in his head.

The wicked are snared by the trap that is set,
But the righteous are spared and shall come out of it.

The wicked shall be caught by his sin and its stings;
The just are delivered from troublesome things.

From the fruit of his words a man is satisfied with good;
He receives the reward of his hands, as he should.

The way of a fool is right in his eyes,
But listening to counsel is what really is wise.

It doesn't take long till a fool's wrath is shown;
Those who cover the shame, by their prudence are known.

When an honest man gives evidence, it is truth you receive;
When a liar gives perjury, you cannot believe.

Rash words, like the piercing of a sword, make their thrust,
But healing and health are the words of the just.

The lips speaking truth will forever endure;
Lies' vanities last for a moment, that's sure.

The counselors of evil are filled with deceit;
The counselors of peace shall have joy that is sweet.

DON'T GET CAUGHT

Proverb:

"The wicked is snared by the transgression of his lips: but the just shall come out of trouble" (Proverbs 12:13).

Precept:

When my brother and I were children, my father would tell us bedtime stories that he made up. We would beg him to tell us the story of "Old Three Toe," one of our favorites. Old Three Toe was a wolf that escaped from a trap. Only one toe had been caught in the trap, and he gnawed it off, leaving him with three toes.

Evil men are caught in a snare—just as surely as the wolf in my dad's story—by their own sinful talk. Just think about those who have a habit of lying. After one lie is told, they have to tell another lie to try to cover up that lie. On and on it goes until the liar finds himself ensnared in a web of lies. The only way to escape the trap of evil communication is to completely disconnect oneself from the cycle of sinful speech. Old Three Toe escaped the trap missing a toe, but he escaped with his life.

However, there is a way to avoid the trap altogether, and that is to be honest and godly in your conversation. A man who always tells the truth does not have to worry about contradicting what he said in a previous conversation. A person who never speaks ill of others does not have to worry about what they have said getting back to the person they spoke about. Learning to control our tongue and speak only things that are pleasing to God will keep us out of many troubles.

David understood the power of his words when he wrote, "Let the words of my mouth, and the meditation of my heart, be acceptable in thy sight, O LORD, my strength, and my redeemer" (Psalm 19:14). He understood the need for divine intervention to direct his words in positive manner. Many temptations of the tongue are presented to us all. However, with the help of God we can escape the trap and triumph over trouble.

Practice:
Make an effort to think before you speak. Do not get involved in idle gossip. Make it a habit to refuse to speak ill of other people. Live a life that is above reproach so that you will not be caught or trapped by your own words.

Prayer:
Lord, set a guard over my mouth. Help me to be slow to speak when I am angry and to think before I speak words that could cause harm to myself or others.

DAY 39: CONQUERORS AND CONFIDENCE (PROVERBS 12:21-28)

No evil can conquer those who in the Lord trust;
Misfortune and trouble overwhelm the unjust.

Lying lips are abominable in the sight of the Lord,
But those who speak truthfully, He delights in their word.

A prudent man's knowledge is by him concealed,
But the foolishness of fools is quickly revealed.

The hand of the diligent is to rule in the earth;
The labor of the slothful is that of a serf.

Depression is caused by anxiety of heart;
To speak words of kindness will gladness impart.

Righteousness surpasses in every way;
The way of the wicked will lead them astray.

The slothful man neglects the catch from his hunt,
But the substance of the diligent will serve for his lunch.

Life in abundance true righteousness imparts,
And in life's pathway, death forever departs.

DON'T THROW IT AWAY

Proverb:

"The slothful man roasteth not that which he took in hunting: but the substance of a diligent man is precious" (Proverbs 12:27).

Precept:

I was born in Oklahoma during the Great Depression. I was one of seven children at home, and commodities were often scarce. Nothing was wasted; everything was appreciated. Store-bought items were a luxury. My "toys" were spools used for horses, pecans used for cattle, a baking powder can used for a well, and a thimble used for a bucket. My mother used empty flour sacks to make clothes for my sisters. Our circumstances were less than desirable, yet I do not remember anything negative from my childhood. I was just a happy boy growing up with my family. However, to this day I do not like to throw anything away, and I enjoy eating leftovers.

I recently heard a young minister say that the first thing he told his wife when they married was, "Don't ever serve me leftovers!" I do not know how my family would have survived without leftovers. However, in today's generation, so many things are taken for granted and are not fully appreciated.

I realize that times have changed, and most people in our country do not live in the dire circumstances dictated by the depression of the 1930s. By those standards, most everyone now would be considered wealthy, with spacious homes, comfortable cars, fashionable clothes, and plentiful food. However, even in our present state of comfort, we should be careful to appreciate the good things God has given to us. We should not be wasteful with our provisions and possessions just because there is no lack or shortage.

The slothful man of the above proverb loved to hunt. He evidently was able to catch something, but when he did, he just threw it away. On the other hand, the diligent man considered everything he had as worth saving. He made a meal of the very thing that the other man threw away, bringing to mind the familiar saying, "One man's trash is another man's treasure." Whatever blessings God has given you, count them as precious and do not throw them away!

Practice:

You are a blessed person. Savor your friendships, your family, your recreation opportunities, and your material blessings. Rejoice in your church, your salvation experience, and your hope of heaven.

Prayer:

Lord, do not let me fall a victim to the mentality of the "throw-it-away" society. Help me to appreciate everything that You have given me and to value it as You intended. Help me to be a good steward of all of the things that You have bestowed upon me.

PROVERBS 13

A wise son heareth his father's instruction: but a scorner heareth not rebuke. A man shall eat good by the fruit of his mouth: but the soul of the transgressors shall eat violence. He that keepeth his mouth keepeth his life: but he that openeth wide his lips shall have destruction. The soul of the sluggard desireth, and hath nothing: but the soul of the diligent shall be made fat. A righteous man hateth lying: but a wicked man is loathsome, and cometh to shame. Righteousness keepeth him that is upright in the way: but wickedness overthroweth the sinner. There is that maketh himself rich, yet hath nothing: there is that maketh himself poor, yet hath great riches. The ransom of a man's life are his riches: but the poor heareth not rebuke. The light of the righteous rejoiceth: but the lamp of the wicked shall be put out. Only by pride cometh contention: but with the well advised is wisdom. Wealth gotten by vanity shall be diminished: but he that gathereth by labour shall increase. Hope deferred maketh the heart sick: but when the desire cometh, it is a tree of life. Whoso despiseth the word shall be destroyed: but he that feareth the commandment shall be rewarded. The law of the wise is a fountain of life, to depart from the snares of death. Good understanding giveth favour: but the way of transgressors is hard. Every prudent man dealeth with knowledge: but a fool layeth open his folly. A wicked messenger falleth into mischief: but a faithful ambassador is health. Poverty and shame shall be to him that refuseth instruction: but he that regardeth reproof shall be honoured. The desire accomplished is sweet to the soul: but it is abomination to fools to depart from evil. He that walketh with wise men shall be wise: but a companion of fools shall be destroyed. Evil pursueth sinners: but to the righteous good shall be repayed. A good man leaveth an inheritance to his children's children: and the wealth of the sinner is laid up for the just. Much food is in the tillage of the poor: but there is that is destroyed for want of judgment. He that spareth his rod hateth his son: but he that loveth him chasteneth him betimes. The righteous eateth to the satisfying of his soul: but the belly of the wicked shall want.

DAY 40: A SENSIBLE SON (PROVERBS 13:1-8)

With a sensible son, no correction is needed,
But a son without sense, no rebuke will be heeded.

A good man will reap the fruit of his goodness,
But the evil man shall eat of his sin to its fullest.

When you guard your lips, it's your life that is saved,
But the man who talks freely, with violence is paid.

The soul of the slothful is hungry but empty;
The soul of the diligent is fat with his plenty.

A good man hates deception and lies;
A wicked man is loathsome and in shame when he dies.

Good men are safeguarded by integrity,
But sinners are overthrown by their iniquity.

Some people act like they're rich, and they're not.
Other people are poor, but, in fact, have a lot.

A rich man can ransom his life with his wealth,
But the poor man has nothing to give but himself.

THE POOR RICH MAN

Proverb:
"There is that maketh himself rich, yet hath nothing: there is that maketh himself poor, yet hath great riches" (Proverbs 13:7).

Precept:
In our current American society, men and women are measured by their net worth. Consequently, many are in a constant state of trying to "keep up with the Joneses." They want to wear expensive clothes, drive luxury vehicles, and live in impressive homes, even if they cannot really afford it. They strive to maintain the appearance of wealth by constantly overspending. Other people are legitimately poor, yet they spend the little money they do have trying to "get rich quick" through lotteries, casinos, or other questionable methods.

Meanwhile, advertisers, credit card companies, and department stores feed on this craving for material wealth. Credit card offers are routinely sent through the mail, offering instant credit. Many people respond to the offers, using the credit to purchase things they do not need with money they do not have. If they are not careful, they will become so overextended that they cannot pay their bills and will end up losing everything in bankruptcy.

Those who think money is the answer to all of life's problems have not realized how quickly riches can disappear. Proverbs 23:5 says, "For riches certainly make themselves wings; they fly away as an eagle toward heaven." Even the majority of those who have won millions of dollars in lotteries have not been able to keep their wealth. Many have ended up broke or bankrupt, and in a worse situation than they were in before they won.

The Bible says, "But they that will be rich fall into temptation and a snare, and into many foolish and hurtful lusts, which drown men in destruction and perdition" (I Timothy 6:9). The Gospel of Matthew also teaches about "the deceitfulness of riches," which will choke the Word and cause people to become unfruitful in the kingdom of God. (See Matthew 13:22.)

It is not wrong to have money, for many great men of the Old Testament (including Abraham, Job, and Solomon, the writer of this proverb) possessed wealth. But it is wrong to trust in your own ability to get wealth. I Timothy 6:17 says, "Charge them that are rich in this world, that they be not high-minded, nor trust in uncertain riches, but in the living God, who giveth us richly all things to enjoy."

The Bible teaches that we should not try to store up wealth in this life where thieves can steal, but that we should store up treasures in heaven. (See Matthew 6:19-20.) If we put our trust in God and His riches, even though we may be poor, we are rich!

Practice:

Commit your finances to the Lord. Understand that everything you have belongs to Him. Be faithful in your tithes and offerings. The more God has blessed you, the bigger responsibility you have to support the work of God.

Prayer:

Lord, help me not to put more trust in finances and material blessings than I do in You. Thank You for what You have given to me and for the promise that You will supply my needs.

DAY 41: A GOOD MAN (PROVERBS 13:9-14)

The light of a good man shines bright through the night;
The lamp of the wicked shall be put out of sight.

The stupid sow discord by insolence and pride,
But wise men are careful their accomplishments to hide.

Wealth that is quickly received will soon go,
But fortune gained wisely continues to grow.

When hope is kept waiting, the heart's sick and it grieves;
When desire is accomplished, it's as a tree with new leaves.

Despising God's Word will cause you destruction,
But fearing God's precepts will bring exaltation.

The law of the wise is life's fountain for all
So we may shun snares that cause us to fall.

KEEP BELIEVING

Proverb:
"Hope deferred maketh the heart sick: but when the desire cometh, it is a tree of life" (Proverbs 13:12).

Precept:
Every person has a secret hope, desire, dream, or longing for their life, whether it is their own inner ambition or drive, or a God-given dream. Whichever the case, if you are to accomplish your desires and dreams, it is important to keep believing.

King David had a deep desire to build a house for God. Initially, the prophet Nathan sanctioned David's desire, but afterward, God sent him back to tell David that he would not be allowed to build the Temple. (See II Samuel 7:1-13.) However, David continued his work of gathering materials of gold, silver, precious stones, wood, and spices. David did not build the Temple, but he could not keep from dreaming about it and longing for it. Because of his dream and desire, he prepared the way for his son Solomon to build the Temple.

Joseph had a dream in which he saw himself standing as a ruler, while his parents and his brothers knelt to him. (See Genesis 37:5-7.) Although his family ridiculed him and did not understand, Joseph's dream was from God. However, it took many years and much hardship before Joseph's dream became an actuality. There were probably many times when Joseph may have doubted if God's plan would ever unfold in his life. However, he continued to live a life of integrity before God, no matter what circumstances he encountered. Acts 7:9-10 sums up Joseph's life, "And the patriarchs, moved with envy, sold Joseph into Egypt: but God was with him, and delivered him out of all his afflictions, and gave him favour and wisdom in the sight of Pharaoh king of Egypt; and he made him governor over Egypt and all his house."

If you have a longing, an ambition, a desire, or more importantly, a God-given dream, do not let it die—keep believing. Be faithful, be patient, be trustworthy, be determined, and keep believing. If God has promised you something, it will happen. Psalm 37:4-5 says, "Delight thyself also in the LORD; and he shall give thee the desires of thine heart. Commit thy way unto the LORD; trust also in him; and he shall bring it to pass."

You may go through challenging times, but when your longing is fulfilled, your promise materializes, or your hope is realized, the desire that was planted as a little seedling will become a full-grown, graceful tree of life!

Practice:

Waiting is hard to do, but sometimes we may have to wait weeks, months, or even years to see God's promises come to pass. Hold on to the dream that God has given you, and wait for the promise to be fulfilled in God's time. "He hath made every thing beautiful in his time" (Ecclesiastes 3:11).

Prayer:

Lord, I believe that the promise You have given to me will become a reality. I place my trust in You, and I wait patiently for You to perform it according to Your will.

DAY 42: MAXIMS (PROVERBS 13:15-25)

A good understanding gives favor's reward,
But the way of transgressors is a way that is hard.

Refusing instruction will cause poverty and shame,
But to take heed to warnings brings respect to your name.

A messenger who's wicked has disaster to tell,
But a faithful ambassador will report all is well.

To refuse wise instruction brings poverty and shame,
But if you accept reproof men will honor your name.

When desire is accomplished, it is sweet to the soul,
So to depart from evil makes no sense to a fool.

When you're walking with wise men you, too, become wise;
When fools are your friends, if you're one—no surprise!

You're pursued by misfortune, when you're following sin;
If you're just and you're righteous, a good
        recompense you'll win.

Good men leave a legacy to their children and heirs;
In the wealth of the sinner, the just sometimes shares.

There is food for the poor, if we till fallow ground,
But through lawsuits and laziness there's none to be found.

Use the rod in correction, or you hate your own son.
If you love him, correct him, or see that it's done.

The righteous man's blessed to have food to satisfy;
The wicked man's empty of the things for his supply.

IT PAYS TO LISTEN

Proverb:
    "Poverty and shame shall be to him that refuseth instruction: but he that regardeth reproof shall be honoured" (Proverbs 13:18).

Precept:
    I listened to the radio the night before Hurricane Katrina struck the Gulf Coast. The news anchor was interviewing people in New Orleans who refused to evacuate. One man, a bar owner, was questioned about his decision to ride out the

storm. He told the news anchor that he had plenty of food and beer, and he was going to be ready to open up for business when the storm cleared. I am certain that with the devastation that came with Katrina, he did not open for business when the storm passed. Without shame, he refused to heed the warnings that were given, and thus he had to endure the consequence of his decision.

An individual who refuses to receive instruction is destined for disaster. How much pain and heartache could be avoided if people would follow the instructions designed to help them? Billions of dollars are spent every year on medical treatment, but how many people follow the instructions given by their doctor? We want to be healthy, wealthy, and wise, but as a culture we don't like taking orders from someone else. The doctor says, "You need to lose weight and exercise," but our flesh says, "Another piece of cake won't hurt me." Those who regard reproof will be blessed by their obedience.

God has given us His Word as a road map for our life. Every question, every dilemma, and every problem have an answer that can be found in God's Word. The psalmist said, "Thy word is a lamp unto my feet, and a light unto my path" (Psalm 119:105). If we hearken to God's instruction for our life, we will be honored for our obedience. However, if we refuse the instruction of God's Word, we are destined for spiritual poverty and shame. It pays to listen to His instruction. One who delights in the law of the Lord "shall be like a tree planted by the rivers of water, that bringeth forth his fruit in his season; his leaf also shall not wither; and whatsoever he doeth shall prosper" (Psalm 1:3).

Practice:

Take time to listen. Be still in the presence of God and hear what He would speak to you. Listen to sermons and Christian songs. Many times God will use them to speak wisdom to you and to give you answers to questions with which you may be struggling.

Prayer:

Lord, I want to listen. Help me to shut out all the noise around me so that I can hear Your still, small voice.

Week 7

PROVERBS 14

Every wise woman buildeth her house: but the foolish plucketh it down with her hands. He that walketh in his uprightness feareth the LORD: but he that is perverse in his ways despiseth him. In the mouth of the foolish is a rod of pride: but the lips of the wise shall preserve them. Where no oxen are, the crib is clean: but much increase is by the strength of the ox. A faithful witness will not lie: but a false witness will utter lies. A scorner seeketh wisdom, and findeth it not: but knowledge is easy unto him that understandeth. Go from the presence of a foolish man, when thou perceivest not in him the lips of knowledge. The wisdom of the prudent is to understand his way: but the folly of fools is deceit. Fools make a mock at sin: but among the righteous there is favour. The heart knoweth his own bitterness; and a stranger doth not intermeddle with his joy. The house of the wicked shall be overthrown: but the tabernacle of the upright shall flourish. There is a way which seemeth right unto a man, but the end thereof are the ways of death. Even in laughter the heart is sorrowful; and the end of that mirth is heaviness. The backslider in heart shall be filled with his own ways: and a good man shall be satisfied from himself. The simple believeth every word: but the prudent man looketh well to his going. A wise man feareth, and departeth from evil: but the fool rageth, and is confident. He that is soon angry dealeth foolishly: and a man of wicked devices is hated. The simple inherit folly: but the prudent are crowned with knowledge. The evil bow before the good; and the wicked at the gates of the righteous. The poor is hated even of his own neighbour: but the rich hath many

*friends. He that despiseth his neighbour sinneth: but he
that hath mercy on the poor, happy is he. Do they not err
that devise evil? but mercy and truth shall be to them
that devise good. In all labour there is profit: but the talk
of the lips tendeth only to penury. The crown of the wise
is their riches: but the foolishness of fools is folly. A true
witness delivereth souls: but a deceitful witness speaketh
lies. In the fear of the LORD is strong confidence: and his
children shall have a place of refuge. The fear of the LORD
is a fountain of life, to depart from the snares of death.
In the multitude of people is the king's honour: but in the
want of people is the destruction of the prince. He that is
slow to wrath is of great understanding: but he that is
hasty of spirit exalteth folly. A sound heart is the life of
the flesh: but envy the rottenness of the bones. He that
oppresseth the poor reproacheth his Maker: but he that
honoureth him hath mercy on the poor. The wicked is
driven away in his wickedness: but the righteous hath
hope in his death. Wisdom resteth in the heart of him
that hath understanding: but that which is in the midst
of fools is made known. Righteousness exalteth a nation:
but sin is a reproach to any people. The king's favour is
toward a wise servant: but his wrath is against him that
causeth shame.*

Day 43: Treasures of Wisdom (Proverbs 14:1-18)

Every wise woman builds her house and it stands,
But fools will tear down their own house with their hands.

If you're walking uprightly with God then you fear Him;
If you're wayward, devious, and perverse, you abhor Him.

In the fool's own mouth is a rod of pride,
But the wise men's lips keep them safe every time.

Where there are no oxen, the crib will be clean,
But the presence of oxen, a great blessing will mean.

A witness who's faithful, the truth will reveal,
But a false one will testify lies very well.

A scorner seeks wisdom but no sense is around,
But by men who have knowledge, it's easily found.

You should go from the presence of a man who's a fool
When you see that he's senseless and without a clue.

The prudent man's wisdom plans the route he should take,
But the folly of fools makes their path a mistake.

The arrogant man makes a joke of his wrongs;
In the house of the just is where favor belongs.

The heart its own bitterness would know or could tell;
No outsider could share in its gladness as well.

The house of the wicked shall be overthrown,
But the tent of the upright shall flourish and grow.

Sometimes a way to a man may seem right,
But it dead ends in death with no hope in sight.

Even in laughter the heart could be breaking,
And semblance of mirth that is seen may be faking.

The backslider is filled with his own ways of sin,
But a good man will be happy with the joy that's within.

The simple believe every word that is said,
But the prudent man looks well to the road up ahead.

A wise man fears and from evil withdraws,
But the fool rages on and his confidence is false.

A man with quick temper plays the fool with his wrath,
But the prudent man takes control of himself.

A crown of folly's the inheritance of fools;
A crown of knowledge is for prudent men's use.

CHECK IT OUT

Proverb:

"There is a way which seemeth right unto a man, but the end thereof are the ways of death" (Proverbs 14:12).

Precept:

Once as I was traveling to Arizona on a major highway through West Texas, I became concerned that I might be going the wrong way. I stopped and asked about the direction I was headed and discovered I was going south toward El Paso and the Mexican border instead of west toward New Mexico and Arizona. I'm sure I am not the only one who has ever been in this predicament. It is not hard to get disoriented, miss the turn, or follow wrong directions and find yourself going the opposite way from which you had intended to go.

The same is true in a spiritual sense. The Bible teaches that there is a way that seems right unto a man (Proverbs 14:12). He may live a certain way, talk a certain way, and act a certain way, thinking that it seems right, without realizing that the path he is on leads to death. It is one thing to intentionally decide not to go the right direction, but it is another thing to think you are going the right way and then find out you were completely wrong.

If you are planning a trip, it makes sense to get out the map and check the route you intend to take. It also makes sense to take the map along, just in case you need to refer back to it. It also makes sense to stop and ask for directions if at any time you become unsure of whether or not you are traveling in the right direction.

God's Word has been given to us as a map, or guidebook, to direct our path. Psalm 119:105 says, "Thy word is a lamp unto my feet, and a light unto my path." We should never presumptuously make a decision or choose a direction just because it seems right to us. We should always check first with God's Word to find out which way is the right way to go. David said, "Direct my footsteps according to your word; let no sin rule over me" (Psalm 119:133, NIV).

Many unfortunate accidents and tragedies have happened because people who thought they were headed the right way have mistakenly traveled into an area of danger. Several years ago, John F. Kennedy Jr. and his wife and sister-in-law were tragically killed in an airplane crash. According to reports, although Kennedy was a non-instrument-rated pilot, he chose to fly on a dark night in a route that would go over a thirty-mile body of water. Authorities determined that the probable cause of the crash was spatial disorientation. Other pilots flying in the same area reported no visual horizon because of the darkness of night and haze. Because Kennedy could not use the instruments designed to fly a plane in those types of conditions, he had to rely on what seemed right to him. However, with no visual horizon, he evidently became confused, and what he thought was up was actually down, causing him to strike the water in a nose-down position, leading to his death.[16]

Do not make the mistake of assuming you are on the right path or making the right choice just because it seems right to you. Take time to find direction from the Word of God and seek godly counsel from people you trust. Check it out!

Practice:

God has promised to lead and guide us into all truth. Rely on Him as you navigate through life. At every turn seek His direction to help you to take the right path.

Prayer:

Let the words found in Psalm 119:133 be your prayer today: "Order my steps in thy word: and let not any iniquity have dominion over me."

DAY 44: INSIGHT (PROVERBS 14:19-35)

The evil will finally bow before good;
The wicked at the gates of righteousness should.

The person next door oftentimes hates the poor;
The rich man has friends who are his more and more.

If you hate your neighbor, there's sin at your door,
But happy is he who is kind to the poor.

Don't those who plot evil usually go astray?
Do good and watch mercy and truth come your way.

In all labor there's profit, so find something to do;
Just to talk about working brings penury to you.

Wise men wear wisdom, as a crown on their head;
As the diadem for folly, fools wear foolishness instead.

An honest witness is a savior, saving souls and saving lives;
A false witness is a traitor, destroying men by telling lies.

The reverent fear of the Lord is strong confidence for me;
A place of refuge for His children shall He always keep.

Worshipful fear of the Lord is a fountain of life,
Where there is escape from the snares of death and strife.

In the multitude of people is the king's honor shown,
And the absence of numbers marks the downfall of
     the throne.

Understanding causes rulers to show mercy from wrath;
He who quickly shows anger finds folly in his path.

A mind that's at ease makes health come, makes it stay;
The rottenness of evil makes your life waste away.

Oppression of the poor mocks and insults your Maker,
But kindness and mercy will bring Him honor and favor.

A bad man is brought down by his own evil deeds;
Integrity is what a righteous man needs.

Wisdom settles in the minds of men of meditation;
Folly takes the place of sense in men without direction.

Righteousness exalts any nation on earth,
But sin's a reproach wherever your birth.

The king's favor goes toward his men who are able;
His wrath is incurred by the servants, unstable.

A GREAT NATION

Proverb:

"Righteousness exalteth a nation: but sin is a reproach to any people" (Proverbs 14:34).

Precept:

A nation that promotes itself, a nation that is belligerent toward its neighbors, a nation that schemes, lies, and continually wars, is not really a great nation, although it may be geographically large and militarily strong. What makes a nation great is its righteousness: morality, justice, honesty, decency, and uprightness. This proverb states that righteousness exalts a nation (Proverbs 14:34). In other words, righteousness will lift a nation up, cause it to prosper, and compel others to laud, acclaim, and pay tribute to it.

The United States of America is a nation that was founded for the cause of religious freedom and has long been considered a Christian nation. Alexis de Tocqueville, a French political thinker and historian of the 1800s, said this about America in his book *Democracy in America*: "America is great because she is good, and if America ever ceases to be good, America will cease to be great."[17]

When a nation takes a stand for righteousness, God is pleased and will exalt that nation. Conversely, sin is a reproach to any people, whether a nation or an individual. When a nation exalts itself and fails to honor God by doing the things that are right, it has become prideful, which marks that nation for a fall. (See Proverbs 16:18). Our country, which has such a wonderful past record of righteousness, should be careful lest we incur the displeasure of God. He, who has bestowed such blessings upon us, could change His attitude because of our sin, and we could be humiliated and brought down as a nation.

The promise of II Chronicles 7:14 gives the people of God

a hope for the salvation of any nation in which they live: "If my people, which are called by my name, shall humble themselves, and pray, and seek my face, and turn from their wicked ways; then will I hear from heaven, and will forgive their sin, and will heal their land." Grant it, almighty God!

Practice:

A nation is righteous because of individuals who are righteous. Humble yourself before God. Repent for the evil deeds of the nation. Pray that men will turn from their wicked ways. Pray for religious and political leaders to make wise decisions based on godly principles and moral values.

Prayer:

Lord, I pray that righteousness will prevail in our nation. I pray for our leaders and people of influence that they will help truth to triumph. Help us to humble ourselves before You and seek Your face so that You will forgive our sin and heal our land. Amen.

PROVERBS 15

A soft answer turneth away wrath: but grievous words stir up anger. The tongue of the wise useth knowledge aright: but the mouth of fools poureth out foolishness. The eyes of the LORD are in every place, beholding the evil and the good. A wholesome tongue is a tree of life: but perverseness therein is a breach in the spirit. A fool despiseth his father's instruction: but he that regardeth reproof is prudent. In the house of the righteous is much treasure: but in the revenues of the wicked is trouble. The lips of the wise disperse knowledge: but the heart of the foolish doeth not so. The sacrifice of the wicked is an abomination to the LORD: but the prayer of the upright is his delight. The way of the wicked is an abomination unto the LORD: but he loveth him that followeth after righteousness. Correction is grievous unto him that forsaketh the way: and he that hateth reproof shall die. Hell and destruction are before the LORD: how much more then the hearts of the children of men? A scorner loveth not one that reproveth him: neither will he go unto the wise. A merry heart maketh a cheerful countenance: but by sorrow of the heart the spirit is broken. The heart of him that hath understanding seeketh knowledge: but the mouth of fools feedeth on foolishness. All the days of the afflicted are evil: but he that is of a merry heart hath a continual feast. Better is little with the fear of the LORD than great treasure and trouble therewith. Better is a dinner of herbs where love is, than a stalled ox and hatred therewith. A wrathful man stirreth up strife: but he that is slow to anger appeaseth strife. The way of the slothful man is as an hedge of thorns: but the way of the righteous is made plain. A wise son maketh a glad father: but a foolish man despiseth his mother. Folly is joy to him that is destitute of wisdom: but a man of understanding walketh uprightly. Without counsel purposes are disappointed: but in the multitude of counsellers they are established. A man hath joy by the answer of his mouth: and a word spoken in due season, how good is it! The way of life is above to the wise, that he may depart from hell beneath. The LORD will destroy the house of the proud: but he will establish the border of the widow. The thoughts of the wicked are an abomination to the LORD: but the words of the pure are pleasant words. He that is greedy of gain troubleth his own house; but he that hateth gifts shall live. The heart of the righteous studieth to answer: but the mouth of the wicked poureth out evil things. The LORD is far from the wicked: but he heareth the prayer of the righteous. The light of the eyes rejoiceth the heart: and a good report maketh the bones fat. The ear that heareth the reproof of life abideth among the wise. He that refuseth instruction despiseth his own soul: but he that heareth reproof getteth understanding. The fear of the LORD is the instruction of wisdom; and before honour is humility.

DAY 45: CORRECTION AND ADMONITION
(PROVERBS 15:1-13)

An answer that's soft will cause wrath to subside,
But grievous words stir up anger inside.

The tongue of the wise uses knowledge aright,
But the mouth of a fool speaks talk that is trite!

The eyes of the Lord are in every spot;
Over wicked and good He is keeping a watch.

A tongue that is wholesome is a tree of life;
A quarrelsome tongue will crush and bring strife.

He's a fool who despises his father's correction,
But he's prudent when he can receive admonition.

In the house of the righteous you'll find so much treasure;
The revenue of wickedness brings wrath in great measure.

A wise man's discourse will much knowledge diffuse;
The heart of the fool is perverse and abused.

The sacrifice of the wicked to the Lord's an abomination,
But the prayer of the upright brings Him great satisfaction.

A wicked man's way is loathsome to the Lord,
But the Lord loves the man who is true to His Word.

Harsh discipline awaits him who abandons God's way;
He who hates His correction is doomed for death
    and will pay.

Destruction and hell are both open to Him,
And much more the hearts of the children of men.

A scorner despises the man who reproves;
The presence of wise men he avoids, too.

The heart of the happy man shows on his face,
But sorrow of heart will the spirit efface.

GOOD THINGS

Proverb:
"A soft answer . . . a wholesome tongue . . . a merry heart
. . . a cheerful countenance" (Proverbs 15:1, 4, 13).

Precept:
Someone has said that life is a battlefield, not a recreation room. In the course of our lives, many unpleasant things happen to us that cause sadness, confusion, and sorrow. Death is ever present. Sickness is a common occurrence. Afflictions and handicaps are endured. Accidents and tragedies happen. Misfortunes and misunderstandings occur.

An old poem says: "Laugh, and the world laughs with you; Weep, and you weep alone. For the sad old earth must borrow its mirth, But has trouble enough of its own."[18] Even Jesus was a man of sorrows and acquainted with grief. (See Isaiah 53:3.) Yet He did not intend for us to live our lives in a state of gloom and despair. He intended that we live life abundantly, in spite of whatever the day may bring.

We should learn that it is not what happens to us that really matters, but how we respond to it. Proverbs 15 gives us several good things to equip us for a proper response:

1. A soft answer (Proverbs 15:1). To be the recipient of someone's cruel and abusive speech is not easy. However, a harsh response might produce a quarrel, perhaps a fight, or maybe even a murder. Those who choose to respond with a soft answer and a pleasant disposition can often diffuse the whole situation.

2. A wholesome tongue (Proverbs 15:4). A person who has a wholesome tongue is one who knows how to speak kindly in a way that will not bring division. An old rule of thumb is that before you speak, ask yourself these questions: Is it true? Is it kind? Is it necessary? If it is not true, do not say it. If it causes someone to be hurt or reveals something that would make him uncomfortable, keep silent. If it really does not add anything to the subject being discussed, then be wise and just listen.

3. A merry heart which brings a cheerful countenance (Proverbs 15:13). Even though life does bring heartache and disappointment, we must still look for reasons to be happy. Sometimes we have to smile when we do not feel like it, and laugh to keep from crying. The Bible teaches that laughter does good like a medicine. (See Proverbs 17:22.)

When faced with life's unpleasantness, remember you choose your response. You will feel much better if you respond with good things: a soft answer, a wholesome tongue, a merry heart, and a cheerful countenance.

Practice:

Check the tone of your voice when you respond to a difficult situation. Are your frustrations with the situation or the person you are addressing evident? Temper your response to give a soft answer. Think before you speak. Speak positive and uplifting things, and do not dwell on the negative. Choose to have a merry heart and bring joy and happiness to those around you. A smile is a small effort that brings rewards. People will find it hard not to respond in kind to your smiling face.

Prayer:

Lord, help me as I speak to others to give a soft answer. Let Your joy be evident in my life, and help me to have a merry heart and a cheerful countenance so I can spread that joy to others.

DAY 46: CRITICISM AND INSTRUCTION (PROVERBS 15:14-21)

Men of wisdom seek for knowledge with their hearts
    and are wise,
But the mouth of the foolish on his folly relies.

Depression causes misery to the greatest or least,
But happiness will make life a continuous feast.

It is better to fear God and have little of worth
Than to have a great fortune and be anxious on earth.

It is better to have nothing and eat vegetables
    throughout life
Than eat meats of the finest, in hatred and strife.

An ill-tempered person will stir up contention;
A temperate man soothes discord and dissension.

Like thorns in a hedge is a life of don't care!
But the path of the upright is a broad thoroughfare.

A son who is wise fills his father with gladness;
A son who is foolish fills his mother with sadness.

A man who is senseless thinks that folly is fine,
But the wise man will take the right path every time.

THE CHOICE

Proverb:
    "Better is little with the fear of the LORD than great treasure
and trouble therewith. Better is a dinner of herbs where love is,
than a stalled ox and hatred therewith" (Proverbs 15:16-17).

Precept:
    Life is full of choices. This proverb tells us that it is better
to choose to fear God and have little than to choose great treasure that is accompanied by trouble. Whichever you prefer is
your choice. And you will be presented with this same choice
throughout your life in a variety of ways.
    Maybe you will have an opportunity to marry someone
wealthy who is unsaved. Although you might never have to
worry about money, if your mate is ungodly and does not agree
with or support your desire to live for God, your life may be
miserable. Maybe you will have an opportunity for a business
deal that will bring a great profit to yourself yet cause others to
be wounded or destroyed in the process.
    The scenarios may be different, but the choice is the same:
Can you be content with what you have in the fear of the Lord?
Or will you seek after money, regardless of what damage it might
do? Will you make your decision based on wisdom, godliness,

and regard for the will of God in your life? Or will it be based on a selfish desire for riches at the expense of your salvation?

Proverbs 15:17 gives an example of the principle stated in the preceding verse: "Better a meal of vegetables where there is love than a fattened calf with hatred" (NIV). Who can enjoy a lavish meal when the atmosphere is filled with hate and animosity? It would be a much better choice to enjoy an inexpensive meal in an atmosphere of love and camaraderie. Some things are worth more than money.

Obviously, it takes money to live, and having extra money helps. But if you had a choice between being right with God with less money or having more money without His love and favor in your life, which would you choose? I hope you will make the right choice!

Practice:

Do not let glamour, fame, or wealth deceive you into making a wrong choice. Understand that none of these things can guarantee happiness. Like Moses, make the choice "to suffer affliction with the people of God, than to enjoy the pleasures of sin for a season" (Hebrews 11:25).

Prayer:

Lord, I want my life to be filled with Your love and favor. Help me to make good decisions and to seek to follow You in all that I do. Help me to remember that this world is not my home and that my goal in life is to live according to Your will so that I can live in heaven with You.

DAY 47: COUNSEL AND DIRECTION (PROVERBS 15:22-33)

Without the right counsel plans will not prevail,
But with counselors many they succeed without fail.

There is joy to be found in the utterance we make;
It is always so good, words in season to speak.

When we prudently live we go upward and on;
We avoid the way downward, that hell we may shun.

The Lord will destroy the proud and their house;
He'll confirm the right border for a surviving spouse.

The thoughts of the wicked by God have been cursed;
The most pleasant speech is the words of the pure.

He who's greedy of gain will to his own house bring sorrow,
But if you hate a bribery, you will live till tomorrow.

The heart of the righteous ponders what he shall say;
The wicked man answers without thought or delay.

The Lord keeps His distance from men who do wrong;
At the prayer of the righteous, He proves Himself strong.

The light of the eyes causes joy in men's hearts;
The bones will grow fat from the good news reports.

The ear that can hear a reproof of correction
Will cause you to walk in the wise man's direction.

He despises his soul who correction disdains;
He'll be counted as wise if his ways he can change.

The fear of the LORD is the start of instruction,
And to learn to be humble is the way to promotion.

TAKE THE HIGH ROAD

Proverb:
    "The way of life is above to the wise, that he may depart
from hell beneath" (Proverbs 15:24).

Precept:
    Every day we are faced with decisions that shape the
course of our lives. All of us have made both right and wrong
decisions. We have felt the benefits when we have made right

decisions and the sting of pain when we made wrong ones. Often it is only with the advantage of hindsight that we are able to look back and analyze the choices we have made.

My son recently went horseback riding in the Sierra Nevada Mountain range that runs along the border of California and Nevada. The area is rich in history with stories of Indians, bandits, the Pony Express, stagecoaches, and the mystique of the untamed West. Many of the trails he traveled were paths that Indians had made many years ago. Indian paintings on the rocks were indications that someone had been on these trails long ago. He told me that the higher he traveled, the more he was able to look back and see that he was on the right path. And by looking below he could see the obstacles and danger he had avoided by staying on a proven path.

Many times we are unwilling to take the high road. Our nature is to take the path of what seems to be the least resistance. We go our own way only to find that what seemed easy is now hard. We sometimes frustrate our faith and waste precious time by trying to navigate through life by our own will.

There are no shortcuts to heaven. You have to be determined to stay on the high road. It is not always easy and there may be some uphill climbs, but it will eventually lead you to your destination. Do not complicate your decisions. Just take the proven path of righteousness, and it will lead you to where you want to go. Many have gone before us, blazing a trail of truth and a highway of righteousness. Isaiah said, "And thine ears shall hear a word behind thee, saying, This is the way, walk ye in it, when ye turn to the right hand, and when ye turn to the left" (Isaiah 30:21).

Jesus said, "I am the way, the truth, and the life" (John 14:6). If you are in doubt as to which road to take, follow Him. He will lead you in the direction you must go. Do not be determined to take the hard road; it only leads to disappointment and hell. Learn from those who have blazed a trail before you, and take the high road. You will gain new heights in God and a fresh vantage point from which you can observe all the obstacles you have avoided.

Practice:

As Christians, we should seek to live a life that is above reproach. My mother was greatly influenced by the classic book, *In His Steps*, by Charles M. Sheldon. In the book, a group of people resolved that with every decision they would ask the question, "What would Jesus do?" This became a popular refrain in our home when we were faced with questions for which we did not know the answer. My mother's reply was always, "What would Jesus do?" Ask yourself this question each time you are faced with a decision. If you respond as Jesus would, you will definitely be on the right road.

Prayer:

Lord, I want to follow the high road that You have for my life. I do not want to take the road that leads to death and hell. Help me to seek Your direction each time I have a difficult decision to make. Let my life bring praise and glory to You.

PROVERBS 16

The preparations of the heart in man, and the answer of the tongue, is from the LORD. All the ways of a man are clean in his own eyes; but the LORD weigheth the spirits. Commit thy works unto the LORD, and thy thoughts shall be established. The LORD hath made all things for himself: yea, even the wicked for the day of evil. Every one that is proud in heart is an abomination to the LORD: though hand join in hand, he shall not be unpunished. By mercy and truth iniquity is purged: and by the fear of the LORD men depart from evil. When a man's ways please the LORD, he maketh even his enemies to be at peace with him. Better is a little with righteousness than great revenues without right. A man's heart deviseth his way: but the LORD directeth his steps. A divine sentence is in the lips of the king: his mouth transgresseth not in judgment. A just weight and balance are the LORD's: all the weights of the bag are his work. It is an abomination to kings to commit wickedness: for the throne is established by righteousness. Righteous lips are the delight of kings; and they love him that speaketh right. The wrath of a king is as messengers of death: but a wise man will pacify it. In the

light of the king's countenance is life; and his favour is
as a cloud of the latter rain. How much better is it to get
wisdom than gold! and to get understanding rather to
be chosen than silver! The highway of the upright is to
depart from evil: he that keepeth his way preserveth his
soul. Pride goeth before destruction, and an haughty
spirit before a fall. Better it is to be of an humble spirit
with the lowly, than to divide the spoil with the proud.
He that handleth a matter wisely shall find good: and
whoso trusteth in the LORD, *happy is he. The wise in*
heart shall be called prudent: and the sweetness of the
lips increaseth learning. Understanding is a wellspring
of life unto him that hath it: but the instruction of fools
is folly. The heart of the wise teacheth his mouth, and
addeth learning to his lips. Pleasant words are as an
honeycomb, sweet to the soul, and health to the bones.
There is a way that seemeth right unto a man, but the
end thereof are the ways of death. He that laboureth
laboureth for himself; for his mouth craveth it of him.
An ungodly man diggeth up evil: and in his lips there
is as a burning fire. A froward man soweth strife: and
a whisperer separateth chief friends. A violent man
enticeth his neighbour, and leadeth him into the way
that is not good. He shutteth his eyes to devise froward
things: moving his lips he bringeth evil to pass. The
hoary head is a crown of glory, if it be found in the way
of righteousness. He that is slow to anger is better than
the mighty; and he that ruleth his spirit than he that
taketh a city. The lot is cast into the lap; but the whole
disposing thereof is of the LORD.

DAY 48: WHAT DOES GOD SAY?
(PROVERBS 16:1-15)

The preparations of the heart, in every man's way,
And the answers he makes are what the Lord has him say.

All a man's ways are clean in his sight,
But the Lord weighs the spirit to see if it's right.

To establish your thoughts and to cause them to stand,
Commit your works to the Lord; place them all in His hand.

For His purpose He made all things that appear;
Without Him no evil man would be here.

It's offensive to God if you're arrogant and proud;
They'll not go unpunished though they may be a crowd.

Mercy and truth will purge guilt from the heart;
If you fear the Lord you'll from evil depart.

When a man pleases God in every way,
He will make all his enemies keep peace all his days.

It is better to have righteousness, with little at home,
Than to tolerate injustice for great revenues to own.

A man plans his own course and thinks it's correct,
And it will be, if God helps his steps to direct.

Even a king needs the help of the Lord,
To give inspiration in judgment and word.

A just balance and scales belong to the Lord;
Injustice is wrong and we're weighed by His Word.

A kingdom's established by justice and right;
Kings who are wicked are a curse in God's sight.

Truth-speaking lips are the delight of a king;
They love men who're honest in everything.

The wrath of a king a death message will send;
A wise man will pacify and cause it to end.

There is life in the light of the look of a king,
For his favor brings blessings like rain clouds in spring.

THE MIRROR

Proverb:

"All the ways of a man are clean in his own eyes; but the LORD weigheth the spirits" (Proverbs 16:2).

Precept:

The mirror is marvelous in its ability to reflect our appearance, but how we see ourselves is not always correct. A man looks at himself in a mirror, but he cannot see what others see. He speaks, but he does not hear himself as others do. He complains about the annoying actions of others, yet he does not realize that he often does the very same thing. Sometimes it is through the eyes of others that we understand the truth about ourselves.

Once, while preaching a revival at a certain church, I noticed a man with extra-long arms. I said to the pastor, "That brother has some of the longest arms I have ever seen!" The pastor replied, "That's what he said about you!" Later, I went to the man and asked him what size sleeve length he wore. Much to my surprise, he wore the same size as I did. Although my arms seemed just right to me, they looked long to him. And although his arms looked just right to him, they seemed long to me.

James said that the Word of God is like a mirror. (See James 1:23-25.) It is a special mirror, for it shows us not how we see ourselves but how God sees us. God is the only one who is able to see us as we really are. Man looks on the outward appearance, but God looks on the heart. (See I Samuel 16:7.)

During King David's reign, he committed adultery with Bathsheba. He then had her husband killed. Heady with his own power, he tried to justify his sinful actions. God sent the prophet Nathan to David to point out the error of his ways. The prophet told him a parable of a wealthy man with many sheep, who took another man's only lamb and killed it for his meal. David became irate and declared that he would punish him for what he had done. When he asked for the man's identity, Nathan replied, "You are the man, David!" (See II Samuel 12:7.)

Just as David did not recognize himself as the one who had sinned, we sometimes cannot see the error of our own ways. God is the only one who is able to weigh our spirit and evaluate us properly. To understand what He sees, we must look in the mirror of His Word. Our prayer should be as David's: "Create in me a clean heart, O God; and renew a right spirit within me" (Psalm 51:10).

Practice:

When you look into a mirror, remind yourself that God is looking at your heart. What does He see? Is there anything that you know will not be pleasing to Him? Decide to make the necessary changes.

Prayer:

Lord, I want my heart to be clean and my spirit to be right. When You look at me, may You see a reflection of Yourself in my life.

DAY 49: EXAMPLES—GOOD AND BAD (PROVERBS 16:16-21)

To get wisdom is better than gold for your wealth,
Or understanding to choose more than silver itself.

The highway of the upright will from evil abstain;
If you safeguard your pathway, your own soul you'll gain.

Pride goes before destruction—like a dead-end street;
He who has a haughty spirit, a great fall will surely meet.

It is better to be humble and walk with lowly men
Than to divide the loot with proud men, who will plunder
    when they can.

If you're wise and are successful, you will first
    devise a plan.
If you really want to prosper, trust the Lord; be a happy man.

For your prudence to be noted, be a wise man in your walk.
Put some sweetness on your lips; have influence
    in your talk.

HAPPINESS IS

Proverb:

"He that handleth a matter wisely shall find good: and whoso trusteth in the LORD, happy is he" (Proverbs 16:20).

Precept:

Everyone wants to be happy. Sadly, few people on earth seem to find that place of total satisfaction. Those who want riches never have enough. Those who are discontent with their life can never be satisfied. Those who are sexually promiscuous go through numerous relationships seeking true love. Those who use pleasure-inducing drugs or alcohol become addicted and have to continually feed their habits. They have not discovered the secret that true happiness comes when we place our trust in God.

One definition of happiness is the enjoyment of pleasure without pain; blessedness, or satisfaction. An old song says, "Happiness is to know the Savior, Living a life within His favor, Having a change in my behavior, Happiness is the Lord!"[19]

God's Word is full of promises of happiness for His people: "Happy is that people, whose God is the LORD" (Psalm 144:15); "Happy is he that hath the God of Jacob for his help, whose hope is in the LORD his God" (Psalm 146:5); "He that keepeth the law, happy is he" (Proverbs 29:18); "Behold, happy is the man whom God correcteth" (Job 5:17); "Behold, we count them happy which endure" (James 5:11); and, "If ye be reproached for the name of Christ, happy are ye" (I Peter 4:14).

Happiness cannot be found in the pleasures that this world has to offer. It can only be found in a relationship with Jesus Christ. The Bible teaches that our pleasure should come from being in His presence. "Thou wilt shew me the path of life: in thy presence is fulness of joy; at thy right hand there are pleasures for evermore" (Psalm 16:11).

Practice:

Your joy is found in Jesus. As you experience His presence and see the ways that He is working in your life, you cannot help but smile.

Prayer:

Lord, thank You for the joy that You give to us in spite of our circumstances or place in life. You are the source of our strength and joy. You give us happiness like no other. For this we give You thanks.

Week 8

DAY 50: THE WAY OF THE WISE
(PROVERBS 16:22-33)

Wisdom springs forth like a fountain at pools,
But instruction is nothing but folly to fools.

The heart of the wise tells his mouth what to say,
Adds learning to his lips, uses persuasion to sway.

Pleasant words are like honey from out of the comb,
Makes them sweet to the taste, and gives health
    to the bones.

There's a way that seems right to a man but go slow,
For that way will lead you to death down below.

The working man labors for himself alone,
For the need of his hunger urges him on.

In order to find evil, a man dirt overturns;
In his lips there's a fire that continually burns.

An intriguer sows strife as a man would sow grain;
A whisperer separates friends, causing pain.

The violent entices his neighbor to wrong
And leads him to places he does not belong.

A wicked man deliberates evil things he can do;
He sets them in motion and carries them through.

The righteous who live to old age, white hair
Like a crown of glory, on his head he will wear.

It is better to be patient than a mighty warrior grow.
One would rather rule his temper, than a city overthrow.

When the lot is cast in the lap, it is still,
The disposing of it, to find the Lord's will.

DON'T LIGHT THAT FUSE!

Proverb:

"He that is slow to anger is better than the mighty; and he that ruleth his spirit than he that taketh a city" (Proverbs 16:32).

Precept:

Both a firecracker and a stick of dynamite are lit by a fuse. Neither will go off unless there is something to ignite it. However, when lit, both will cause an explosion. Likewise, anger can be as mild as a small firecracker, or it can be as explosive as a stick of dynamite. The Bible teaches that we should be slow to anger and learn to rule our own spirit.

The first murder occurred when Cain became angry with his brother, Abel. Instead of trying to control his anger, he gave way to it, then attacked his brother and killed him. (See Genesis 4:8-9.) A fit of rage can cause a parent to injure a child, a husband to strike his wife, or a man or woman to assault his or her neighbor or friend. Your anger can cause you to hurt someone you love, commit crimes you did not intend, and do things that would not have happened if you had been in control of your own spirit.

So how can a person control his or her temper and keep the anger fuse from being lit? The Bible is very helpful in teaching us what we should do.

1. We learn to "keep cool" by training. Proverbs 22:6 says, "Train up a child in the way he should go: and when he is old, he will not depart from it." From early childhood, a child should be disciplined to avoid outbursts of temper that cause him to strike out at those around him. Training should continue through adulthood until a man or woman has learned this valuable lesson.

2. We learn to appeal to authority. God has instituted human government for our own benefit, and we learn that

instead of fighting, we can appeal to parents, teachers, and other authorities for judgment that will resolve our differences. Leave the law enforcement to the authorities and the vengeance to God. Do not try to take it into your own hands.

3. We become mature. As adults, and especially as Christians, we learn to put away anger, wrath, malice, and all other things that will bring us into conflict with others. (See Colossians 3:8.) While the actions and words of others may anger us, we are advised to "be angry, and sin not." (See Ephesians 4:26.) We are to allow God's Spirit to control the evil reactions of the flesh. (See Galatians 5:19-21.)

If you can gain control of your own emotions, you are a hero. It is better than if you had conquered a city in warfare. You may have a short fuse, but just make sure that you do not light it!

Practice:

Don't let your anger rule you. Use discussion, proper authority, and the laws of the land to resolve your issues rather than taking matters into your own hands. If you struggle with anger, discover ways to control that anger. You will grow in maturity as you learn to control your anger, rather than letting that anger control you and your actions.

Prayer:

Lord, I do not want my anger to cause me to sin. Help me to control my anger. Help me to find the right way to deal with issues that upset me and would cause me to lose control of my emotions.

PROVERBS 17

Better is a dry morsel, and quietness therewith, than an house full of sacrifices with strife. A wise servant shall have rule over a son that causeth shame, and shall have part of the inheritance among the brethren. The fining pot is for silver, and the furnace for gold: but the LORD trieth the hearts. A wicked doer giveth heed to false lips; and a liar giveth ear to a naughty tongue.

Whoso mocketh the poor reproacheth his Maker: and he that is glad at calamities shall not be unpunished. Children's children are the crown of old men; and the glory of children are their fathers. Excellent speech becometh not a fool: much less do lying lips a prince. A gift is as a precious stone in the eyes of him that hath it: whithersoever it turneth, it prospereth. He that covereth a transgression seeketh love: but he that repeateth a matter separateth very friends. A reproof entereth more into a wise man than an hundred stripes into a fool. An evil man seeketh only rebellion: therefore a cruel messenger shall be sent against him. Let a bear robbed of her whelps meet a man, rather than a fool in his folly. Whoso rewardeth evil for good, evil shall not depart from his house. The beginning of strife is as when one letteth out water: therefore leave off contention, before it be meddled with. He that justifieth the wicked, and he that condemneth the just, even they both are abomination to the LORD. Wherefore is there a price in the hand of a fool to get wisdom, seeing he hath no heart to it? A friend loveth at all times, and a brother is born for adversity. A man void of understanding striketh hands, and becometh surety in the presence of his friend. He loveth transgression that loveth strife: and he that exalteth his gate seeketh destruction. He that hath a froward heart findeth no good: and he that hath a perverse tongue falleth into mischief. He that begetteth a fool doeth it to his sorrow: and the father of a fool hath no joy. A merry heart doeth good like a medicine: but a broken spirit drieth the bones. A wicked man taketh a gift out of the bosom to pervert the ways of judgment. Wisdom is before him that hath understanding; but the eyes of a fool are in the ends of the earth. A foolish son is a grief to his father, and bitterness to her that bare him. Also to punish the just is not good, nor to strike princes for equity. He that hath knowledge spareth his words: and a man of understanding is of an excellent spirit. Even a fool, when he holdeth his peace, is counted wise: and he that shutteth his lips is esteemed a man of understanding.

DAY 51: REFRAINING FROM RIDICULE (PROVERBS 17:1-6)

Life is better with quietness (though the crust may be dry)
Than a house of contention, with a good food supply.

Save the brother's inheritance from a worthless son's rule;
Set a servant with sense to provide for them all.

There's refining for silver or for gold and its parts,
But the Lord is the only refiner of hearts.

A man who is evil gives heed to wicked lips
And gives ear to falsehood from a mischievous tongue's slips.

If you make fun of the poor of the land,
You are bringing reproach to the Master of men.

If you rejoice in the harm that others have known,
You're asking for punishment for yourself to be shown.

Children's children are a crown to your head when
    you're old;
Children's glory is their father, when they do as
    they're told.

FAMILY TREASURES

Proverb:
"Children's children are the crown of old men; and the glory of children are their fathers" (Proverbs 17:6).

Precept:
Best-selling author Lois Wyse said, "If I had known how wonderful it would be to have grandchildren, I'd have had them first."[20] And I tend to agree. God has blessed my wife and me with ten beautiful grandchildren, whom we love dearly. Each of them is unique and brings a special joy to our lives.

Grandchildren are the crown of old men (and women as well) and are a great treasure to any family. A friend of mine, whose children are unmarried professionals, will shake his head sadly as he laments his lack of grandchildren. I, on the other hand, am continually amused, delighted, and thrilled with the antics, anecdotes, and accomplishments of my children's children. I find myself repeating them often to anyone who will listen.

Recently, my son, told a humorous story while preaching. The audience responded with laughter. After the laughter died down, my two-year-old granddaughter shouted out, "Funny, Daddy. Funny!" And the audience laughed again.

I am separated from most of my grandchildren by many miles, so the times we spend together are very precious to me. Thankfully, we have made some wonderful memories of special times together in California, Missouri, and Virginia. I look forward to their phone calls, letters, and e-mails and try to keep up with what is happening in their lives.

Parents are also a great treasure to the family, for the "glory of children are their fathers." My own father was the best man and Christian I have ever known. He has been, and will always be, my hero. His life was prematurely taken as a result of injuries he received while carrying burning curtains out of the church he pastored in Hennepin, Oklahoma. The building survived, but my father did not. Throughout his life and in his death, he taught me by example how to live unselfishly, always putting the needs of others ahead of my own.

Do you have parents? Children? Grandchildren? Great-grandchildren? If so, stop to consider what each one of them means to your life. You will find that they are some of your greatest treasures.

Practice:

Connect with your family today. Call, write, or email your loved ones and share with them your love and concern for their welfare. Do not let the miles that separate you from your family form a wall that hinders your relationship. No matter how far away you are, you can still remain close in your hearts and have a relationship that distance or time cannot steal away.

Prayer:

Lord, bless my family today. Help me to show them how much I love and appreciate them. If there are emotional distances that have formed, please help me to find a way to bridge the gap and restore that relationship.

DAY 52: KEEPING THE PEACE (PROVERBS 17:7-17)

A fool is a fool though he makes a good speech;
Princes are not princes when they lie through their teeth.

To the man who receives, a gift is to him,
Wherever it turns, a valuable gem.

If you cover a wrong for the love of a friend,
Don't repeat it to others, lest your friendship would end.

A reproof helps a wise man, for he feels the sting,
More than one hundred stripes on a fool's back could bring.

A man in rebellion's so evil, it seems to me,
That nothing can stop him, but one crueler than he.

I would rather a bear meet, that is robbed of her whelps,
Than a fool in his folly, whom no one can help.

The law of the harvest means giving evil for good
Will cause evil on your house forever, as it should.

When you start up a quarrel, you will find there's no end,
Like a hole that is punched in a dike or a dam.

Therefore leave off contention, and try making peace,
Before the meddling gets muddy and the water's released.

To justify the wicked is a shame and disgrace;
To vilify the just is an abomination in God's face.

Why would a fool pay a price to be wise,
When his heart is not in it, however he tries?

A friend is the one who will love you always;
A brother is born to stand firm, come what may.

A TRUE FRIEND

Proverb:
"A friend loveth at all times, and a brother is born for adversity" (Proverbs 17:17).

Precept:
I had only one brother—and five sisters. You would have thought that my brother and I would have been the best of buddies, as well as comrades and allies against the female forces. However, he was four years older than I, and a lot bigger and tougher.

Bob was 6'4" by the age of fourteen, and I was still a scrawny ten-year-old with glasses. He did not want to live for God and left home at a young age to join the armed forces. He later married and relocated to another city. Although we loved one another and visited when we could, we had very little in common except our kinship.

But just as David, the youngest of eight brothers, found a special friend in Saul's son, Jonathan (I Samuel 18:1), I, too, found a friend, who became like a brother to me. I had already left home to attend college but returned one weekend to visit. My parents told me about a young couple who recently had graduated from Bible school and who had moved to Oklahoma to pastor their first church. I later met them, and a friendship began that developed into a lifelong bond that is still strong today.

One of the greatest privileges in life is to have a true friend who will love you for who you are and will stick with you through the good times and the bad. Jonathan and David were that kind of friend to each other. Even when Jonathan's own father turned against David, Jonathan stood by his friend. He warned David of the impending danger, then tried to reason with his father on David's behalf. (See I Samuel 19:1-6.) Years later, after Jonathan's death, David, who was then king, showed great kindness to Jonathan's crippled son because of his friendship with the boy's father (II Samuel 9:6-7).

Although my brother and I were not close, I prayed for him throughout the years. When he was fifty-nine years old, he called and asked if he could drive from where he lived in Texas to my home in Missouri so that I could baptize him in Jesus' name. I will never forget the thrill of that day. My brother later received the Holy Ghost and lived for God until his death at age seventy-seven. Our relationship changed during those years; although already brothers, we became friends as well.

I am thankful for the many friends God has given to me. A true friend and a brother is a wonderful thing to have!

Practice:

Do you have a close friend? Do you have a friendship that has been neglected? Find a way to connect with a friend today. If you don't have many friends, seek to build a new relationship. A person who shows himself a friend to others will be blessed.

Prayer:

Lord, I thank You for the friendships I have and for the way they bless my life. Help me to be the kind of friend to them that I need to be, and help me to seek opportunities to be a friend to those around me.

DAY 53: THE CHOICE BETWEEN FOLLY AND WISDOM (PROVERBS 17:18-28)

It's a man with no wisdom who will pledge to make bail
For the crime of a friend or a neighbor in jail.

He who treasures transgression and loves to have strife
Is marked for destruction and the loss of his life.

Nothing good will a man with a wayward heart get;
A contrary tongue leads to calamity's net.

Begetting a son who is stupid is sad;
A father with a fool for a son is not glad.

A merry heart is like a medicine to you,
But a spirit that's broken makes your bones feel bad, too!

A man who is wicked takes a gift as a bribe
To circumvent justice and turn it aside.

If you have understanding, keep your sight on the goal;
The ends of earth are in the eyes of a fool.

A son who is foolish brings grief to his dad,
And his mother is bitter for the son whom she had.

It's unfair that the innocent are fined, pay a fee,
Or that princes are beaten, while the guilty go free.

He who limits his words is a man of good sense,
And a good spirit shows a man's intelligence.

If a fool keeps his mouth shut, no one knows he's not bright,
So keep silent and see, you'll be thought sensible and right.

Can You Keep a Secret?

Proverb:

"He that hath knowledge spareth his words: and a man of understanding is of an excellent spirit. Even a fool, when he holdeth his peace, is counted wise: and he that shutteth his lips is esteemed a man of understanding" (Proverbs 17:27-28).

Precept:

Father's Day was approaching, and my five-year-old grandson knew what his mother had bought for his dad. However, she had instructed him not to tell anyone what the present was because it was a secret. During the days leading up to Father's Day, I asked him to tell me the secret, but he refused. He wanted to show that he could keep a secret.

I believe that keeping a secret is one of the greatest challenges for mankind because it involves controlling the tongue. James said, "The tongue can no man tame; it is an unruly evil, full of deadly poison" (James 3:8). We can tame wild animals and train vicious beasts, but what a challenge it is to bring the tongue under submission! Wisdom is just as much about knowing when to be silent as it is about knowing when to speak.

Some people just do not know when to be quiet. They seem to fall in love with the sound of their own voice. Someone said, "It is better for men to think you a fool, than to open your mouth and prove it!" A man with knowledge understands that words are powerful and that they are to be used with discretion. Even a foolish man who holds his peace can be credited with wisdom simply by his silence.

When our children are born, we spend several years teaching them to talk. They will then spend the rest of their lives learning how to be quiet. Knowing when to speak and knowing when to be silent is a mark of wisdom and maturity. Can you keep a secret? Can you resist the impulse to blurt something out at a time when nothing should be said? Can you exercise vocal restraint when your passions demand otherwise? James said, "If any man offend not in word, the same is a perfect man, and able also to bridle the whole body" (James 3:2).

Practice:

Keep the secrets that have been entrusted to you. Just because you know something does not give you the right to share it with others. Learn to be a "safe" person whom others can trust.

Prayer:

Lord, I want to guard my tongue. Give me the wisdom to know when to speak and when to be silent. Help me to keep the secrets that have been entrusted in my care.

PROVERBS 18

Through desire a man, having separated himself, seeketh and intermeddleth with all wisdom. A fool hath no delight in understanding, but that his heart may discover itself. When the wicked cometh, then cometh also contempt, and with ignominy reproach. The words of a man's mouth are as deep waters, and the wellspring of wisdom as a flowing brook. It is not good to accept the person of the wicked, to overthrow the righteous in judgment. A fool's lips enter into contention, and his mouth calleth for strokes. A fool's mouth is his destruction, and his lips are the snare of his soul. The words of a talebearer are as wounds, and they go down into the innermost parts of the belly. He also that is slothful in his work is brother to him that is a great waster. The name of the LORD is a strong tower: the righteous runneth into it, and is safe. The rich man's wealth is his strong city, and as an high wall in his own conceit. Before destruction the heart of man is haughty, and before honour is humility. He that answereth a matter before he heareth it, it is folly and shame unto him. The spirit of a man will sustain his infirmity; but a wounded spirit who can bear? The heart of the prudent getteth knowledge; and the ear of the wise seeketh knowledge. A man's gift maketh room for him, and bringeth him before great men. He that is first in his own cause seemeth just; but his neighbour cometh and searcheth him. The lot causeth contentions to cease, and parteth between the mighty. A brother offended is harder to be won than a strong city: and their contentions are like the bars of a castle. A man's belly shall be satisfied with the fruit of his mouth; and with the increase of his lips shall he be filled. Death and life are in the power of the tongue: and they that love it shall eat the fruit thereof. Whoso findeth a wife findeth a good thing, and obtaineth favour of the LORD. The poor useth intreaties; but the rich answereth roughly. A man that hath friends must shew himself friendly: and there is a friend that sticketh closer than a brother.

DAY 54: DON'T BE A FOOL (PROVERBS 18:1-8)

Through desire, a man can consecrate and separation make,
To start the search for wisdom, whatever it will take.

A fool has no desire for learning or to understanding find;
He only wants to express himself, whatever's on his mind.

Vice leads a man to wickedness and the contempt it brings;
Ignominy will bring reproach with all its hateful stings.

The words of wise men all are like waters of a pool;
They flow deep, they spring high, and the words refresh
      and cool.

It is not good to accept a man of wickedness, I know,
For righteousness and judgment he will try to overthrow.

A fool's talk will bring contention and cause trouble on
      his track;
By his tongue he causes anger, brings a beating to his back.

For his mouth is his destruction and his lips will
      weave a snare
For a fool to be caught in it, and his soul will soon be there.

A talebearer's words are as wounds that remain;
They go deep in your heart and cause lingering pain.

STAY WITH THE GROUP

Proverb:
      "Through desire a man, having separated himself, seeketh
and intermeddleth with all wisdom" (Proverbs 18:1).
      "A man who isolates himself seeks his own desire: He rages
against all wise judgment" (Proverbs 18:1, NKJV).

Precept:
      We were not created to be isolated from mankind. Everyone,
regardless of personality and personal preference, has a need to
connect with someone else. Adam, the first man, was created by
the very hands of God and received from Him the breath of life.
However, God said, "It is not good that the man should be alone;
I will make him an help meet for him" (Genesis 2:18). We are
inextricably linked to others by our Creator. "None of us liveth to

himself, and no man dieth to himself" (Romans 14:7). Therefore, we cannot separate ourselves from our need to connect and communicate with those around us.

It is perilous to follow one's own ways. I recently heard about a young Pentecostal lady who was on a tour in a foreign country. During a lull in the touring schedule, she decided to walk by herself into the local market. While there, a man pulled her into his carpet store with the promise to "fix her some apple tea." She forced her way out of the shop and ran back to the hotel and the tour group. She was sharply rebuked for taking such great risk and was admonished to stay with the group. She had disregarded all the warnings about going out alone because she wanted to seek her own desire.

We must be careful that we do not cast off wise judgment in order to pursue our own agenda. There is safety in numbers. No one is wise enough or strong enough to seek his own path away from healthy relationships with others.

David said, "Know ye that the LORD he is God: it is he that hath made us, and not we ourselves; we are his people, and the sheep of his pasture" (Psalm 100:3). Sheep were not designed by their Creator to abide alone, but they were created to stay with the flock under the watchful eye of the shepherd. Jesus told the story of a shepherd who left ninety-nine sheep safely in the fold and went looking for the one sheep that had separated itself from the others. When the shepherd found the lost sheep, he put him on his shoulder and came home rejoicing (Luke 15:4-5).

If you are still in the group, stay in the group. If you have separated yourself to seek your own desire, come back to the fold. If you have divested your life of godly influences and wise counsel, beware. If you are lost and want to come home, the Shepherd is searching.

Practice:

Do not be an island and isolate yourself from others. The best thing that you can do for yourself is to surround yourself with people in your life who will give you support and encouragement. Connect with your church, your community, your family, your friends, and your neighbors. Stay with the group.

Prayer:

Lord, help me to seek the safety of a group. Help me to stay connected with my church body, family, and friends. Help me to reach out to those around me who may be isolated and include them in my group.

DAY 55: REMINDERS (PROVERBS 18:9-14)

A man who is slack in his work day by day
Is as bad as the one who wastes his substance away.

The name of the Lord is a strong and mighty tower;
The righteous run in it and are safe every hour.

The rich man's wealth is as a city that's strong;
It is a wall of protection when something goes wrong.

After destruction a man's pride will tumble.
Before he gets honor, he has to be humble.

He who answers a matter without the whole score,
Reaps folly and a shame if he answers before.

The spirit of man will his infirmity sustain;
If his spirit is wounded, it's hard to bear pain.

THE COST OF LOST LABOR

Proverb:

"He also that is slothful in his work is brother to him that is a great waster" (Proverbs 18:9).

Precept:

The New Testament parables of the talents (Matthew 25:15-29) and of the pounds (Luke 19:11-26) have many similarities. One is that the "one-talent man" and the "one-pound man" both did *nothing* with what had been given to them. While the others multiplied their talents or pounds, the one-talent and one-pound receivers did not utilize the chance they had to become productive. They felt good about the fact that they had just held on to what they had been given. However, in the end they both lost what they had, and their negligence cost them. The talent or pound they lost was what they would have gained if they had put it to use.

It is always better to do whatever you can with whatever you have! The Bible teaches that we should work while it is day, for the night will come when no man can work. (See John 9:4.) Ecclesiastes 9:10 says, "Whatsoever thy hand findeth to do, do it with thy might; for there is no work, nor device, nor knowledge, nor wisdom, in the grave, whither thou goest."

When a man is being paid a wage for his labor, there is an even greater obligation to be productive. If he is lazy and unproductive, he is actually stealing from the man for whom he is working! This proverb says that "one who is slack in his work is brother to one who destroys" (Proverbs 18:9, NIV). The lost labor is a cost to the employer just as deliberate destruction would be. So the two men—the lazy man and the destructive man—are brothers.

Most people would not intentionally want to be destructive and destroy someone else's property, but they may not think anything of being a little slack in their employment responsibilities or obligations. If we are being paid to do a particular job, we should do it to the best of our ability.

Proverbs 3:27 says, "Withhold not good from them to whom it is due, when it is in the power of thine hand to do it." This would include the work for which you are being paid. In the New Testament, Paul urged slaves not to withhold their service but to "do it heartily, as to the Lord, and not unto men" (Colossians 3:23).

In the parables of the talents and the pounds, those who worked hard and were productive were commended by their master and rewarded for their efforts. "His lord said unto him, Well done, thou good and faithful servant: thou hast been faithful over a few things, I will make thee ruler over many things: enter thou into the joy of thy lord" (Matthew 25:21). We should work in such a way that our efforts bring praise and rewards instead of incurring costs to our employer for our lost labor.

Practice:

Whatever you have been asked to do, do it to the best of your ability. Take pride in your accomplishments. Be a good steward of the time and responsibilities that have been given to you.

Prayer:

Lord, I want to give my best to You and to those for whom I work. Help me to give my whole heart to my job and to do the job well.

DAY 56: OPTIONS (PROVERBS 18:15-24)

A thoughtful mind more knowledge desires;
It is that for which a wise man aspires.

If you take a gift to an important man,
It will help you gain access and be part of his plan.

A man who speaks first will make his cause sound right,
Until his rival speaks and you hear the other side.

To cast the lot will make an end to controversial strife
Between powerful contenders and their disputes in life.

Quarrels among brothers are like cities under siege,
And like bars upon a castle, are contentions among these.

As the belly must be satisfied with what mouth and lips
    give way,
So our conscience must be pleased with what we do and say.

Death and life are in our tongue's power to wield.
We must wisely use our words; we eat the fruit of what
    they yield.

He who finds a good wife, a good thing he has found;
He's obtained the Lord's approval and His favor
    will abound.

Men made humble by their poverty use entreaties when
   they speak.
Rich men will speak with roughness; they think politeness
   makes them weak.

A man who would have friends must friendly be as well;
There's a friend who sticks more closely than a brother
   would himself.

A LITTLE HONEY

Proverb:

"The poor useth intreaties; but the rich answereth roughly"
(Proverbs 18:23).

Precept:

An old adage says, "You can catch more flies with honey
than you can with vinegar." Behind the crude saying is a great
truth. The way you approach an individual or group has a great
deal to do with the kind of answer you will receive.

If you were trying to catch flies, a saucer of honey would
catch a lot more than a saucer of vinegar. Honey is sweet,
savory, and sticky, as opposed to vinegar, which is sour, smelly,
and not at all sticky. Flies are first attracted by the pleasant
scent, then they taste the sweet syrup, and before you know it,
they are caught in the sticky substance.

On the other hand, flies are not attracted at all to the sour
smell of vinegar. After one bitter taste, they are ready to fly
away. And the watery liquid has no power to entrap them.

The obvious moral to this story is that you can attract more
people to your side by gentle persuasion and compliments than
you can by bitter barbs and hostile words. Without being dishonest or deceitful, people need to learn to use the "honey"
approach instead of the "vinegar" approach, regardless of their
wealth or station in life.

This proverb states that "the rich answer roughly." Their
self-sufficiency makes them feel that they do not need to make
any concessions in their attitude or speech in order to get what
they need. So they arrogantly make their demands and are
ready to rebuke anyone who stands in their way.

The poor, on the other hand, must use a different approach. They cannot claim wealth or privilege, but they do wish their petition to be heard. So they speak pleasantly and do not demand but implore. They do not threaten; rather, they plead, request, and entreat.

God always recognizes the humble approach. Psalm 9:12 says, "He forgetteth not the cry of the humble." Matthew 23:12 says, "And whosoever shall exalt himself shall be abased; and he that shall humble himself shall be exalted." James 4:6 says, "God resisteth the proud, but giveth grace unto the humble."

So whether you are rich or poor, if you need to convince a friend, persuade an enemy, or even petition God, put away the vinegar and use a little honey!

Practice:

A demand is often met with resistance, but a request is usually acknowledged. With respect and humility make your requests known to those around you. A little "honey" can be used in your favor to obtain the favor and grace that you seek.

Prayer:

Lord, let me speak kindly and respectfully as I make my requests known to others. Grant me favor so that I can accomplish things for Your kingdom.

Week 9

PROVERBS 19

Better is the poor that walketh in his integrity, than he that is perverse in his lips, and is a fool. Also, that the soul be without knowledge, it is not good; and he that hasteth with his feet sinneth. The foolishness of man perverteth his way: and his heart fretteth against the LORD. Wealth maketh many friends; but the poor is separated from his neighbour. A false witness shall not be unpunished, and he that speaketh lies shall not escape. Many will intreat the favour of the prince: and every man is a friend to him that giveth gifts. All the brethren of the poor do hate him: how much more do his friends go far from him? he pursueth them with words, yet they are wanting to him. He that getteth wisdom loveth his own soul: he that keepeth understanding shall find good. A false witness shall not be unpunished, and he that speaketh lies shall perish. Delight is not seemly for a fool; much less for a servant to have rule over princes. The discretion of a man deferreth his anger; and it is his glory to pass over a transgression. The king's wrath is as the roaring of a lion; but his favour is as dew upon the grass. A foolish son is the calamity of his father: and the contentions of a wife are a continual dropping. House and riches are the inheritance of fathers: and a prudent wife is from the LORD. Slothfulness casteth into a deep sleep; and an idle soul shall suffer hunger. He that keepeth the commandment keepeth his own soul; but he that despiseth his ways shall die. He that hath pity upon the poor lendeth unto the LORD; and that which he hath given will he pay him again. Chasten thy son while there is hope, and let not thy soul spare for his crying. A man of great wrath *shall suffer punishment: for if thou deliver him, yet thou must do it again. Hear counsel, and receive instruction, that thou mayest be wise in thy latter end. There are many devices in a man's heart; nevertheless the counsel of the LORD, that shall stand. The desire of a man is his kindness: and a poor man is better than a liar. The fear of the LORD tendeth to life: and he that hath it shall abide satisfied; he shall not be visited with evil. A slothful man hideth his hand in his bosom, and will not so much as bring it to his mouth again. Smite a scorner, and the simple will beware: and reprove one that hath understanding, and he will understand knowledge. He that wasteth his father, and chaseth away his mother, is a son that causeth shame, and bringeth reproach. Cease, my son, to hear the instruction that causeth to err from the words of knowledge. An ungodly witness scorneth judgment: and the mouth of the wicked devoureth iniquity. Judgments are prepared for scorners, and stripes for the back of fools.*

DAY 57: PERSONAL PROVERBS (PROVERBS 19:1-8)

Better is the poor who is honest in his walk
Than the fool who is stubborn and perverse when he talks.

To be without sense for your soul is not good,
So ponder the path of your feet, as you should.

The foolishness of man has perverted his way;
He frets at the Lord and with Him will not stay.

Because of your wealth, many friends you may make,
But when poverty comes, every one will forsake.

A false witness unpunished, I don't think you will see,
And a liar will not escape his penalty.

A prince will be entreated by all in his sway;
We'll all be his friend if he gives gifts away.

Poor people are not in their brethren's good favor.
Nobody wants them, but God is their Savior.

He who gains wisdom is his own best friend;
He who loves learning will succeed in the end.

On Fire

Proverb:
"Also, that the soul be without knowledge, it is not good;
and he that hasteth with his feet sinneth" (Proverbs 19:2).

Precept:
Zeal is a word that literally means "heat" and is taken from
the Greek word *zelos*, which means "to boil."[21] It is synonymous
with the word fervor, which is taken from the Latin word *zelus*,
which also means "to boil." So when you have zeal, it is like a
fire that is burning inside. However, as with real fire, it must be
kept under control and used with wisdom. It is good to have
zeal, to be excited and enthused, and to be passionate about
your cause or beliefs; but zeal without knowledge is like a fire
that is burning out of control.

Many mistakes have been made by people who were zealous
to accomplish a task but were lacking the needed knowledge to
do it. In the early 1700s, an accepted medical practice was for
doctors to "bleed" their patients. They mistakenly thought that
taking some of a person's blood would also take away the sickness. When George Washington became ill, he was treated in
this way. He died, not as a result of his illness, but because of
the loss of blood.

Sometimes zeal without knowledge also causes erroneous
spiritual practices. Romans 10:2-3 says, "For I bear them
record that they have a zeal of God, but not according to knowledge. For they being ignorant of God's righteousness, and
going about to establish their own righteousness, have not submitted themselves unto the righteousness of God."

The Pharisees thought they would be heard for their much
speaking, so they prayed long prayers in order to impress God
(and those listening) with their zeal. (See Matthew 23:14.) They
thought outward washings would make them pure on the

inside, so they made countless ceremonies of washings, while inside they were rotten to the core. (See Mark 7:4-8.) They were so zealous about keeping the Sabbath that they criticized Jesus because He healed and cast out devils on the Sabbath. (See Luke 13:14.) He reminded them that if their ox fell in the ditch on the Sabbath, they would get it out. Likewise, it was more necessary for a person to be delivered of sicknesses and afflictions than it was to pull the ox out of the ditch. (See Luke 13:15-16.)

Zeal combined with knowledge can be a powerful thing. Paul wrote to the church at Corinth and commended them for their zeal in giving and their enthusiasm that had stirred many to action. (See II Corinthians 2:9.) In Colossians 4:13 he recounted the zeal of one of his fellow workers, a fervent prayer warrior for the saints at Colosse.

Do not let your zeal be a raging fire that is out of control. Combine it with wisdom and knowledge to accomplish great things for God.

> You need knowledge to know the right thing to do;
> You need zeal to take action that's best.
> You need facts put together, to know which and
>   know whether;
> You need plenty of zeal for the rest.
> So keep your zeal bold, and let passion unfold
> To ignite you and make you aflame;
> Let knowledge direct you in doing your part,
> With both zeal and with knowledge, the same!
>
> –W. C. PARKEY

Practice:

Being excited about an idea or a project is a good thing. But take some time before you begin to think it through and determine your best plan of action.

Prayer:

Lord, I want to have the passion and fervor to accomplish the tasks that are before me. I want to have wisdom to know the right approach. Give me the knowledge I need to use my zeal in the best way.

DAY 58: PRACTICAL PRECEPTS (PROVERBS 19:9-19)

A false witness shall not unpunished go,
And a man speaking lies will perish I know.

Delight is not seemly when done by a fool;
Much less for a servant over princes to rule.

A good man's discretion helps defer his wrath;
It is part of his glory o'er transgression to pass.

The king's wrath scares like the lion's roar,
But his favor refreshes like the dew on the moor.

A foolish son ruins his father, in truth.
A nagging wife is like a leak in the roof.

Houses and riches are inherited from your dad.
A prudent wife from the Lord will make you glad.

Laziness will put you into a deep sleep,
And idleness will cause you to hunger and weep.

He who keeps the commandments keeps his soul just as well,
But who is careless of his conduct will end up in hell.

He who pities the poor to the Lord loves to lend,
And the Lord will repay what he owes in the end.

Chasten your son while there's hope he'll repent;
Do not let his crying cause you to relent.

A man who will sin finds punishment and pain.
Do not pay his fine, for he'll do it again.

LENDING TO THE LORD

Proverb:
"He that hath pity upon the poor lendeth unto the LORD; and that which he hath given will he pay him again" (Proverbs 19:17).

Precept:

God has always been concerned about the poor, so much so that the Old Testament law included provisions for them. Those who owned fields were instructed not to plow in the corners so that the poor could go in and glean. (See Leviticus 2:23.) In the year of Jubilee, all debts were forgiven, and those who had been sold into slavery were to be redeemed. (See Leviticus 25.)

When Jesus came to the earth as God manifest in the flesh, He paid particular attention to the poor. "The Spirit of the Lord is upon me, because he hath anointed me to preach the gospel to the poor" (Luke 4:18). As He ministered to the multitudes, He was moved with compassion (Matthew 9:36) for them because of their various needs.

We must let our eyes see the multiplied millions who are in need not only in our country but around the world. God must touch our hearts with feelings of mercy, love, and grace for them. We must realize that "but for the grace of God there [go I]."[22] We must put ourselves in their place until compassion and empathy fill our heart.

We must also look for ways in which our feelings of compassion can be turned into action. In Mark 6:34, Jesus again had compassion upon the multitude and began to teach them many things. As the day progressed and the people grew hungry, the disciples wanted to send them away to find their own bread, but Jesus told the disciples to feed them. (See Mark 6:36-37.) Of course, it was only through Christ's miracle that they could be fed. While we cannot take on the personal burden of the whole world, we can share our blessings with those around us as God enables us to do it.

Finally, as we recognize the needs of the poor, we must remember that our primary responsibility is to share the gospel with them. The saving gospel of Jesus Christ is able to help those who are unfortunate and without hope to take a new lease on life, develop a work ethic, and have a reason for existing that will cause them to move to a new level.

When we are assisting the poor, we are lending to the Lord. He has promised that whatever we give to them, He will repay us. When Jesus Christ returns, He will be coming back for His people, and He will remember those who have lent to the Lord by giving to the poor.

Practice:

Find ways that you can give to the needy. Give a basket of food to a family who might be struggling. Is there a college student or a single mother who might be blessed by a home-cooked meal? Donate food items to the drives that are available in your community through local shelters, schools, libraries, and government offices.

Prayer:

Lord, help me to be sensitive to the needs of those around me. Help me to share the blessings that You have given to me with those who are less fortunate.

DAY 59: LIFE AT ITS BEST (PROVERBS 19:20-29)

If you will accept counsel and receive correction,
In time you will be wise from others' instruction.

Men devise their plans with their crafty designs,
But God's eternal purposes prevail every time!

A man is known by the thing he desires;
It is better to be poor than be known as a liar.

The fear of the Lord leads to life at its best.
With that life we're satisfied; in safety we'll rest.

A man who is slothful in his pocket keeps his hands;
He wants you to feed him, that's just one of his demands.

Smite a scorner in public and the simple will beware.
Reprove a man of wisdom; he'll believe you and take care.

The son who berates his dad and forsakes his mother
Will cause a reproach and bring shame to the others.

My son, cease to listen to instruction that's bad;
It will cause you to err from the lessons you've had.

Both judgment and justice a rascal will scorn;
Perjury pours from every scoundrel who's born.

Scoffers are judged by the punishment of rules;
A rod is prepared for the back of the fools.

READ THE INSTRUCTIONS

Proverb:

"Cease, my son, to hear the instruction that causeth to err from the words of knowledge" (Proverbs 19:27).

Precept:

Instructions are important. If you have ever tried to assemble anything, you know this to be true. One missed step in the process will cause everything thereafter to be flawed. However, many people do not even look at the instructions but think they can proceed without them. After several hours of frustration, they usually end up right back where they started and concede that they should have read the instructions.

A teacher friend of mine has told me how he sometimes distributes to his class a quiz with specific instructions. If a student does not first read the instructions but skips over them and attempts to take the test, he or she will answer the test completely wrong. He then writes on the student's paper, "FFI," for "failure to follow instructions."

Wisdom is gained by listening to instruction. As long as you follow instructions, you will do the right thing the right way. It is when we cease listening to instruction that we err in whatever we attempt to do.

In the Old Testament, the moral law that God gave to Moses was written on tables of stone. These laws were not the "ten suggestions"—they were the Ten Commandments. Though centuries have gone by, the principles that were engraved there are still instructions for right living. The world would do well to follow the instructions of wisdom, for when they stop following, they start straying.

If you are following a line and you start to diverge from that line, at that point you are just barely different from the correct line. However, the farther you travel from that divergence, the wider the separation from the correct line becomes. You may just be off an inch when you first leave the line, but then it becomes off one foot, then one yard, then one mile, and finally it may be miles and miles off the course.

If you are assembling a toy for your children, please read the instructions. If you are taking a trip to an unfamiliar destination, please follow directions. If you have a serious illness, please follow your doctor's prescription. If you are trying to live a godly life, please read God's Word and follow the instruction that it gives.

Practice:

The Bible is our instruction manual. Do not set it aside and try to live your life without following the advice and admonition that it gives. Take time each day to read God's Word.

Prayer:

Lord, help me to follow the instructions You have given me through Your Word. Help me to follow You closely and to renew my mind in the Holy Ghost so that I will know Your will.

PROVERBS 20

Wine is a mocker, strong drink is raging: and whosoever is deceived thereby is not wise. The fear of a king is as the roaring of a lion: whoso provoketh him to anger sinneth against his own soul. It is an honour for a man to cease from strife: but every fool will be meddling. The sluggard will not plow by reason of the cold; therefore shall he beg in harvest, and have nothing. Counsel in the heart of man is like deep water; but a man of understanding will draw it out. Most men will proclaim every one his own goodness: but a faithful man who can find? The just man walketh in his integrity: his children are blessed after him. A king that sitteth in the throne of judgment scattereth away all evil with his eyes. Who can say, I have made my heart clean, I am pure from my sin? Divers weights, and divers measures, both of them are alike abomination to the LORD.

Even a child is known by his doings, whether his work be pure, and whether it be right. The hearing ear, and the seeing eye, the LORD hath made even both of them. Love not sleep, lest thou come to poverty; open thine eyes, and thou shalt be satisfied with bread. It is naught, it is naught, saith the buyer: but when he is gone his way, then he boasteth. There is gold, and a multitude of rubies: but the lips of knowledge are a precious jewel. Take his garment that is surety for a stranger: and take a pledge of him for a strange woman. Bread of deceit is sweet to a man: but afterwards his mouth shall be filled with gravel. Every purpose is established by counsel: and with good advice make war. He that goeth about as a talebearer revealeth secrets: therefore meddle not with him that flattereth with his lips. Whoso curseth his father or his mother, his lamp shall be put out in obscure darkness. An inheritance may be gotten hastily at the beginning; but the end thereof shall not be blessed. Say not thou, I will recompense evil; but wait on the LORD, and he shall save thee. Divers weights are an abomination unto the LORD; and a false balance is not good. Man's goings are of the LORD; how can a man then understand his own way? It is a snare to the man who devoureth that which is holy, and after vows to make inquiry. A wise king scattereth the wicked, and bringeth the wheel over them. The spirit of man is the candle of the LORD, searching all the inward parts of the belly. Mercy and truth preserve the king: and his throne is upholden by mercy. The glory of young men is their strength: and the beauty of old men is the gray head. The blueness of a wound cleanseth away evil: so do stripes the inward parts of the belly.

DAY 60: FOOD FOR WISE THOUGHT
(PROVERBS 20:1-10)

Wine is a mocker, it is wise to believe.
Strong drink is raging, so don't let them deceive.

The wrath of a king is like a lion when he's caged;
Your life is in danger, when he's loose and enraged.

It's an honorable thing when a man stops a fight;
A ruckus any fool can start, although it's not right.

Because of the cold, a sluggard won't plow;
He will beg during harvest, if he will not work now!

Counsel in a man's heart is like a deep water well,
But a man who is clever will draw it out still.

Many a man will insist that he's kind,
But a trustworthy man is difficult to find.

The righteous is upright and wise in his talk;
His children are blessed if they follow his walk.

A monarch who rules in justice is wise
And scatters the evil that appears to his eyes.

Who can say, "My heart is made clean of all sin,
I am pure and I'm perfect, there is no fault within?"

Different weights and different measures for two kinds of men
Are the Lord's abomination; they're dishonest to Him.

DRAWING OUT DEEP WATER

Proverb:
"Counsel in the heart of man is like deep water; but a man of understanding will draw it out" (Proverbs 20:5).

Precept:
I grew up on a farm that did not have running water. We did not even have a well. However, I remember the day that my dad took a willow branch and went "witching" for water. He found water, and a well was dug on our farm.

In order to get water out of our well, we would let down a skinny bucket and listen for a gurgling sound. When we heard the gurgling sound, we knew that the bucket was full and we would pull it back up to the surface. Getting water out of that well was not easy, but how rewarding it was to get a clear, cool, refreshing drink! We relied on the well to provide the water that we needed for everyday living.

Wisdom is not a common commodity that is available without a concerted effort. If wisdom was readily available, everyone would have it and life would be grand. Wisdom is like the underground stream that ran beneath our farm that a man of understanding had to find. Wisdom is something that must be discerned, desired, and sought after.

Have you ever noticed that it is the person who knows the least about the subject who wants to talk about it the most? Those who are qualified to talk on the subject are usually reticent and do not offer their opinion without it being solicited. Solomon said, "A fool uttereth all his mind: but a wise man keepeth it in till afterwards" (Proverbs 29:11). Wisdom runs in the heart of a man like deep water, and it is not offered casually to every passerby. A man with wisdom does not stand on the street corner shouting his observations, but he usually hides them in his heart.

A man with understanding learns to locate the sources of wisdom in his life. Once a source has been identified, there can be a careful "drawing out" of godly counsel. Have you ever been with someone with whom you were only casually acquainted and discovered that they had a depth of knowledge of which you were completely unaware? When you discover how much someone knows about a particular subject, you mark them as someone you can seek out when you need advice. Counsel runs deep in the heart of a man, but it may be closer than you think.

Practice:

Are there people in your life to whom you can turn when you need wise counsel? Make it a point to seek their advice. Ask them questions about the specific things you need to know. Take time to listen to what they have to say. Do not let their wisdom go unheeded. Be a person of understanding who will listen and learn.

Prayer:

Lord, help me to properly acknowledge the wise people You have placed in my life. I thank You for the things they have learned and the experiences they have had that they can use to help me. Help me to take time to receive the wisdom they have to share.

DAY 61: TIPS FOR LIVING (PROVERBS 20:11-20)

Even a child is known by his doing.
Is it right? Is it pure? Their fruits will be showing.

The hearing ear, and the seeing eye, the LORD knows them
    quite well.
He created them both, and He their story can tell.

Do not love excessive sleep, lest you sleep and be poor;
If you open your eyes, you'll find bread outside your door.

"Oh, it's really good for nothing," cries the buyer as he leaves,
But you'll find him boasting later of the bargain he receives.

There is gold and there are rubies, other riches of their kind,
But the greatest jewel ever is the knowledge you will find.

Take the garment that is given to provide a stranger's bail.
Make it pay for something useful; he'll just spend it,
    never fail!

Bread received by some deception, to a man will seem
    so sweet,
But it will taste like eating gravel, when you pay for
    what you eat.

To establish wise decisions for a battle, if you can;
Call your counselors together; by wise counsel,
    make your plan.

He who goes as a talebearer will reveal all secrets shown.
Don't associate with gossips; with their lips they're
    quite well-known.

Those who despise their parents will then curse them
    at the last.
Their lamps will be extinguished; darkness deep will
    hold them fast.

A Clean Slate

Proverb:

"Who can say, I have made my heart clean, I am pure from
my sin?" (Proverbs 20:9).

Precept:

The answer to the question posed by this proverb is, no
one. Romans 3:23 says, "For all have sinned, and come short of
the glory of God." Sin is not just a mistake. It is not just a wrong
choice. It is not just the result of a sickness. Sin is a transgression of the law of God. (See James 2:10.) It is not just a
municipal offense, a state offense, or a federal offense, but it is
an offense toward God. David said, "Against thee, and thee only
have I sinned" (Psalm 51:4).

So if sin is an offense against God and all have sinned, how
can a man be cleansed of his guilt and sins? God foresaw the problem before man ever sinned. He provided a substitute system that
allowed man to offer an animal sacrifice that would cause his sins
to be rolled ahead for one year. Each year a new sacrifice could
be made that would roll the sin ahead for another year. This was
only a temporary system, somewhat like paying a bail bond that
allows an accused man to go free until his trial date.

Fortunately, God did away with the temporary sacrificial
system and made a way for our sins to be completely abolished
through the supreme sacrifice of His Son, Jesus Christ, at
Calvary. Jesus Christ was "the Lamb slain from the foundation
of the world"! (See Revelation 13:8.) When Jesus died on
Calvary, He died for the sins of the whole world. I Peter 1:18-
19 says, "Forasmuch as ye know that ye were not redeemed
with corruptible things, as silver and gold, from your vain con-

versation received by tradition from your fathers; but with the precious blood of Christ, as of a lamb without blemish and without spot."

Salvation is no longer a temporary thing. "And if any man sin, we have an advocate with the Father, Jesus Christ the righteous: and he is the propitiation for our sins: and not for ours only, but also for the sins of the whole world" (I John 2:1-2). I John 1:9 says, "If we confess our sins, he is faithful and just to forgive us our sins, and to cleanse us from all unrighteousness."

No man can say, "I have made my heart clean!" No man can escape from giving an account of his sins to God. However, we can say, "Jesus Christ has made me free from the guilt and the shame of my sins."

Do not try to become clean of your sins by yourself. You cannot do it. Do not try to use heathen sacrifices or religious rituals to try to keep yourself pure. Repent of your sins, ask God for forgiveness, be baptized in the name of Jesus for the remission of sins, and receive His Spirit. (See Acts 2:38.) He will give you a clean slate!

Practice:

Repentance is the key for maintaining a clean slate. Ask God to forgive you for any sin that you have committed. Ask Him to give you a clean heart.

Prayer:

Lord, I ask You to search my heart and cleanse me from any wickedness that may be there. I thank You for forgiving me of my sins. Help me to continually seek Your forgiveness so that I can be clean before You.

DAY 62: THE LAMP OF THE LORD (PROVERBS 20:21-30)

Money you have received without anything to pay
Is not usually lasting but will soon fade away.

Do not say, "I will recompense sin." Never doubt!
Just wait on the Lord, and He'll work it all out!

A double standard in your weights is one of
    God's abominations;
When your scales are set up falsely, He is filled
    with detestation.

It is God who directs a man's steps where he's going;
It's no wonder that the future, man has no way of knowing.

It is a snare for a man to quickly make a vow,
Before considering if he can fulfill it and how.

A wise king sifts out the wicked and punishes his crime;
He starts the wheels rolling for judgment each time.

The lamp of the Lord is the spirit of man;
It searches the innermost parts when it can.

Mercy and truth will sustain a king's power
And uphold his kingdom and keep it each hour.

The glory of a young man is the prowess he shows,
But the splendor of an old man is the white hair he grows.

Evil men sometimes won't listen till they're beaten
    black and blue;
Let your chastening bring you healing to your soul
    and body, too.

THE INNER VOICE

Proverb:
    "The spirit of man is the candle of the LORD, searching all
the inward parts of the belly" (Proverbs 20:27).

Precept:
    God has been very good to mankind. Man was nothing but
a lump of clay and a heap of dust when God formed him. God
took nothing and made something out of it. Not only was it
something, but it was somebody. Man was made in the image
of God.

Man was given dominion over the fowls of the air, the fish of the sea, and all the earthly creation. (See Genesis 1:26.) A fear of man is in every animal. When they smell man, they will steer clear of him. However, because of man's dominion, he can make animals submit to his will. Man has conquered the land, the sea, the air, and space. God has made man ruler of the world.

Not only did God give man dominion over the earth, but He also placed a spirit within him. Genesis 2:7 says, "And the LORD God formed man of the dust of the ground, and breathed into his nostrils the breath of life; and man became a living soul." The spirit of a man is the breath of God. It is a constant presence and reminder to let him know that he has an obligation to do right. It is the inner voice of his conscience.

God has not only given His breath to be the conscience of mankind, but He has also placed eternity in our hearts and minds (Ecclesiastes 3:11, NIV). God has given man a hope of future destiny beyond the realm of time.

All of these things combine to make man what he is. He has a life and existence that correspond to the animal kingdom but man is not an animal; he is a living soul! He has been given a spirit, which is the breath of God. God has equipped his mind with a built-in eternity. And he has the knowledge that he is a creature made in God's image. This combination makes him not only able to appreciate a sunrise and know how to love, laugh, weep, or pray, but it allows him to be sensitive to the voice of God. Man's spirit becomes like a candle to the Lord, which lights up all the dark places of his life and senses.

David said, "I will praise thee; for I am fearfully and wonderfully made: marvellous are thy works; and that my soul knoweth right well" (Psalm 139:14). He understood that God's creation of man was a marvelous thing. He also understood the relationship between the spirit of man and the breath of God that creates a God-given conscience—that inner voice. At the conclusion of Psalm 139, he prayed, "Search me, O God, and know my heart: try me, and know my thoughts: and see if there be any wicked way in me, and lead me in the way everlasting" (Psalm 139:23-24).

Practice:

We would do well to follow the advice David gave his son Solomon: "And thou, Solomon my son, know thou the God of thy father, and serve him with a perfect heart and with a willing mind: for the LORD searcheth all hearts, and understandeth all the imaginations of the thoughts: if thou seek him, he will be found of thee; but if thou forsake him, he will cast thee off for ever" (I Chronicles 28:9).

Prayer:

Lord, thank You for giving me a sensitivity to the urging of Your Spirit. Help me to sense when You are speaking to me, and enable me to answer the call.

PROVERBS 21

The king's heart is in the hand of the LORD, as the rivers of water: he turneth it whithersoever he will. Every way of a man is right in his own eyes: but the LORD pondereth the hearts. To do justice and judgment is more acceptable to the LORD than sacrifice. An high look, and a proud heart, and the plowing of the wicked, is sin. The thoughts of the diligent tend only to plenteousness; but of every one that is hasty only to want. The getting of treasures by a lying tongue is a vanity tossed to and fro of them that seek death. The robbery of the wicked shall destroy them; because they refuse to do judgment. The way of man is froward and strange: but as for the pure, his work is right. It is better to dwell in a corner of the housetop, than with a brawling woman in a wide house. The soul of the wicked desireth evil: his neighbour findeth no favour in his eyes. When the scorner is punished, the simple is made wise: and when the wise is instructed, he receiveth knowledge. The righteous man wisely considereth the house of the wicked: but God overthroweth the wicked for their wickedness. Whoso stoppeth his ears at the cry of the poor, he also shall cry himself, but shall not be heard. A gift in secret pacifieth anger: and a reward in the bosom strong wrath. It is joy to the just to do judgment: but destruction shall be to the workers of iniquity. The man that wandereth out of the way of understanding shall remain in the congregation of the dead. *He that loveth pleasure shall be a poor man: he that loveth wine and oil shall not be rich. The wicked shall be a ransom for the righteous, and the transgressor for the upright. It is better to dwell in the wilderness, than with a contentious and an angry woman. There is treasure to be desired and oil in the dwelling of the wise; but a foolish man spendeth it up. He that followeth after righteousness and mercy findeth life, righteousness, and honour. A wise man scaleth the city of the mighty, and casteth down the strength of the confidence thereof. Whoso keepeth his mouth and his tongue keepeth his soul from troubles. Proud and haughty scorner is his name, who dealeth in proud wrath. The desire of the slothful killeth him; for his hands refuse to labour. He coveteth greedily all the day long: but the righteous giveth and spareth not. The sacrifice of the wicked is abomination: how much more, when he bringeth it with a wicked mind? A false witness shall perish: but the man that heareth speaketh constantly. A wicked man hardeneth his face: but as for the upright, he directeth his way. There is no wisdom nor understanding nor counsel against the LORD. The horse is prepared against the day of battle: but safety is of the LORD.*

DAY 63: THE RIGHT ROAD (PROVERBS 21:1-10)

The king's heart, like the rivers, is in the Lord's hands;
It will turn a direction, as the Lord shall command.

A man's way that he chooses in his own eyes is best,
But the Lord will determine if it passes God's test.

To do justice and judgment is the best way to go;
They're more acceptable than sacrifice to the Lord,
    this I know.

A high look and a proud heart, both are known as sin;
The plowing of the wicked will also do him in.

The thoughts of the diligent make them toil for their gain,
But the rash man's impatience brings him poverty and pain.

Treasures gotten by lies, by fraud and much worse,
Are tossed to and fro like a bubble that bursts.

The dishonesty of the wicked shall judge them at last;
They're undone by their villainy, destroyed by their past.

The course of the culprit is crooked and a blight,
But the way of the innocent is straight and it's right.

'Tis better to live upstairs in the halls
Than to live in a wide house with a woman who brawls.

The soul of the wicked desires that evil be done;
There's no favor for friends or a neighbor, not one.

MASTER CONTROL

Proverb:
"The king's heart is in the hand of the LORD, as the rivers of water: he turneth it whithersoever he will" (Proverbs 21:1).

Precept:
Do not ever forget that God is still in control. He has instituted human government and does not intervene in every situation, but when God desires, He can overrule the edicts of governors, mayors, captains, and kings.

When wickedness and evil were in every imagination of men's heart, God sent the Flood. (See Genesis 7.) When men built the Tower of Babel to make themselves a name and to try to reach the stars, God stopped it. (See Genesis 11:4-9.)

When the Israelites were slaves to Egypt's pharaoh, God sent Moses to tell him to "Let my people go!" (See Exodus 7.) But God hardened Pharaoh's heart so that he would not agree. When Pharaoh resisted, God sent the miraculous plagues that wreaked havoc on the Egyptians. Then with a mighty hand He delivered them from the tyrant's grasp by parting the waters of the Red Sea. (See Exodus 14.)

The nation of Judah was carried captive to Babylon. Their brightest and best young men were selected to be educated and to work in the Babylonian system. Daniel 3 tells the story of Shadrach, Meshach, and Abednego, who refused to break one of God's commandments by bowing down to King Nebuchadnezzar's image, even though it meant that they would be thrown into the fiery furnace. Although the king meant to punish them by death, God had other plans. Miraculously, when they reached the fire, it only burned off their bonds, and they walked freely in the fire. When they were called out of the fire, they were not burned and did not even smell like smoke. (See Daniel 3:27.)

Daniel 3:28 clearly indicates how the king's heart was changed: "Then Nebuchadnezzar spake, and said, Blessed be the God of Shadrach, Meshach, and Abednego, who hath sent his angel, and delivered his servants that trusted in him, and have changed the king's word, and yielded their bodies, that they might not serve nor worship any god, except their own God."

Some things occur by happenstance and others by circumstance, but when the providence of God is involved, it overrules everything else. When Jesus was threatened by Pilate, who said, "Don't you know what I could do to you?" Jesus said, "You have no power at all except what is given to you."

God can change the rule of the city council or the Supreme Court. If you are wrestling with a problem with authorities, remember that God can change the situation just like He can change the course of the river. Remember, He is the Master, and He is in control.

Practice:

You may not understand God's methods (Isaiah 55:8), but no matter what situation you might be facing in your life know this: God is in control.

Prayer:

Lord, I trust You with my life and with the circumstances I am facing that are out of my control. Thy will be done, I pray. In Jesus' name. Amen.

Week 10

DAY 64: LEARNING THE LESSON
(PROVERBS 21:11-20)

When a scoffer gets a beating, the fool gets the lesson,
But a man of good sense learns by knowledge's impression.

The righteous observe when the wicked's house is gone;
The wicked see nothing until they're overthrown.

He who closes his ears to the cry of the poor
Has his own cry rejected when he knocks at the door.

A gift made in secret will pacify wrath;
A reward in your bosom causes anger to pass.

When justice is done, it gives righteous men joy,
But the evil men's work that same justice destroys.

The man who strays has a place he can go;
He can stay in his wanderings till he goes down below.

He who lives for his pleasure shall be poor in the end;
To love oil and wine and sin's dainties won't win.

The wicked and transgressors shall their penalty pay,
But the upright and righteous are ransomed always.

It is better to live in a wilderness place
Than with a woman who gripes and quarrels in your face.

There are treasures in the house of the just, and to spare,
But the fool spends it all and has nothing to share.

BETTER THAN SACRIFICE

Proverb:

"To do justice and judgment is more acceptable to the LORD than sacrifice" (Proverbs 21:3).

Precept:

In Old Testament times, many sacrifices and offerings were made on the brazen altar of the Temple. The offerings and sacrifices were symbolic of the people's offering of themselves to God with humility, as they exhibited the principles of justice and judgment that were taught in the law of Moses.

A problem developed when the people continued to offer blood sacrifices but did not do the works of justice and judgment that were prescribed in the law. The prophet Micah said, "And what doth the LORD require of thee, but to do justly, and to love mercy, and to walk humbly with thy God?" (Micah 6:8). He was emphasizing what this proverb states, that doing the right thing is more acceptable to God than offering sacrifices.

King Saul learned this lesson firsthand. In I Samuel 15, God told Saul to go to the city of Amalek and utterly destroy everything. He was to leave nothing alive. However, Saul disobeyed and kept the king alive, as well as the best sheep, oxen, and everything that was good. (See I Samuel 15:9.)

Saul told the prophet Samuel to meet him at an appointed time for sacrifice. But when Samuel did not come, Saul, who was not a prophet or a priest, took over the assembly and made the sacrifice, which only the priest was supposed to do. God was displeased with Saul and told Samuel, "It repenteth me that I have set up Saul to be king: for he is turned back from following me, and hath not performed my commandments" (I Samuel 15:11).

When Samuel came, he rebuked Saul for his actions saying, "Hath the LORD as great delight in burnt offerings and sacrifices, as in obeying the voice of the LORD? Behold, to obey is better than sacrifice, and to hearken than the fat of rams. For rebellion is as the sin of witchcraft, and stubbornness is as iniquity and idolatry. Because thou hast rejected the word of the LORD, he hath also rejected thee from being king" (I Samuel 15:22-23). Saul's sacrifice was meaningless because he was in complete disobedience with what God had commanded.

Centuries later, religious people are still struggling to grasp this concept. Sacred rituals and ceremonies, attending church, carrying a Bible, and other outward displays of Christianity are not the things that please God the most. God is most pleased when we are obedient to His Word. He would rather we obey the truths of the Bible through our words, attitudes, and actions than go through any sort of religious motions. He does not want just lip service; instead, He wants a heart that is truly submitted to the will of God.

Do not let your sacrifices for God substitute for obedience, faithfulness, love, and humility. Obey God. It is better than sacrifice.

Practice:

Jesus said in John 14:15, "If ye love me, keep my commandments." No amount of outward conformity and sacrifice will save you. It all comes down to being obedient to God and His commandments.

Prayer:

Lord, I want to follow Your commandments. Help me to love You with my whole heart, mind, body, soul, and strength, and to offer my life unto You as a sacrifice of praise.

DAY 65: REAPING THE RESULTS (PROVERBS 21:21-31)

If you're following righteousness and mercy, you'll find
Honor, righteousness, and life every time.

A wise man can capture a city that's strong;
He can conquer the strongholds to which they belong.

If you would keep your soul from both troubles and strife,
Watch your tongue and your mouth; keep them safe,
    keep them right.

There's a man who is arrogant, haughty, and proud.
Scoffer's his name; if you say it, speak it loud!

The sluggard's propensity causes his death;
He refuses to work, till he runs out of breath.

Some folks are consumed by their money and greed,
But the just man will always help someone in need.

The sacrifice of the wicked's an abomination, I know;
How much more when their offerings are made for a show?

A false witness shall perish and to judgment will come,
But a good man's words shall be told on and on.

A wicked man hardens his face—he's to blame;
A good man speaks truth with no fear of shame.

There is no understanding or counsel that can stand
Against the Lord's face or escape from His hand.

The horse is prepared for the battle's great day,
But deliverance is God's and He'll have His own way.

HORSEPOWER

Proverb:
    "The horse is prepared against the day of battle: but safety is of the LORD" (Proverbs 21:31).

Precept:
    War is a terrible thing, but it has long been a part of man's history. In primitive battles of the past, men fought with staves, spears, swords, bows, and arrows, but the horse was one of the most feared and prized elements of warfare. In this proverb, the power of the horse in winning a battle is compared to the power of the Lord.
    James Watt, an inventor in the late 1700s, wanted to measure the power of a horse and consequently originated the term "horsepower." He needed a way to rate the capabilities of the steam engine he was trying to sell, so he came up with a formula based on how much force a horse could pull multiplied by the speed it traveled per minute, which equaled thirty-three

thousand foot-pounds per minute, the standard "horsepower" measurement still used today.[23]

Although Watt's figure was probably a bit optimistic, it highlighted the strength and power of a horse. But God's power far outnumbers any amount of horsepower anyone or anything might have. The psalmist said, "Some trust in chariots, and some in horses: but we will remember the name of the LORD our God" (Psalm 20:7). Proverbs 18:10 says, "The name of the LORD is a strong tower: the righteous runneth into it, and is safe." Granted, in a time of conflict it is wise to try to match forces with the forces that are coming against you, but our best defense is a reliance on the Lord. I Timothy 2:2 admonishes us to pray "for kings, and for all that are in authority; that we may lead a quiet and peaceable life in all godliness and honesty." It does not matter how equipped our nation is for war; our safety and security is of the Lord.

Throughout the history of mankind, God has used some unusual ways to win battles. He has used lightning (II Samuel 22:14-15), thunder (I Samuel 7:10), and hail (Joshua 10:10-11) to cause the enemy to scatter. One time He instructed the army to send the singers out first (II Chronicles 20:16-22). Then there was the time when God told the army to dig ditches, and He sent water to fill the ditches. When the enemy saw it, they thought it looked like rivers of blood and fled (II Kings 3:16-24). When the four leprous men marched into the camp of the enemy, God magnified their footsteps until they sounded like a great host, and once again the enemy fled (II Kings 7:3-7).

God does not need horsepower. He just needs men and women who will put their trust in Him. "For the battle is not yours, but God's" (II Chronicles 20:15).

Practice:
What battle is raging in your life? What war of circumstances, sickness, financial setback, or family difficulties are you fighting? Ask the Lord to fight your battles, and He will give you the victory!

Prayer:
Lord, I do not want to fight my battles by myself. Please fight my battles for me and help me to be victorious.

PROVERBS 22

A good name is rather to be chosen than great riches, and loving favour rather than silver and gold. The rich and poor meet together: the LORD is the maker of them all. A prudent man foreseeth the evil, and hideth himself: but the simple pass on, and are punished. By humility and the fear of the LORD are riches, and honour, and life. Thorns and snares are in the way of the froward: he that doth keep his soul shall be far from them. Train up a child in the way he should go: and when he is old, he will not depart from it. The rich ruleth over the poor, and the borrower is servant to the lender. He that soweth iniquity shall reap vanity: and the rod of his anger shall fail. He that hath a bountiful eye shall be blessed; for he giveth of his bread to the poor. Cast out the scorner, and contention shall go out; yea, strife and reproach shall cease. He that loveth pureness of heart, for the grace of his lips the king shall be his friend. The eyes of the LORD preserve knowledge, and he overthroweth the words of the transgressor. The slothful man saith, There is a lion without, I shall be slain in the streets. The mouth of strange women is a deep pit: he that is abhorred of the LORD shall fall therein. Foolishness is bound in the heart of a child; but the rod of correction shall drive it far from him. He that oppresseth the poor to increase his riches, and he that giveth to the rich, shall surely come to want. Bow down thine ear, and hear the words of the wise, and apply thine heart unto my knowledge. For it is a pleasant thing if thou keep them within thee; they shall withal be fitted in thy lips. That thy trust may be in the LORD, I have made known to thee this day, even to thee. Have not I written to thee excellent things in counsels and knowledge, that I might make thee know the certainty of the words of truth; that thou mightest answer the words of truth to them that send unto thee? Rob not the poor, because he is poor: neither oppress the afflicted in the gate: for the LORD will plead their cause, and spoil the soul of those that spoiled them. Make no friendship with an angry man; and with a furious man thou shalt not go: lest thou learn his ways, and get a snare to thy soul. Be not thou one of them that strike hands, or of them that are sureties for debts. If thou hast nothing to pay, why should he take away thy bed from under thee? Remove not the ancient landmark, which thy fathers have set. Seest thou a man diligent in his business? he shall stand before kings; he shall not stand before mean men.

DAY 66: GAINS AND LOSSES (PROVERBS 22:1-12)

A good name should be chosen before riches untold;
Loving favor choose rather than silver or gold.

The rich and the poor meet in one place;
With the Lord as their Maker, they are the same.

A wise man sees trouble ahead and will hide;
The wicked pass on and are punished besides.

When a man's fear of God and humility are recorded,
With honor, long life, and success he's rewarded.

A hard man's way grows up with thorns and with snares;
He who guards his soul's pathway will none of this share.

Train up a child the right way, make it plain,
And when he is old, in the same way he'll remain.

Just as the rich can rule over the poor,
So the borrower is slave to the lender, for sure.

He who iniquity sows will have sorrow indeed,
For the rod of his anger will fail in his need.

The friendly man's blessed and has friends at his door,
For he shares of his substance and gives to the poor.

Get rid of the scoffer and your strife will then cease,
For the arrogant sow discord and disturb the peace.

He with grace in his speech and with purity of heart,
Is beloved of the Lord, and the king takes his part.

The Lord preserves knowledge and men who do right,
But their words are ruined who transgress in His sight.

A Good Name

Proverb:
"A good name is rather to be chosen than great riches, and
loving favour rather than silver and gold" (Proverbs 22:1).

Precept:
The Book of Proverbs has a lot to say about riches. The Bible
says, "For the love of money is the root of all evil" (I Timothy
6:10). That does not mean that riches in themselves are bad, but
they have a bad reputation, they have a bad connotation, and
they present a constant temptation. The message Solomon reit-
erated throughout his writings is that many things in life are
more valuable than riches. One of those things is the value of a
good name.

Although my father did not leave me riches in this life, he
did give me the heritage of a good name. I have always been
interested in genealogy and the history of my family. Whenever
I travel, I usually look in the phone book to see if there are any
Parkeys in that city.

Once when I was in a Midwestern city, I looked in the phone
book and found someone named Parkey who owned a business
in that town. I called the man, introduced myself, and told him
that I was always glad to meet one of the Parkeys and to find
out to which part of the family he or she belonged. The man did
not respond quite like I had expected. He said he was not sure
that he wanted to be associated with any more Parkeys. He told
me about his particular family—how he had no respect for his
father, who had divorced his mother, or his grandfather, who
claimed to be religious but was a hypocrite.

I apologized for all the trouble he had experienced and
went on to tell how my family was far different. My father was
a minister and my grandfather was a kindly Christian gentle-
man with a testimony that I long remembered.

After I had returned home and a few weeks had passed, I received a call from the distant relative I had contacted. The first thing he said was, "I want to apologize to you. I know I was rude to you when you called to talk about the Parkeys."

He went on to tell me that later that same week a customer had walked into his business and said, "I know you must be proud that you are a Parkey. Some of the finest people I know are named Parkey."

He then asked the customer if he happened to know a W. C. Parkey. The customer replied, "Oh, yes! I have known him since we were both young men in his father's church. In fact, his father was a wonderful man and performed my wedding ceremony."

The man then said to me, "I want to tell you that I was wrong about what I said, and I do want to be associated with the Parkeys."

A good name is equated with a good reputation. And a good reputation is kept by living a life that is blameless and above reproach. I Thessalonians 5:22 teaches that we should "abstain from all appearance of evil." A good name is worth more than riches, so it is worth protecting.

Practice:

Conduct yourself in a manner that will bring respect rather than reproach to your name. Remember that your actions reflect not only on you but also on the others of your family who bear your name.

Prayer:

Lord, thank You for the family of which I am a part. Let me always conduct myself with honor so that our name can be respected and well thought of. Let me also remember that I am a part of Your family as well and that my actions should reflect that.

DAY 67: FOOLISH THINGS (PROVERBS 22:13-16)

The sluggard's excuse is "There's a lion in the street.
I can't go outside; I'd be killed if we meet!"

A harlot's a trap for a man, a deep pit;
You are cursed of the Lord if you fall into it.

Foolishness is bound in a child's heart to stay,
But a rod of correction will drive it away.

He who oppresses the poor for himself to get gain
Will for bribery be sentenced to poverty and pain.

EXCUSES

Proverb:

"The slothful man saith, There is a lion without, I shall be slain in the streets" (Proverbs 22:13).

Precept:

Excuses are as old as man. In the very beginning, Adam and Eve both gave excuses for their sin. Adam said, "It was all the fault of this woman whom You gave me." Eve said, "It was the devil's fault that I sinned." (See Genesis 3:12-13.) A friend of mine says, "An excuse is the skin of a reason stretched over a lie."

The slothful man of this proverb loves to sleep and does not want to work. Since he does not have a real reason to justify his lack of gainful employment, he invents the story that there is a lion in the streets.

If there were a lion in the streets, then why was not someone attempting to rid the town of such a grave danger? Everyone else seemed to be going about their business, except for this lazy man who used the excuse that he was afraid of being hurt.

As a young man, I remember an individual who was intellectually brilliant but was not inclined to be gainfully employed. He spent all his time in the pool hall playing games and never seemed to work. If someone else needed a job, he was full of advice about where to go to get one and the best methods to use. But he always had an excuse for why he was not working.

In speaking of the excessive sins committed by the Gentile nations in Romans 1, Paul said, "They are without excuse" (Romans 1:20). There is no excuse for being shiftless and negligent in your attempts to provide for the necessities of life. I Timothy 5:8 says, "But if any provide not for his own, and specially for those of his own house, he hath denied the faith, and is worse than an infidel."

There are situations where men do not have the opportunity to work or the means to accomplish the task of providing for their families. The soup lines of depression days and the horrible experiences of not being able to find work or food are very real for some. Victor Hugo's story of Jean Valjean, in *Les Miserables*, is a widely known account of a man who was sent to prison for stealing a loaf of bread for his hungry family.[24] The Bible admonishes us to have pity on those who have to steal to eat. "Men do not despise a thief, if he steal to satisfy his soul when he is hungry" (Proverbs 6:30).

However, if you are able, don't make an excuse. Just get to work.

Practice:

Stop making excuses and start making plans. Figure out ways that you can accomplish goals, and act on those plans.

Prayer:

Lord, help me to avoid excuses and to begin the change that is needed in my life. Give me the courage to face my failures and inadequacies and the wisdom not to give excuses for why I have not fulfilled my calling in life.

DAY 68: SAYINGS OF THE SAGES (PROVERBS 22:17-29)

Open your mind and incline your ears,
Apply your hearts and my words you shall hear.

They'll give you delight in your heart if you'll keep them;
They will be pleasant indeed if you will speak them.

So that your trust then can be in the Lord,
That's why I tell you these things for your good.

Have I not written to you long ago
Excellent things for you to know?

You may then know that with certainty I speak,
That you may give others answers they seek.

Don't rob a poor man because he has failed
Or oppress the afflicted because he's been jailed.

For the Lord will defend them and their cause He will plead;
And He'll rob him who robs them of something they need.

Never make friends with an unfriendly man,
Or keep company with ill-tempered ones, lest you sin.

For you may learn of his ways and will find out too late
That your friendship with him will a snare for you make.

Do not be one of those who for bond give a bail
Or who sign for a note for somebody in jail.

For if you don't have the means to pay them what you owe,
You will lose all your goods and have no place to go.

Remove not the old landmarks which our fathers have set;
They are stones set for markers, we should never forget.

When a man loves his work and excels in his skill,
He's not someone common, but a king's work he'll fill.

FIXED FENCES

Proverb:
   "Remove not the ancient landmark, which thy fathers have
set" (Proverbs 22:28).

Precept:
   "Good fences make good neighbors" is a proverb taken
from Robert Frost's poem, "Mending Wall."[25] The poem is about
the mending of a stone wall or fence dividing two farms. In ear-
lier times, it was common to use the stones taken from one's
field to make a fence along the edge of one's property so that
all would know where the boundaries were. The stone fences
were landmarks that defined the owner's property, protected
his livestock from straying, and kept unwanted, potentially dangerous creatures out.

The principles in the Word of God are like a fixed fence that should not be removed. If we adhere to them, they will define who we are in Christ and mark the promises we have been given. They will protect us from straying from our Chief Shepherd and will keep unwanted, potentially dangerous things out of our lives.

On my mother's land, which she received as part of her Indian allotment, giant pecan trees grew along the property line. A fence ran around the property on the outside of the trees. When a new neighbor received possession of his land, he replaced the fence on the property line. He could not remove the trees, so he removed the fence wire and fastened it to the side of the trees inside our property. This maneuver changed the fence line to exclude three feet or more from our land, placing it on the neighbor's side.

Proverbs 22:28 admonishes us not to move the ancient landmarks that our fathers set up. It is to our benefit to protect the boundaries of our spiritual heritage and not allow anyone or anything to move them. If we are not careful, others can come along who will move our boundaries ever so slightly and slyly without us even realizing we are losing territory. Or, sometimes, by our own negligence, the boundary lines can become blurred.

In Robert Frost's poem, the stone walls crumbled in some places because of soil changes throughout the seasons. It was a springtime ritual to mend the broken places in the wall to preserve his relationship with his neighbor.

To protect the integrity of our relationship with God, we, too, should be concerned about preserving the fixed fences in our lives.

Practice:

Tried and true building blocks of prayer, fasting, Bible reading, church attendance, and personal devotions should not be neglected. Do not be so obsessed with the "newest" and "best" that you lay aside the things of value that have passed the test of time.

Prayer:

Lord, in this world that is ever-changing, help me to hold fast to the truths that have been passed down to me and to the fences that have been established in my life.

PROVERBS 23

*When thou sittest to eat with a ruler, consider dili-
gently what is before thee: and put a knife to thy throat,
if thou be a man given to appetite. Be not desirous of
his dainties: for they are deceitful meat. Labour not to
be rich: cease from thine own wisdom. Wilt thou set
thine eyes upon that which is not? for riches certainly
make themselves wings; they fly away as an eagle
toward heaven. Eat thou not the bread of him that hath
an evil eye, neither desire thou his dainty meats: for as
he thinketh in his heart, so is he: Eat and drink, saith
he to thee; but his heart is not with thee. The morsel
which thou hast eaten shalt thou vomit up, and lose thy
sweet words. Speak not in the ears of a fool: for he will
despise the wisdom of thy words. Remove not the old
landmark; and enter not into the fields of the fatherless:
for their redeemer is mighty; he shall plead their cause
with thee. Apply thine heart unto instruction, and thine
ears to the words of knowledge. Withhold not correction
from the child: for if thou beatest him with the rod, he
shall not die. Thou shalt beat him with the rod, and
shalt deliver his soul from hell. My son, if thine heart be
wise, my heart shall rejoice, even mine. Yea, my reins
shall rejoice, when thy lips speak right things. Let not
thine heart envy sinners: but be thou in the fear of the
LORD all the day long. For surely there is an end; and
thine expectation shall not be cut off. Hear thou, my son,
and be wise, and guide thine heart in the way. Be not
among winebibbers; among riotous eaters of flesh: for
the drunkard and the glutton shall come to poverty:
and drowsiness shall clothe a man with rags. Hearken
unto thy father that begat thee, and despise not thy
mother when she is old. Buy the truth, and sell it not;
also wisdom, and instruction, and understanding. The
father of the righteous shall greatly rejoice: and he that
begetteth a wise child shall have joy of him. Thy father
and thy mother shall be glad, and she that bare thee
shall rejoice. My son, give me thine heart, and let thine
eyes observe my ways. For a whore is a deep ditch;*

and a strange woman is a narrow pit. She also lieth in wait as for a prey, and increaseth the transgressors among men. Who hath woe? who hath sorrow? who hath contentions? who hath babbling? who hath wounds without cause? who hath redness of eyes? They that tarry long at the wine; they that go to seek mixed wine. Look not thou upon the wine when it is red, when it giveth his colour in the cup, when it moveth itself aright. At the last it biteth like a serpent, and stingeth like an adder. Thine eyes shall behold strange women, and thine heart shall utter perverse things. Yea, thou shalt be as he that lieth down in the midst of the sea, or as he that lieth upon the top of a mast. They have stricken me, shalt thou say, and I was not sick; they have beaten me, and I felt it not: when shall I awake? I will seek it yet again.

DAY 69: DOS AND DON'TS (PROVERBS 23:1-14)

When with a ruler you sit down to eat,
Carefully consider what is set for your meat.

Put a knife to your throat; make sure you do right,
If you are one with a huge appetite.

Be not desirous of the dainties you've seen,
For delicacies are deceitful, if they make you act mean.

Do not toil for great riches; they will leave you in grief.
So renounce your ambition; let your wisdom give relief.

Wealth is here then it's gone; set your eyes not on things.
They will soon fly away, like an eagle with wings.

Don't consort with a miser, don't eat of his bread,
Don't desire what he has, nor repeat what he's said.

For as he thinks in his heart, so will he do;
He'll invite you to dinner but begrudge you, too.

The things that you eat make your stomach to heave,
For he fed you to fool you and sweetly spoke to deceive.

In the ears of a fool, words of wisdom don't say,
For he will despise them; you'll just throw them away.

The landmarks of yesterday please keep in their place,
And do not encroach on an orphan's estate.

Their Redeemer is strong, and here's what He'll do—
He'll defend all their rights, plead their cause against you.

Turn your heart to instruction, and your ears to
    knowledge bend.
Don't withhold your child's chastisement; let him know
    that you're his friend.

If you chasten him with switches, it won't kill him;
    he won't die.
But if you'll give him a good whipping, it may save
    him by and by.

THE CARROT AND THE STICK

Proverb:
   "Withhold not correction from the child: for if thou beatest
him with the rod, he shall not die. Thou shalt beat him with the
rod, and shalt deliver his soul from hell" (Proverbs 23:13-14).

Precept:
   Hebrews 12:6 teaches that the Lord disciplines those He
loves. Therefore, if we love our children, it is necessary that we
discipline them.
   I never had any doubt that my parents loved me. They,
being loving parents, punished me at times. My mother used a
twig off the lilac bush or the peach tree. My father, who did not
punish as often as my mother, used a belt (which would not be
acceptable to most folks these days). I can assure you that
words are meaningful and threats are sometimes useful, but if
you have felt the sting of a lilac limb, it is much more effective.

However, in disciplining children, it is often necessary to use various methods. The story is told of a man who tied a carrot in front of his donkey to entice him to keep him going. But if the carrot did not work, he used a stick to prod him along.

Concerning children, Paul said that we should "bring them up in the nurture and admonition of the Lord" (Ephesians 6:4). In order for children to be respectful and grow up to be responsible adults, they must receive needful instructions. When the admonition is given, it must be reinforced with actions that indicate that you really mean what you say.

But along with admonition, children also need to be nurtured. Some children get only criticism, reprimands, and punishment. Children need to know that they are loved unconditionally. They need sympathy, tenderness, encouragement, and comfort.

Once when my daughter was spanking my grandson, he began to beg for mercy. In a frustrated tone, she asked him, "Do you think you really deserve mercy?" He quickly answered, "Yes, seventy times seven!"

You should chastise your children, but don't be cruel. You should give admonition, but do not turn it into persecution. If you use both the carrot and the stick, you will end up with a well-adjusted child who will become a responsible and mature adult.

Do not withhold discipline from your child. You will save him or her, and yourself as well, from a lot of mistakes and heartaches. You may also save a soul from death!

Practice:

Show your children that you love them by giving them the discipline they need. Although they may resist your instruction and test your boundaries, they do it intentionally to see what you will do. Knowing you have set boundaries and will discipline them for misbehavior gives them a sense of security. It makes them feel safe and loved.

Prayer:

Lord, only You can give me the wisdom I need to train up my child in the way he should go. Give me the courage to say no when I need to be firm. Help me to show loving discipline. Help me to communicate to my children the reason why I am taking a stand so that they will be better equipped to make decisions on their own as they grow. Help me to instill biblical values in their hearts.

DAY 70: FATHERLY ADVICE (PROVERBS 23:15-28)

My son, if you are wise, I'll be glad with you.
My heart shall rejoice, and your heart will, too.

Let not your heart envy sinners in any way,
But stay in the fear of the Lord every day.

For there is a hereafter, of this we are sure,
And the hope that you have will forever endure.

Hear, my son, and be wise, as your father shall tell.
Guide your heart, keep your way, everything will go well.

Don't run with the riotous or with winebibbers dine,
Don't eat with the gluttonous, and you will be fine.

For the drunkard and glutton come to an end that is bad,
As a lazy man who's given to sleep ends in rags.

Listen, my son, to what your father has told;
Resent not your mother just because she is old.

Buy the truth, buy instruction, buy wisdom without fail,
Buy discernment, then mark it all, "Not for Sale!"

A father who is righteous and will truth to you tell
Can rejoice in his soul to know you are well.

Let your parents have joy as you strive to be true.
She who bore you will rejoice, and your father will, too.

My son, I'll be glad if your heart can be won;
Then let your eyes follow what I have done.

For a harlot is a deep ditch, you had better not doubt.
A strange woman's a pit, and most men can't get out.

She will lie low in wait, like a lion for his prey;
She increases transgression with men every day.

TRUE VALUE

Proverb:

"Buy the truth, and sell it not; also wisdom, and instruction, and understanding" (Proverbs 23:23).

Precept:

In 1932, gold was devalued, and the United States went off the gold standard. For many years, the price of gold stood around $30 an ounce. Today, gold is twice as valuable. People have realized that it is worth much more than they thought.

Truth is worth having. It is worth saving. It is worth keeping. Many are selling truth cheaply. Some are just giving it away. Some are trying to water it down. Some may not consider it to be of any value. But like gold, it is worth much more than they realize.

Thomas Jefferson, one of our country's founding fathers, wrote in the Declaration of Independence, "We hold these truths to be self-evident that all men are created equal; that they are endowed by their Creator with certain unalienable rights; that among these are life, liberty, and the pursuit of happiness."[26]

The famous line "We hold these truths to be self-evident," was originally written as such in rough draft: "We hold these truths to be sacred and undeniable."[27] It is clear that Thomas Jefferson understood that truth is sacred and valuable. We, as a country, have proudly protected the democratic truths that were penned in his historical document. They are truths that we have not allowed anyone to take away from us.

Far greater than the truth of the Declaration of Independence is the truth of the Word of God. In John 14:6 Jesus said, "I am the way, the truth, and the life: no man cometh unto the Father, but by me." In John 8:32, He said, "And ye shall know the truth, and the truth shall make you free."

Eternal truth and eternal life are in Jesus Christ. To know

Him is to know truth. To have Him is to have truth. To believe in Him is to believe the truth.

You do not have to know the price of gold to be saved. You do not have to believe all men are created equal to be saved. But you do have to believe in Jesus Christ to be saved, for that is saving truth.

"And we know that the Son of God is come, and hath given us an understanding, that we may know him that is true, and we are in him that is true, even in his Son Jesus Christ. This is the true God, and eternal life" (I John 5:20). Recognize the true value of this truth and hang on to it. Do not sell it or let anyone take it away from you.

Practice:

Do you treasure your walk with God? Having riches, gold, silver, houses, land, cars, investments, or businesses cannot compare to the treasure that is found in Him. Remember that "where your treasure is, there will your heart be also (Matthew 6:21).

Prayer:

Lord, may I always value Your Word and Your commandments. May they always be more precious to me than silver or gold.

Week 11

DAY 71: THE DANGER OF STRONG DRINK (PROVERBS 23:29-35)

Who has sorrows? Who has wounds without cause?
    Who has woe?
Who has babblings? Who has contentions? Can't you tell?
    Don't you know?

Who has eyes filled with redness? Here's the
    answer, you see:
Those addicted to wine; from mixed wine they're not free!

Don't look at red wine when it moves in your cup,
When it sparkles with color as so smoothly you sup.

See your wine at the last, when as a serpent it bites;
It will sting like a poisonous adder that strikes.

It will cause you to see strange women and ways;
Your lips are confused and your mind's in a daze.

You'll be tossed like a man who's asleep on the deck;
You'll take hold of the mast but end up as a wreck.

Crying, "They beat me, but I don't feel a blow!"
You can't feel when they strike you; you're too
    stupid to know.

Saying, "Wait till the night has come to an end;
When the morning is come, let me get drunk again!"

Take Another Look

Proverb:

"Look not thou upon the wine when it is red, when it giveth his colour in the cup, when it moveth itself aright. At the last it biteth like a serpent, and stingeth like an adder" (Proverbs 23:31-32).

Precept:

The billboard shows a beautiful woman holding a crystal glass of sparkling wine to her lovely lips. The captivating color caption scrolls over the top, inviting you to join her as you rest, relax, and enjoy a delicious drink of the intoxicating beverage. How captivating, how enticing, how inviting, but how deceiving, and how deadly! Everything looks so appealing at the first glance, but the first glance does not tell the whole story.

Millions of people are drawn into the trap of alcoholism every year when they buy into the promise of false advertisement. The ads show pretty pictures that depict men and women in the prime of life, filled with vitality and vigor. They suggest a mountaintop experience accompanied by happiness, friendship, and success, but that is not a complete picture.

Let me show you another picture of a heap of twisted metal that was once the car of a teenager who just wanted to be cool. Or of a hospital room where those who have been crippled or maimed from the accident are recovering from their terrible wounds. Perhaps the picture could be of a family that was looking forward to a birthday, a holiday, or a special event but had to do without because the paycheck had gone to a liquor store or a bar. The picture may be of a courtroom where a mother and father are divorcing because of the stresses and strains of a drunken father or an alcoholic mother. This picture shows us how alcohol "biteth like a serpent, and stingeth like an adder" (Proverbs 23:32).

As a student in college, my roommate had an addiction to liquor that he satisfied by bringing gallon jars of bootleg whiskey to keep in our room. The only time he offered to go to church with me was when he was inebriated. I had to lock him in the room, for he was in no shape to be in the room with me, much less go to church with me.

The writer of the proverb tried to warn us of the deceptive picture of the cup of wine when he pleaded with us not to look on the wine when it is red, when it moves and sparkles in the cup (Proverbs 23:31). He went on to talk about all of the shameful effects of the cup of wine on one's life. The proverb challenges us to look at the end result and not be deceived by the sensuous appeal of strong drink.

The apostle Paul admonished us with these words: "And be not drunk with wine, wherein is excess; but be filled with the Spirit" (Ephesians 5:18). The Spirit of God provides the joy, the excitement, the thrill, and the pleasure for which the wine drinker is seeking. This produces, not a headache, a hangover, or an accident, but righteousness, joy, and peace in the Holy Ghost.

Practice:

Satan paints a beautiful picture, but if you could see behind the scenes, you would see the life of misery. Do not be deceived by the enticements of Satan. If you choose what he has to offer, you will reap addictions, sickness, immorality, financial ruin, prison, and even death. Jesus invites you to accept His offering of righteousness, peace, joy, and life everlasting.

Prayer:

Lord, do not let me be deceived by the pleasures of sin for a season. Help me to realize the devastating effects they will have on me and my family.

PROVERBS 24

Be not thou envious against evil men, neither desire to be with them. For their heart studieth destruction, and their lips talk of mischief. Through wisdom is an house builded; and by understanding it is established: and by knowledge shall the chambers be filled with all precious and pleasant riches. A wise man is strong; yea, a man of knowledge increaseth strength. For by wise counsel thou shalt make thy war: and in multitude of counsellers there is safety. Wisdom is too high for a fool: he openeth not his mouth in the gate. He

that deviseth to do evil shall be called a mischievous
person. The thought of foolishness is sin: and the scorner
is an abomination to men. If thou faint in the day of
adversity, thy strength is small. If thou forbear to
deliver them that are drawn unto death, and those that
are ready to be slain; if thou sayest, Behold, we knew it
not; doth not he that pondereth the heart consider it?
and he that keepeth thy soul, doth not he know it? and
shall not he render to every man according to his
works? My son, eat thou honey, because it is good; and
the honeycomb, which is sweet to thy taste: so shall the
knowledge of wisdom be unto thy soul: when thou hast
found it, then there shall be a reward, and thy expecta-
tion shall not be cut off. Lay not wait, O wicked man,
against the dwelling of the righteous; spoil not his rest-
ing place: for a just man falleth seven times, and riseth
up again: but the wicked shall fall into mischief. Rejoice
not when thine enemy falleth, and let not thine heart be
glad when he stumbleth: lest the LORD *see it, and it dis-*
please him, and he turn away his wrath from him. Fret
not thyself because of evil men, neither be thou envious
at the wicked; for there shall be no reward to the evil
man; the candle of the wicked shall be put out. My son,
fear thou the LORD *and the king: and meddle not with*
them that are given to change: for their calamity shall
rise suddenly; and who knoweth the ruin of them both?
These things also belong to the wise. It is not good to
have respect of persons in judgment. He that saith unto
the wicked, Thou art righteous; him shall the people
curse, nations shall abhor him: but to them that rebuke
him shall be delight, and a good blessing shall come
upon them. Every man shall kiss his lips that giveth a
right answer. Prepare thy work without, and make it fit
for thyself in the field; and afterwards build thine
house. Be not a witness against thy neighbour without
cause; and deceive not with thy lips. Say not, I will do
so to him as he hath done to me: I will render to the man
according to his work. I went by the field of the slothful,
and by the vineyard of the man void of understanding;
and, lo, it was all grown over with thorns, and nettles

had covered the face thereof, and the stone wall thereof was broken down. Then I saw, and considered it well: I looked upon it, and received instruction. Yet a little sleep, a little slumber, a little folding of the hands to sleep: so shall thy poverty come as one that travelleth; and thy want as an armed man.

DAY 72: YOUR FORTUNE AND FUTURE (PROVERBS 24:1-14)

Don't ever be envious of evil men's ways,
Nor desire to be friends or to hear what they say.

For their heart is concerned with violence and gore,
And their lips speak of mischief and trouble and more.

For wisdom will build you a house; that's not all.
Understanding will keep it secure; it won't fall.

By knowledge its chambers will be filled with supply,
With things precious and pleasant your money will buy.

A wise man is better than a strong man can be,
And a man who has knowledge will his power increase.

For it is by wise guidance a man wages war
And victory shall come; that's what counselors are for.

Wisdom is too high for fools who don't know
To be silent in judgment so their folly won't show.

He who plots to do evil gets intrigue for his name.
He's a maker of mischief; watch out for his scheme.

The plan of a fool is the devising of sin,
And the scoffer is cursed both by God and by men.

If you faint in the day of adversity, you'll know
That your strength is small, and your weakness you'll show.

Deliver all those who are destined for death,
For if you don't rescue, they'll take their last breath.

If you say, "We forgot!" or "We didn't know!"
God sees your soul, and the truth He will show.

My son, you can taste of the honey that's sweet;
And the honeycomb, also, is given to eat.

Make wisdom your own; when you find it, don't swerve
From the future ahead and the reward you deserve.

A WISE BUILDER

Proverb:

"Through wisdom is an house builded; and by understanding it is established" (Proverbs 24:3).

Precept:

Everyone knows the story of the three little pigs who were sent out into the world by their mother to live on their own. They each built a house: one of straw, one of sticks, and one of bricks. The first two pigs were both eaten by the wolf, who huffed and puffed and blew both of their houses down. But the third pig built a house so sturdy that the wolf could not blow it down. Furthermore, when the wolf tried to trick him, he outsmarted the wolf at every turn and ended up capturing him in a pot of boiling water and eating him for supper.

It takes wisdom to build a house that will last. Jesus illustrated this point in Matthew 7, when He spoke about the differences between the foolish man's house and the wise man's house. The foolish man built his house upon the sand, and when the rains came and the winds blew, the house fell. But the wise man built his house upon the rock. And when the rains came and the winds blew, his house stood firm (Matthew 7:24-27).

Whether you are erecting a building, a family, a church, a dynasty, or a nation, you need wisdom to build it. Anyone can hammer nails into a board, but it takes wisdom to build a useable structure. Anyone can get married, but it takes wisdom to make the relationship work. Proverbs 14:1 says, "Every wise woman buildeth her house: but the foolish plucketh it down with her hands." (And the same holds true for men.) Anyone can have children, but it takes wisdom to raise them. Anyone can start a church, but it takes wisdom to establish it.

Like the wolf in the story of the three little pigs, there is an enemy who will try to destroy what you have built. It is imperative that you establish your life, your home, your family, or your church on Jesus Christ, the solid rock. With His help, you will be able to build something that will last. Psalm 127:1 says, "Except the LORD build the house, they labour in vain that build it."

I Corinthians 3:9 says, "For we are labourers together with God: ye are God's husbandry, ye are God's building." When you choose to work together with God and to follow His counsel, you are a wise builder, indeed.

Practice:

Build up instead of tearing down. Build your family by showing love and forgiveness to one another. Build your church by serving in capacities that match your ability. Build your community by working together for a common cause. Build the kingdom of God by offering your finances and your prayers to further the cause of Christ around the world.

Prayer:

Lord, I thank You for the home that we have established. Help us to build one another up and to work together to be a closer family. Thank You for the church that I attend. Help me to do my part to build it up. Help me to pray for my pastor and to support the church with my finances. Do not let me be guilty of tearing down what has been established.

DAY 73: FORBIDDEN FRUIT (PROVERBS 24:15-22)

Do not lie in wait like a felon to plan
For the fall of the house of a righteous man.

For a just man can fall seven times and then rise,
But the wicked will fall and remain where he lies.

Do not rejoice when your enemies fall;
Don't be glad at the sinner who stumbles at all.

Lest the Lord should see it and show you His displeasure,
And instead pour His wrath out on you without measure.

Do not stew and fret because of evil men,
And do not be envious of them or their kin.

For the evil shall have no reward; without doubt,
The candle of wicked men is completely put out.

My son, fear the Lord and the king every day;
Don't associate with those who refuse to obey.

For they shall be destroyed by their Lord and their master,
Who can both involve you in all kinds of disaster.

DOWN BUT NOT OUT

Proverb:
"For a just man falleth seven times, and riseth up again: but
the wicked shall fall into mischief" (Proverbs 24:16).

Precept:
When a baby learns to walk, he will fall. When a child
learns to skate or ride a bicycle, he or she will experience a few
falls. Even as adults, whether skating, riding a bicycle, or walking, we, too, will sometimes fall. To fall is humiliating and
sometimes harmful, but in order to continue what you are
doing, you have to get up.

As Christians, our relationship with God is often referred to
as a walk. In the New Testament, we are instructed to walk "in
the newness of life" (Romans 6:4); "not after the flesh, but after
the Spirit" (Romans 8:1); "honestly" (Romans 13:13); "by faith,
not by sight" (II Corinthians 5:7); "in the Spirit" (Galatians
5:16); "in love" (Ephesians 5:2); "as children of light" (Ephesians 5:8); "circumspectly" (Ephesians 5:15); "worthy of the
Lord" (Colossians 1:10); "in wisdom" (Colossians 4:5); and "in
truth" (III John 4).

Although we do our best to please God and obey Him, there will be times in our Christian walk that we stumble and fall. But to fall does not mean that we are finished. It just means that we are temporarily down but not out. We must brush ourselves off, get up, and continue walking.

The only person who has not fallen or made mistakes in his spiritual walk is the person who is sitting still and attempting nothing for God. Fortunately, God understands our human frailties and weaknesses. He does not expect us to be perfect. He just wants us to be willing to get up and try again. Psalm 145:14, says "The LORD upholdeth all that fall." Psalm 37:23-24 says, "The steps of a good man are ordered by the LORD: and he delighteth in his way. Though he fall, he shall not be utterly cast down: for the LORD upholdeth him with his hand."

The apostle Peter experienced the promise of this verse in a unique way. One night while he and the other disciples were riding in a storm-tossed ship, they saw Jesus walking toward them on the water. Peter asked the Lord to bid him to come, then he stepped out of the boat and began walking on the water toward Jesus. When Peter got distracted by the storm, he began to sink. Immediately Jesus stretched forth His hand, caught him, and then took him safely to the ship. (See Matthew 14:25-32.)

Peter experienced the miraculous by walking on the water, yet he later openly denied his association with Jesus. (See Luke 22:55-62.) Peter was humiliated by his spiritual fall and wept bitterly. But his story does not end there. At some point, he must have gotten up and brushed himself off, for after Jesus' resurrection, Peter was one of the first to the tomb. And on the Day of Pentecost in Acts 2, Peter was the one who preached the salvation message.

When you fall down, do not be like the wicked and remain in your unfortunate state, but rise up and try one more time. Make this verse of Scripture your motto:

"Rejoice not against me, O mine enemy: when I fall, I shall arise" (Micah 7:8).

Practice:

Notice that the verse of Scripture does not say *if* I fall, but it says *when* I fall. No one is perfect, and it is guaranteed that at some point in your life you will fall. You will fall down, but you must get up. That is the only way to be an overcomer.

Prayer:
Lord, I am thankful that failure is not final with You. Thank You that when we fall, You help us to get back up and try again. Your grace is sufficient for us.

Day 74: Good Sense (Proverbs 24:23-34)

The sayings of the wise men, let us hear what they wrote:
It isn't fair for you to favor one side in a suit.

A judge who calls a man "right" when he's wrong
Is cursed by all men, nations, and throngs.

But if you will punish the guilty, you will find all is well;
The people will bless you and have good things to tell.

A straightforward answer with honest intent
Is better than friendship and a kiss that's well meant.

If you're building a house and a home, if you can,
Prepare your work in the field, and then finish your plan.

Don't bear witness against your neighbor, unless your
cause is just.
When you witness, tell the whole truth; do not betray his trust.

Do not say, "I will treat him in the same way that I have
been treated;
I'll repay him for all the bad things to me he has meted."

I passed by the slothful man's field, and I saw
The vineyard of a man with no wisdom at all.

It was grown up with nettles and weeds everywhere.
There were thorns, there were thistles; where I looked
they were there.

Its stone wall was broken, and a lesson I learned;
I received my instruction as my eyes to it turned.

Just a little more slumber, a little more rest,
Just a little more sleep, with hands folded on my breast.

So, like a robber, shall your poverty come,
And your need will come on you, like a thief with a gun.

FIRST THINGS FIRST

Proverb:

"Prepare thy work without, and make it fit for thyself in the field; and afterwards build thine house" (Proverbs 24:27).

Precept:

I remember sitting in the business session of the General Conference of the United Pentecostal Church International as we discussed the need to plant churches in North America. The specific question on the floor concerned the priority of the home missionary. Should a home missionary secure a building first and then gather a congregation? Or should he gather a congregation and then secure a building? The debate carried on until a seasoned old preacher, who had built several churches, took the conference floor. The old preacher said, "Prepare thy work without, and make it fit for thyself in the field; then when you have a congregation, build your building."

When one endeavors to build anything that is lasting, he must keep first things first. A decision is a good one only if it is made at the right time. Everything must proceed in a proper sequence if it is to succeed. A newly married couple would be foolish to overextend themselves financially to live at a level that took their parents a lifetime to achieve. Patience, planning, and proper priorities will allow good things to develop in time.

Some ministers who have the proper training and support may be an instant success, but most of the great success stories started with a time of limited opportunities, small beginnings, and ministry development.

One minister spent time training in Bible college until his graduation. Then, his home district offered him an opportunity to pastor a church with a small congregation, some income, and a three-bedroom parsonage. With disdain, the minister refused. He said, "I didn't spend four years in Bible school to come to something like this!"

Ministers have started churches in their living rooms, with just their family in attendance. However, those churches have grown into large congregations with fine buildings. Others have started next to bars or in buildings that were formerly goat sheds and have built established churches. Missionary works that were begun with no adherents have grown into a membership of thousands with hundreds of ministers. Many great things start with small beginnings.

Whatever your endeavor and wherever you labor, do not hesitate to begin your operation of a family, a church, a ministry, or a mission field with proper priorities and preparation. Learn to work with whatever resources you have. Remember that your time for expansion, growth, and fulfillment will come. "Who hath despised the day of small things?" (Zechariah 4:10).

Practice:
At what stage are you? Are you at the place of humble beginnings, the middle of the road, or have you achieved greatness? No matter where you are, it is always good to look back and reminisce about the places from which God has brought you and the blessings that He has given you along the way.

Prayer:
Lord, I thank You for the way You have provided for me in the past, and the plans that You have for me for my future.

PROVERBS 25

These are also proverbs of Solomon, which the men of Hezekiah king of Judah copied out. It is the glory of God to conceal a thing: but the honour of kings is to search out a matter. The heaven for height, and the earth for depth, and the heart of kings is unsearchable. Take away the dross from the silver, and there shall

come forth a vessel for the finer. Take away the wicked
from before the king, and his throne shall be established
in righteousness. Put not forth thyself in the presence of
the king, and stand not in the place of great men: for
better it is that it be said unto thee, Come up hither;
than that thou shouldest be put lower in the presence of
the prince whom thine eyes have seen. Go not forth
hastily to strive, lest thou know not what to do in the
end thereof, when thy neighbour hath put thee to shame.
Debate thy cause with thy neighbour himself; and discover not a secret to another: lest he that heareth it put
thee to shame, and thine infamy turn not away. A word
fitly spoken is like apples of gold in pictures of silver. As
an earring of gold, and an ornament of fine gold, so is
a wise reprover upon an obedient ear. As the cold of
snow in the time of harvest, so is a faithful messenger
to them that send him: for he refresheth the soul of his
masters. Whoso boasteth himself of a false gift is like
clouds and wind without rain. By long forbearing is a
prince persuaded, and a soft tongue breaketh the bone.
Hast thou found honey? eat so much as is sufficient for
thee, lest thou be filled therewith, and vomit it.
Withdraw thy foot from thy neighbour's house; lest he
be weary of thee, and so hate thee. A man that beareth
false witness against his neighbour is a maul, and a
sword, and a sharp arrow. Confidence in an unfaithful
man in time of trouble is like a broken tooth, and a foot
out of joint. As he that taketh away a garment in cold
weather, and as vinegar upon nitre, so is he that
singeth songs to an heavy heart. If thine enemy be hungry, give him bread to eat; and if he be thirsty, give him
water to drink: for thou shalt heap coals of fire upon his
head, and the LORD shall reward thee. The north wind
driveth away rain: so doth an angry countenance a
backbiting tongue. It is better to dwell in the corner of
the housetop, than with a brawling woman and in a
wide house. As cold waters to a thirsty soul, so is good
news from a far country. A righteous man falling down
before the wicked is as a troubled fountain, and a corrupt spring. It is not good to eat much honey: so for men

to search their own glory is not glory. He that hath no
rule over his own spirit is like a city that is broken
down, and without walls.

DAY 75: SOLOMON'S PROVERBS COPIED
BY MEN OF HEZEKIAH
(PROVERBS 25:1-14)

These are the proverbs of Solomon the king;
Men of King Hezekiah have copied these things.

God's glory is a mystery that He has concealed;
The king's glory is to search out, hidden meanings reveal.

The earth is for depth, the heaven is for height,
So unsearchable are the kings' hearts and minds.

Remove the dross from silver; there is no dross inside.
Remove the sin from men's hearts; they're
        completely purified.

Remove the wicked from the presence of the king;
His throne will be better with righteousness in everything.

Claim no honor in the king's presence when you
        have come in;
Strive not to be seated in the place of great men.

For it would be better for you that you've higher to go
Than from a place with the prince, be demoted down low.

Don't go hastily to court or have charges to make,
Lest you be shamed and admit that you made a mistake.

In a dispute with a neighbor or friend, don't fuss;
Keep it secret from all and debate if you must,

Lest he who hears it exposes your shame,
Your reputation is ruined, and you are to blame.

A word fitly spoken is like apples of gold,
In settings of silver, at the right time when it's told.

Like an ornament of gold that is placed in one's ear
Is a rebuke wisely made to a man who will hear.

Like the coolness of snow, in a harvest's dry heat,
Is the news by a messenger whom his master repeats.

Like wind without water and clouds without rain,
Is the boasting of one who false gifts will proclaim.

LOOK AT ME!

Proverb:

"Put not forth thyself in the presence of the king, and stand not in the place of great men" (Proverbs 25:6).

Precept:

The lesson of humility is taught often in the Bible, but it is not often practiced in the lives of individuals. There are social climbers who try to rise to a higher level by cultivating the rich, the famous, and the influential. There are employees who try to rise to the top by "buttering up" the management. Even some church members and ministers go to unusual lengths to be noticed by the leadership of their church, district, or organization. Unfortunately, some people feel that it is appropriate to scheme and maneuver in order to promote themselves and make themselves known to men in authority and power.

I remember a college classmate who joined a prestigious church with a large and influential membership for the purpose of being accepted into medical school. He knew that one of the church members was also a member of the committee that selected students for acceptance into the medical school that he wanted to attend. He thought that by joining the church and becoming acquainted with this particular member, he would have a better chance of being accepted.

Such reasoning runs contrary to the teaching of the above proverb. Instead of promoting oneself in the presence of the king, the writer advised that an individual take the lowest seat, which is better than taking the highest seat and then being sent to a lower place. It is better to be honored by being elevated to a higher position than to be humiliated by being demoted to a lower position (Proverbs 25:7).

Psalm 75:6-7 says that "promotion cometh neither from the east, nor from the west, nor from the south. But God is the judge: he putteth down one, and setteth up another." God will promote someone to fulfill His purpose, and He will demote for the same reason.

Abraham Lincoln said, "I will prepare myself, and the opportunity will come!"[28] Prepare yourself, and your opportunity will come. Let promotion come to you instead of promoting yourself. You will not be sorry that you did.

Practice:

Do not try to force your advancement. Let God prepare the way before you. If you prepare yourself and wait patiently on Him, He will open doors and make a way for you.

Prayer:

Lord, I do not want to exalt myself and try to seek a promotion that would put me ahead of where You want me to be. Help me to prepare myself.

DAY 76: BE SOFT AND BE SWEET (PROVERBS 25:15-28)

By patience is a ruler persuaded to give in;
A soft tongue, like lightning, breaks the bone but not the skin.

Have you found honey? Eat only that which you need.
Too many sweets will cause sickness; watch out
     for your greed!

Be friendly with your neighbor, but make your visits few,
Lest he become weary and learn to hate you.

To testify falsely against your neighbor causes woe.
It's like a club or a sword; it's like an arrow and bow.

To place confidence in an unfaithful man when
    you're strained
Causes pain like a toothache or a foot that's been sprained.

To be forced on a winter day with your garments to part
Is as vinegar on nitre or songs to a heavy heart.

If your enemy is hungry, give him something to eat;
If your enemy is thirsty, give him water to drink.

You'll heap coals of fire on his head, that's what you'll do.
Your action may make him think, and the Lord
    will reward you.

The wind from the north will the rain drive away;
In the presence of anger, backbiters won't stay.

It is better in a corner of the housetop to stay
Than to live in a wide house with a nagging wife always.

Like cold water refreshes a throat when it's dry,
So good news brought from a distant land will
    a blessing supply.

For a righteous man to fall down to the wicked is sad;
It's a corrupted spring, a polluted well, and
    everything that's bad.

To eat a surfeit of honey is not a good call;
To promote your own glory is not glory at all.

He who over his spirit has no more command
Is like a broken-down city with no walls that can stand.

THE LETDOWN

Proverb:
    "Confidence in an unfaithful man in time of trouble is like
a broken tooth, and a foot out of joint" (Proverbs 25:19).

Precept:

Have you ever leaned on something for support, only to have it give way? Have you ever trusted someone only to find that they were unfaithful? Then join the crowd. Most everyone has had this kind of experience, and it hurts! It is like a broken tooth or a foot out of joint.

Many years ago, I read a sermon by Robert G. Lee, one of the preaching greats. His opening statement was, "The mule that was under him went away! It always does." He spoke of Absalom, the son of David who rode a mule under a giant oak tree whose branches seemed to reach out and grab Absalom's long hair. The mule kept going, and Absalom, who was trying to usurp his father's throne, was left dangling from the tree. Joab, the captain of David's army, rode by and killed Absalom with three darts to his heart. (See II Samuel 18:14.)

Ahithophel was David's counselor and one of his most trusted men. When they counted to see who was still with David, Ahithophel was not there. He had gone over to Absalom's side. Absalom had lost his life when the mule that was under him rode away, but it was not that mule that left David hanging in a maze of uncertainty. It was the desertion of Ahithophel, David's trusted counselor and grandfather of his wife Bathsheba.

Jesus was let down when Judas Iscariot, one of His twelve disciples, sold Him to the Jews for thirty pieces of silver. (See Matthew 26:14-15.) Paul had his disappointment when he wrote, "Demas hath forsaken me, having loved this present world" (II Timothy 4:10).

It is painful when close friends betray us or choose to turn their back and walk away from truth. Yet David, Paul, and even Jesus Himself were let down by unfaithful men. It is to be expected that we will also be betrayed or let down at some point in our lives by a friend who is unfaithful.

In that event, we should not blame God foolishly. It is not who to blame but what to do about it. We cannot become vindictive. We should pray for those who have betrayed us, as did Jesus: "Father, forgive them; for they know not what they do" (Luke 23:34).

When people fail us, then God helps us. When Paul lamented the defection of Demas, he added, "Notwithstanding the Lord stood with me, and strengthened me" (II Timothy 4:17). Although others will sometimes let us down, we can trust in a God who never fails.

Practice:

Learning to forgive someone who has betrayed you is painful and does not usually happen overnight. Forgiveness is often achieved over a period of time as you continually take the need to God in prayer. As we release our hurt, anger, and bitterness to God, He can then equip us with the love and grace needed to forgive the unfaithful friend. The measure of mercy and forgiveness we are able to give is the measure that we will receive. (See Luke 6:36-38.)

Prayer:

Lord, help me to give all of the pain of betrayal to You. Do not let me allow it to cause a root of bitterness to grow in my life. Help me to forgive those who trespass against me.

PROVERBS 26

As snow in summer, and as rain in harvest, so honour is not seemly for a fool. As the bird by wandering, as the swallow by flying, so the curse causeless shall not come. A whip for the horse, a bridle for the ass, and a rod for the fool's back. Answer not a fool according to his folly, lest thou also be like unto him. Answer a fool according to his folly, lest he be wise in his own conceit. He that sendeth a message by the hand of a fool cutteth off the feet, and drinketh damage. The legs of the lame are not equal: so is a parable in the mouth of fools. As he that bindeth a stone in a sling, so is he that giveth honour to a fool. As a thorn goeth up into the hand of a drunkard, so is a parable in the mouth of fools. The great God that formed all things both rewardeth the fool, and rewardeth transgressors. As a dog returneth to his vomit, so a fool returneth to his folly. Seest thou a man wise in his own conceit? there is more hope of a fool than of him. The slothful man saith, There is a lion in the way; a lion is in the streets. As the door turneth upon his hinges, so doth the slothful upon his bed. The slothful hideth his hand in his bosom; it grieveth him to bring it again to his mouth. The sluggard is wiser in his own conceit than seven men that can render a reason. He that passeth by, and meddleth with strife belonging not to him, is like one that taketh a dog by the ears. As a mad man who casteth firebrands, arrows, and death, so is the man that deceiveth his neighbour, and saith, Am not I in sport? Where no wood is, there the fire goeth out: so where there is no talebearer, the strife ceaseth. As coals are to burning coals, and wood to fire; so is a contentious man to kindle strife. The words of a talebearer are as wounds, and they go down into the innermost parts of the belly. Burning lips and a wicked heart are like a potsherd covered with silver dross. He that hateth dissembleth with his lips, and layeth up deceit within him; when he speaketh fair, believe him not: for there are seven abominations in his heart. Whose hatred is covered by deceit, his wickedness shall be shewed before the whole congregation. Whoso diggeth a pit shall fall therein: and he that rolleth a stone, it will return upon him. A lying tongue hateth those that are afflicted by it; and a flattering mouth worketh ruin.

Day 77: Comparisons (Proverbs 26:1-9)

Like snow in the winter or the harvest time rain,
To give a stupid man honors is entirely in vain.

Like a sparrow by wandering can find a new home,
So a curse that is causeless will surely not come.

A bridle for donkeys and for horses a quirt;
There's nothing but a rod that will make a fool work.

Do not answer a fool according to his mistake,
For you surely will of yourself a fool make.

You may answer a fool according to his fun,
But to make him think he's wise just should not be done.

If you send out a message by a fool whom you meet,
You drink to your damage and you cut off your feet.

The legs of the lame are not equal in size,
Nor the meaning of a parable which a fool's mouth applies.

Like one who entangles a stone in a sling
Is a man who to a fool would great honor bring.

CRIPPLED COMPARISONS

Proverb:
"The legs of the lame are not equal: so is a parable in the mouth of fools" (Proverbs 26:7).

Precept:
The Book of Proverbs consists of the sayings of wise men of the past, such as Solomon and Hezekiah. They are given in comparison form; they compare the actions of folly and wisdom to some natural event or object. The purpose of the proverb is to instruct the reader in the way of wisdom. Jesus often taught by telling parables that used an earthly situation to illustrate a heavenly meaning. Proverbs and parables are valid methods of illuminating truth. However, a fool will use stories, proverbs, and parables not to confirm or validate truth, but rather to refute or confuse the facts.

One time I was talking to a lady about the negative aspects of smoking cigarettes. I pointed out that it had been proven by many medical authorities that smoking cigarettes is hazardous to one's health. She responded by telling me a story about a relative who smoked cigarettes for years and was never sick. I have no doubt that her story was legitimate, but it did not change the fact that cigarettes are harmful to one's health. Her single example did not carry nearly as much weight as the evidence that was presented against her.

A story in the mouth of a fool is as reliable as the stunted legs of the lame. Therefore, we must consider the credibility of the speaker when determining the value of a story. Just because it is spoken as truth does not confirm the authenticity of the story. A fool will twist and contort a parable to promote his own agenda and acquire his own desire. The proverb of the fool will never go the distance, but it will always be stranded by the revelation of internal inadequacies.

Paul told Titus to "avoid foolish questions, and genealogies, and contentions, and strivings about the law; for they are unprofitable and vain" (Titus 3:9). A fool will have a story for everything, but it will not be confirmed by truth. Refuse to listen to a fool, because, like his story, he is crippled by his own stupidity.

Practice:

In the mouth of two or three witnesses let every word be established (Matthew 18:16). Do not believe every story that you hear without first determining the origin and confirming the validity. Follow the advice of Philippians 4:8: "Finally, brethren, whatsoever things are true, whatsoever things are honest, whatsoever things are just, whatsoever things are pure, whatsoever things are lovely, whatsoever things are of good report; if there be any virtue, and if there be any praise, think on these things."

Prayer:

Lord, I don't want my words or actions to be based on a story that is untrue. Help me to follow after truths that have been established by Your Word and confirmed to me by godly sources.

Week 12

DAY 78: MEN TO AVOID (PROVERBS 26:9-17)

Like a thorn bush brandished by a drunkard's strong arm,
So a proverb told by a fool causes someone harm.

Like an archer who shoots everyone, left or right,
Is someone who hires a drunk fool at first sight.

As a dog returns to his vomit and eats,
Is a fool who his folly continually repeats.

There's more hope of a fool than one who's not right
But thinks that he is and is wise in his sight.

The slothful man uses excuses to say,
"There's a lion that waits in the street by the way."

Like a door uses hinges to swing and to sway,
On his bed, the sluggard turns day after day.

A sluggard puts a hand in the dish for a bite,
But then he's too lazy to lift it upright.

A sluggard is wiser in his own estimation
Than seven wise men with a good education.

Like a man who catches a dog by the ears
Is a man who meddles in other men's wars.

HARD TO HANDLE

Proverb:
   "He that passeth by, and meddleth with strife belonging not to him, is like one that taketh a dog by the ears" (Proverbs 26:17).

Precept:

It is not wise to get involved in someone else's disagreement. It is best to live peaceably and leave other people's problems alone. This proverb compares becoming involved in someone else's argument to taking a dog by the ears. Have you ever taken a dog by the ears? If you have not, do not! Especially if the dog is angry and trying to bite you. You have hold of him, but you cannot turn loose because if you do, you are going to get hurt.

Notice that the man in the proverb was just passing by. He was not part of the quarrel, the disagreement, or the angry argument. Some people find it hard to mind their own business. If they see trouble brewing, they gravitate toward the problem. Proverbs 20:3 says, "It is an honour for a man to cease from strife: but every fool will be meddling." Christians are told not to be "as a busybody in other men's matters" (I Peter 4:15). If there is strife and it does not belong to you, then avoid it.

Once my son-in-law saw a man and a woman having a disagreement in the parking lot of the apartment complex where he lived. The man was very big and bulky and the woman was small. As their disagreement escalated, the man began to beat the woman. She began screaming for help. My son-in-law ran across the lot and jumped between the man and the woman. The woman escaped to safety, but the man began beating up my son-in-law! He did not want to fight with the angry man, so he deflected the blows and backed away. A few minutes later the woman came out from where she had been hiding, and she and the man got in their vehicle and drove away. Although his intentions were good, my son-in-law was left a little ruffled and scuffed from getting involved in someone else's quarrel.

Do not be tempted to get involved in other people's conflicts. It may turn into something too hard for you to handle—like taking a dog by the ears!

Practice:

Many people may act like they want advice or help but then do not receive it when it is given. Be available to help others who are in need, but do not force yourself into other people's conflicts.

Prayer:

Lord, help me to avoid getting involved in conflicts that are not my business. Give me the wisdom to know when I should intervene and how I should do so.

DAY 79: PEOPLE TO WATCH (PROVERBS 26:18-28)

He who deceives another and says, "It's just play!"
Is a madman who shoots deadly arrows each way;

So is the man whom his neighbor deceives
And then tries to say he was just out to tease.

For lack of new fuel a fire will die down;
When a talebearer's gone, there is no strife around.

As bellows for coals and as wood is for flame,
A contentious man's wrath is to strife just the same.

A talebearer's words are as wounds to the soul;
They go down, they go deep, and they hurt as they go.

When sweet talk from a heart that's deceitful shall come,
It's cheap pottery covered with silvery scum.

He who hates a person, with his lips will tell lies;
He is filled with his falsehood, can't be true if he tries.

While he promises friendship, he's seven times worse,
For his heart's filled with wickedness and he's under a curse.

His hatred is covered by treachery and stealth;
His deceit shall be shown before everyone else.

To prepare a pit for others means that you'll fall in, too;
Stones rolled toward your enemy will roll right back on you.

A slandering tongue hates those about whom he lies;
A flattering mouth ruins—a man is kissed, then he dies.

BOOMERANG

Proverb:

"Whoso diggeth a pit shall fall therein: and he that rolleth a stone, it will return upon him" (Proverbs 26:27).

Precept:

While I was president of Gateway College of Evangelism in St. Louis, Missouri, a student from Australia presented me with a boomerang as a gift. I still have it and treasure it as a keepsake, but I have never tried to throw it. It is a flat, sharp, curved stick of hardwood. When it is thrown correctly, it curves and spins and returns to the person who threw it.

The boomerang was originally used by the aborigines of Australia for hunting. Because of its unique design, which causes it to return to the thrower, the word *boomerang* has become synonymous with the meaning "to backfire."[29] Anything that recoils on the person who is doing it is called a boomerang. Anything done that results in harm to the doer is said to boomerang.

The writer of Proverbs did not know the Australian word *boomerang*, but he knew the principle of it. He warned that if you try to plan something that will injure someone else, you probably will end up injuring yourself as much or more than the other person.

In Esther 5, Haman became angry at Mordecai, the cousin of Queen Esther, because he would not bow to him. He hated him so much that he called his friends and his wife together to discuss what could be done. Haman's wife suggested that he build a gallows and have Mordecai hanged. Haman liked the idea and ordered the gallows to be built. But before the story was through, the king of Persia grew angry with Haman, and he ended up hanged, along with his ten sons, on the same gallows he had built for someone else. (See Esther 9.) The revenge that Haman planned for Mordecai backfired. The boomerang not only came back on Haman but on his family as well.

Be careful what kind of revenge you are planning for others. The thing you think will cause injury to others may be the very thing that causes injury to you. If you dig a pit, you may fall in it. If you roll a rock to crush someone else, it may crush you.

The Golden Rule teaches us to do unto others as we would have them do unto us. This principle will safeguard you from the boomerang of a negative action. The Bible also teaches that "whatsoever a man soweth, that shall he also reap" (Galatians 6:7). Whatever you give, you will get. If you sow kindness, that's what you will reap. If you choose to forgive rather than seek revenge, compassion and mercy will be returned to you.

You can choose your own punishment or your own blessing. Whatever you do will boomerang!

Practice:

It is a natural reaction to want to give back whatever is being given to you, whether it be anger, unkind words, or harsh actions. You must resist responding in kind. Instead, when there is strife, give peace; when there is anger, give a soft answer; when there is hatred and envy, give love and forgiveness. Remember that what you give is what you will get in return.

Prayer:

Lord, help me treat others in the way that I would want to be treated. Help me to understand when I have been mistreated that any revenge could backfire and harm me as well. Help me to give my problems to You and let You solve them.

PROVERBS 27

Boast not thyself of to morrow; for thou knowest not what a day may bring forth. Let another man praise thee, and not thine own mouth; a stranger, and not thine own lips. A stone is heavy, and the sand weighty; but a fool's wrath is heavier than them both. Wrath is cruel, and anger is outrageous; but who is able to stand before envy? Open rebuke is better than secret love. Faithful are the wounds of a friend; but the kisses of an enemy are deceitful. The full soul loatheth an honeycomb; but to the hungry soul every bitter thing is sweet. As a bird that wandereth from her nest, so is a man that wandereth from his place. Ointment and perfume rejoice the heart: so doth the sweetness of a man's friend by hearty counsel. Thine own friend, and thy father's friend, forsake not; neither go into thy brother's house in the day of thy calamity: for better is a neighbour that is near than a brother far off. My son, be wise, and make my heart glad, that I may answer him that reproacheth me. A prudent man foreseeth the evil, and hideth himself; but the simple pass on, and are punished. Take his garment that is surety for a stranger, and take a pledge of him for a strange woman. He that blesseth his friend with a loud voice, rising early in the morning, it shall be counted a curse to him. A continual dropping in a very rainy day and a contentious woman are alike. Whosoever hideth her hideth the wind, and the ointment of his right hand, which bewrayeth itself. Iron sharpeneth iron; so a man sharpeneth the countenance of his friend. Whoso keepeth the fig tree shall eat the fruit thereof: so he that waiteth on his master shall be honoured. As in water face answereth to face, so the heart of man to man. Hell and destruction are never full; so the eyes of man are never satisfied. As the fining pot for silver, and the furnace for gold; so is a man to his praise. Though thou shouldest bray a fool in a mortar among wheat with a pestle, yet will not his foolishness depart from him. Be thou diligent to know the state of thy flocks, and look well to thy herds. For riches are not for ever: and doth the crown endure to every generation? The hay appeareth, and the tender grass sheweth itself, and herbs of the mountains are gathered. The lambs are for thy clothing, and the goats are the price of the field. And thou shalt have goats' milk enough for thy food, for the food of thy household, and for the maintenance for thy maidens.

DAY 80: SIMPLE SUGGESTIONS (PROVERBS 27:1-10)

Boast not thyself what tomorrow will hold,
For you know not what the day may unfold.

Don't let your own lips sing praise for you;
Let a neighbor, a friend, or stranger that do.

It's a task to pick up a stone or some sand,
But a fool's wrath is heavier than both in your hand.

Anger and wrath tend to make your heart break,
But envy and jealousy are harder to take.

Sometimes when we're wrong and receive open correction,
It is better for us than someone's secret affection.

Faithful indeed are the wounds of a friend,
But the kisses of enemies are what wound in the end.

When you're full, even sweet things aren't good to your taste;
If you're hungry, you'll eat what's been put on your plate.

As a wild bird that wanders from a familiar nest,
For a man who's been gone, his home is the best.

Both ointment and perfume make your heart to rejoice,
But much sweeter is the fellowship with friends
    of your choice.

Love your faraway relatives, love your parent's friends
    you've known,
But when your tough times come, have some friends
    of your own!

THE CERTAINTY OF UNCERTAINTY

Proverb:
    "Boast not thyself of to morrow; for thou knowest not what
a day may bring forth" (Proverbs 27:1).

Precept:
    If anything is certain about life it is that tomorrow is uncer-
tain. Life has a way of lulling us into a sense of false expectation
that all of our tomorrows will be like we planned them. However,

life is full of surprises. Change and unexpected happenings are to be expected. Only God knows the end from the beginning. He is the only one who really knows what is going to happen tomorrow.

The writer of Proverbs cautioned us not to take pride in the certainty of our plans, because our plans are subject to change without notice. He did not condemn planning, but rather condemned the spirit of invincibility. James cautioned his readers in James 4 against making plans without factoring in the will of God. James said, "Whereas ye know not what shall be on the morrow. For what is your life? It is even a vapour, that appeareth for a little time, and then vanisheth away. For that ye ought to say, If the Lord will, we shall live, and do this, or that" (James 4:14-15).

Many times my plans were changed by unexpected circumstances. I remember one year my wife and I made plans to go to the General Conference in Milwaukee, Wisconsin. We planned to leave on Monday morning and drive the distance to the conference. By Sunday night the bags were packed, the arrangements were made, and we were ready to leave. However, on our way into the house after Sunday night church, my wife caught her shoe on the curb and badly sprained her ankle. Needless to say, all our plans came to a screeching halt, and we did not attend the conference.

You never know what a day will bring forth. The eighteenth-century poet Robert Burns described the fleeting nature of our plans when he wrote, "The best laid schemes o' mice an' men, Gang aft a-gley," or the best-laid plans of mice and men often go awry.[30] Therefore, a wise man makes his plans for tomorrow but does not boast of their certainty. He proceeds only with caution and only in the will of God.

Practice:

Your tomorrows are in the hand of the Lord. He knows the ending from the beginning. Make your plans, but when circumstances arise that alter them, remember that God is in control and you can trust your tomorrows to Him.

Prayer:

Lord, I thank You for the assurance that You hold my tomorrows in Your hand and that You are faithful to bring me through whatever circumstance I might face. I thank You for Your promise to be with me wherever I go.

DAY 81: WORDS OF WISDOM (PROVERBS 27:11-20)

If you'll be wise, my son, you'll bring joy to my heart,
And I won't have to worry when criticism starts.

A prudent man sees trouble and prepares for the worst;
The simple pass on and are punished the first!

Take the garment that's given for the pledge of a stranger
And hold it for when he needs pledge for his danger.

When you meet someone who greets you loudly with flattery,
Beware lest he's using some form of hypocrisy.

As the waters drip continually on a dreary, rainy day,
A contentious woman's gripes sound just that very way.

He who lives with that woman expects the storm
    winds to blow,
Will they come from the north or the south? You don't know!

Iron sharpens iron, so a man can depend;
You can sharpen a countenance when a friend
    meets with friend.

He who keepeth a fig tree with its fruit will be fed;
He who serves a great man shall be honored and led.

As in water a reflection appears with the light,
There are mirrors that show a man's heart in his sight.

For hell and destruction nothing satisfies or fills;
A heart of a man is not satisfied until. . . !

STORM WARNINGS

Proverb:

"A prudent man foreseeth the evil, and hideth himself; but the simple pass on, and are punished" (Proverbs 27:12).

Precept:

Being raised in Oklahoma where tornados and storms are frequent, my father was very storm conscious. During the spring months, many nights he would send our family to the storm cellar, then would go back to the house to "watch the cloud." When I asked him why he sent us to the storm cellar so often, he said, "I have seven children, and if a storm were to come, I couldn't get you all in the cellar quick enough to save you."

Once I stood on the front porch of our house in Oklahoma and watched a tornado as it came towards us. I saw the funnel-shaped cloud and watched it hit the ground. I saw the dirt and debris swirling as it plummeted through the sky. I grabbed my mother's hand and I took her on the fastest run she had ever taken, as we fled for the cellar.

I realize that you cannot spend all your life in a place of safety just because of the possibility of a storm. You have to live, work, and enjoy life. But you should be watchful and ready to take cover when you see the possibility of danger.

Jesus said to the Pharisees and Sadducees, "O ye hypocrites, ye can discern the face of the sky; but can ye not discern the signs of the times?" (Matthew 16:3). When Jesus spoke of the signs of His coming and the end of the world, He spoke of natural things that tell us how we know that something is about to happen. He said, "Now learn a parable of the fig tree; When his branch is yet tender, and putteth forth leaves, ye know that summer is nigh: so likewise ye, when ye shall see all these things, know that it is near, even at the doors" (Matthew 24:32-33).

The Bible plainly states that no man knows the day or the hour when the Lord will come (Matthew 25:13). But there are things that tell the righteous man, the observant man, the thinking man, that the coming of the Lord is near. Paul said, "But of the times and the seasons, brethren, ye have no need that I write unto you. For yourselves know perfectly that the day of the Lord so cometh as a thief in the night" (I Thessalonians 5:1-2).

The above proverb teaches that a cautious man will foresee evil and prepare himself for it, in contrast to the reckless or inattentive man who will overlook it and end up being punished. God has given us His Word and many other signs that point to the death and destruction that will come to those who do not heed His warnings. He has also given us safe places to hide from the storms of life. "For in the time of trouble he shall hide me in his pavilion: in the secret of his tabernacle shall he hide me; he shall set me up upon a rock" (Psalm 27:5). We need to watch for the storm warnings and get ready to take advantage of the escape that God has prepared for us.

Practice:

Many people face the storms of this life with nowhere to turn. We can be thankful that we know that "God is our refuge and strength, a very present help in time of trouble" (Psalm 46:1).

Prayer:

Lord, You are our refuge and strength. Thank You that we can hide ourselves under Your protection and that Your arms uphold us in times of distress. "He that dwelleth in the secret place of the most High shall abide under the shadow of the Almighty. I will say of the LORD, He is my refuge and my fortress: my God; in him will I trust" (Psalm 91:1-2).

DAY 82: FACING THE FACTS (PROVERBS 27:21-27)

The refining pot's for silver, and the furnace for gold,
So a man will be valued by what about him is told.

Take a mortar and pestle, grind up foolishness and grain,
A man's foolishness would still be there; it would
        all be in vain.

Look well to the state of your flocks and your herds.
Pay attention to business, right at the first,

For riches are not forever. There's no guarantee they'll stay.
Does a crown always endure? Each generation pays its way.

So bring the hay from the meadow, gather herbs
    from the field,
Let the green grass grow back, and the earth give her yield.

Your sheep will provide you with clothing as well;
The goats that are surplus, and what's left, you can sell.

You shall have ample goat's milk to feed all who come
To your household, and maintenance for maidens at home.

PAY ATTENTION

Proverb:
"Be thou diligent to know the state of thy flocks, and look
well to thy herds" (Proverbs 27:23).

Precept:
I do not know many people who still measure their wealth
by how many sheep or cows they possess. However, throughout
history the number and quality of a man's flocks and herds
greatly determined his wealth. The Bible in several places
describes the wealth of men and countries by their livestock. To
lose one's animals to war, to theft, to famine, or to disease was
to suffer a serious financial setback. (Losing your livestock
would be the modern-day equivalent of losing your car, your
house, your savings, or your job.) The state of the flock was
serious business to a shepherd. When David went to the battlefield to check on his brothers' welfare, he left his sheep with a
"keeper" (I Samuel 17:20). Why? Because David was protecting
his father's assets.

This proverb teaches us that we need to be good stewards
of the things God has placed within our control. We must be
diligent in the management of our time, our money, our possessions, our family, and our relationship with God. If we neglect
these things, we may find them slipping from our grasp. How
many things have been destroyed simply because someone was
not paying attention? A son becomes wayward because he was

neglected by his father. The engine locks up because the oil was not changed. A marriage disintegrates because neither spouse was paying attention to the needs of the other. A person who once was on fire for God becomes cold and distant because a personal relationship with God was put on the back burner. If we fail to give the proper attention to the things of value in our life, we may wake up one day to find them missing.

Peter said, "Wherefore the rather, brethren, give diligence to make your calling and election sure: for if ye do these things, ye shall never fall" (II Peter 1:10). He identified our relationship with God as the most valuable asset we possess and stressed the necessary effort that it requires to be maintained. Beyond our relationship with God, we should identify what is truly valuable in our life and diligently care for it. As good stewards, we must take care of everything God places in our lives: our possessions, our family, and our relationships. With proper attention and oversight they will flourish and be a continued blessing.

Practice:

Be careful not to neglect those who are closest to you. In this hectic world, we sometimes fail to give the proper attention to those we hold most dear. Make time for your family. Let them know that they are an important part of your life. Do not become so busy with outside activities and responsibilities that you neglect your responsibilities to your home, family, finances, and your walk with God. He wants us to be good stewards of our time and our finances, and not to neglect the gift of our family and friends that He has given to us.

Prayer:

Lord, forgive me if I have neglected to take proper care of those people and things that You have entrusted into my care. Help me to plan my days, focus my energy, and manage my finances in a way that will bring glory and honor to You. This I pray, in Jesus' name. Amen.

PROVERBS 28

The wicked flee when no man pursueth: but the righteous are bold as a lion. For the transgression of a land many are the princes thereof: but by a man of understanding and knowledge the state thereof shall be prolonged. A poor man that oppresseth the poor is like a sweeping rain which leaveth no food. They that forsake the law praise the wicked: but such as keep the law contend with them. Evil men understand not judgment: but they that seek the LORD understand all things. Better is the poor that walketh in his uprightness, than he that is perverse in his ways, though he be rich. Whoso keepeth the law is a wise son: but he that is a companion of riotous men shameth his father. He that by usury and unjust gain increaseth his substance, he shall gather it for him that will pity the poor. He that turneth away his ear from hearing the law, even his prayer shall be abomination. Whoso causeth the righteous to go astray in an evil way, he shall fall himself into his own pit: but the upright shall have good things in possession. The rich man is wise in his own conceit; but the poor that hath understanding searcheth him out. When righteous men do rejoice, there is great glory: but when the wicked rise, a man is hidden. He that covereth his sins shall not prosper: but whoso confesseth and forsaketh them shall have mercy. Happy is the man that feareth alway: but he that hardeneth his heart shall fall into mischief. As a roaring lion, and a ranging bear; so is a wicked ruler over the poor people. The prince that wanteth understanding is also a great oppressor; but he that hateth covetousness shall prolong his days. A man that doeth violence to the blood of any person shall flee to the pit; let no man stay him. Whoso walketh uprightly shall be saved: but he that is perverse in his ways shall fall at once. He that tilleth his land shall have plenty of bread: but he that followeth after vain persons shall have poverty enough. A faithful man shall abound with blessings: but he that maketh haste to be rich shall not be innocent. To have respect of persons is

not good: for for a piece of bread that man will transgress. He that hasteth to be rich hath an evil eye, and
considereth not that poverty shall come upon him. He
that rebuketh a man afterwards shall find more favour
than he that flattereth with the tongue. Whoso robbeth
his father or his mother, and saith, It is no transgression; the same is the companion of a destroyer. He that
is of a proud heart stirreth up strife: but he that putteth
his trust in the LORD shall be made fat. He that trusteth
in his own heart is a fool: but whoso walketh wisely, he
shall be delivered. He that giveth unto the poor shall not
lack: but he that hideth his eyes shall have many a
curse. When the wicked rise, men hide themselves: but
when they perish, the righteous increase.

DAY 83: THE LAND AND THE LAW
(PROVERBS 28:1-10)

Though none pursues him, the wicked will flee,
But the righteous is bold as a lion would be.

A land filled with rebellion will its leader depose;
United and stable, a nation prospers and grows.

When a man takes charge and oppresses the poor,
Like a flood, he leaves them hungry once more.

Those who neglect the law give the bad rulers praise;
Those who uphold the law declare war on their ways.

Evil men do not understand justice and law,
But those who follow the Lord see it all.

It is better to be poor and in righteousness walk
Than be rich and perverse in your action and talk.

A wise son will keep the law whether God's or
        man's, the same;
Friends of troublemakers all will bring their parents to shame.

Wealth you gained by fraud that should not to you belong
Will to the poor return, if you're proved you're doing wrong.

When you turn your ear from hearing God's Word,
Your prayer is perverse and it will not be heard!

Who fashions a trap to cause the upright to falter
Will end up in the snare, while the innocent prosper.

No Fear

Proverb:
"The wicked flee when no man pursueth: but the righteous
are bold as a lion" (Proverbs 28:1).

Precept:
The story of David and Goliath is one of the best-known
stories in the Bible. It is amazing how a shepherd boy, who was
not a soldier, could come against a nine-foot-tall giant when
everyone else was terrified! His trust in God helped him to conquer any fear. He wrote in Psalm 56:3-4, "What time I am
afraid, I will trust in thee. In God I will praise his word, in God
I have put my trust; I will not fear what flesh can do unto me."
In verse 11 he repeated, "In God have I put my trust: I will not
be afraid what man can do unto me."

Those who live righteously and put their trust in God can
be bold as a lion in the face of danger. Jesus taught that we
should "fear not them which kill the body, but are not able to
kill the soul: but rather fear him which is able to destroy both
soul and body in hell" (Matthew 10:28).

The wicked live in continual fear of being found out, being
caught, being punished, or being killed for the deeds they have
done. William Shakespeare said, "Cowards die many times
before their deaths; the valiant never taste of death but once."[31]

Those who are righteous can live in peace without fear,
knowing God will preserve them and protect them. They know
that death will come eventually, but they are not afraid of it.

II Timothy 1:7 says, "For God hath not given us the spirit
of fear; but of power, and of love, and of a sound mind."
Hebrews 13:6 is a promise that, like David, those who are right-

eous can claim, "The Lord is my helper, and I will not fear what man shall do unto me."

Practice:

Do not allow fear to conquer you or control you. Claim the promises in the Word of God. "Fear not: for I have redeemed thee, I have called thee by thy name; thou art mine. When thou passest through the waters, I will be with thee; and through the rivers, they shall not overflow thee: when thou walkest through the fire, thou shalt not be burned; neither shall the flame kindle upon thee" (Isaiah 43:1-2).

Prayer:

Lord, I thank You for the assurance that I have in You, and that I do not have to be afraid of whatever may come my way.

DAY 84: PEOPLE UNDER THE LAW (PROVERBS 28:11-28)

The rich man is wise in his own selfish look;
The poor man with discernment reads his life like a book.

When good people triumph, the bells can be pealed;
When the wicked ones rule, men stay concealed.

He who covers his sins shall not prosper, but fails;
Sins confessed and forsaken shall find mercy avails.

Happy the person, always ready to start,
But you'll get into trouble, if you harden your heart.

Like a bear that is ravenous or a lion hunting prey
Is a ruler who's wicked and his poor people pay.

Brutal and destructive are the ways of a prince;
He could prolong his days, if he had any sense.

With blood on his hands, a man speeds to the pit;
No one should support him, so stay out of it.

Those walking uprightly can expect to be saved;
The dishonest and froward shall fall into the grave.

You may expect the harvest if you tend to your land;
Idle dreams, empty schemes leave naught in your hand.

Many blessings will come to the faithful and true;
A desire to get rich will bring nothing to you.

It is wrong to be partial in judgment, take sides;
Some will transgress for a loaf, as a bribe.

If you're a servant to money, try a get-rich-quick scheme,
Poverty will come quickly; it is only a dream.

Rebuking someone gets more thanks in the end
Than with flattering words on your tongue to begin.

You cannot rob father and mother and say,
"There's no sin." Brother, you're going to pay!

If your heart's proud, then you will be stirring up strife.
Put your trust in the Lord; He'll add weight to your life.

If you trust in your own heart, then you are a fool.
Walk wisely with God; He'll deliver you.

When you give to the poor, all your needs will be met;
If your eyes turn from them, it'll be worse, don't forget.

When the wicked rise up, it is time to lie low;
When the wicked die out, then the righteous can grow!

MERCY

Proverb:
　　"He that covereth his sins shall not prosper: but whoso confesseth and forsaketh them shall have mercy" (Proverbs 28:13).

Precept:

The mercy of God is a wonderful thing! It is especially wonderful, because we all need mercy. The Bible says, "All have sinned and come short of the glory of God" (Romans 3:23). When you have done wrong, you do not need judgment or sympathy; you need mercy!

When I was in high school, one day my class decided to stage a "strike" against the substitute teacher who knew nothing about the subjects we were being taught. When she came in the room, our heads were on our desks, and we pretended to be asleep. We quickly woke up when she left the room and returned with the principal!

That day when I went home, I repeated what had happened to my mother. She said, "Son, you can't do that! You owe the teacher an apology." The next day I apologized to the teacher, told her that I was wrong, and asked for her forgiveness. Later when all the other students were punished, I was not. Because I confessed, I found mercy!

Admitting that we are wrong is often difficult. It is always easier to point out someone else's faults and failures but difficult to admit our own. Before there can be forgiveness there must be confession. "If we say that we have no sin, we deceive ourselves, and the truth is not in us. If we confess our sins, he is faithful and just to forgive us our sins, and to cleanse us from all unrighteousness" (I John 1:8-9).

Before a doctor can treat a patient there must be a revealing of the nature of the problem. We would never play a guessing game with the doctor to see if he could magically figure out what our problem was. We would "confess" where the pain was coming from. Why should it be any different with God, who is the Great Physician? We should willingly confess our sins and shortcomings so that we may be healed and find the soothing salve of His mercy.

Do not hide your past; confess it. Do not mask your inadequacy; admit it. Do not miss the miracle of mercy; receive it. "But God, who is rich in mercy, for his great love wherewith he loved us" (Ephesians 2:4). An old song says it this way, "It's not my brother, not my sister, but it's me, O Lord, standin' in the need of prayer." Confess, forsake, and receive God's mercy today.

Practice:

We need the mercy and grace that the Lord has to offer. Do not allow your faults and failures to separate you from God's love and mercy that He freely offers to you.

Prayer:

Lord, have mercy upon me. Forgive me of my sins. Help me to triumph over the failures that would try to keep me from accepting what You have to offer me.

Week 13

PROVERBS 29

He, that being often reproved hardeneth his neck,
shall suddenly be destroyed, and that without remedy.
When the righteous are in authority, the people rejoice:
but when the wicked beareth rule, the people mourn.
Whoso loveth wisdom rejoiceth his father: but he that
keepeth company with harlots spendeth his substance.
The king by judgment establisheth the land: but he that
receiveth gifts overthroweth it. A man that flattereth his
neighbour spreadeth a net for his feet. In the transgres-
sion of an evil man there is a snare: but the righteous doth
sing and rejoice. The righteous considereth the cause of
the poor: but the wicked regardeth not to know it. Scornful
men bring a city into a snare: but wise men turn away
wrath. If a wise man contendeth with a foolish man,
whether he rage or laugh, there is no rest. The blood-
thirsty hate the upright: but the just seek his soul. A fool
uttereth all his mind: but a wise man keepeth it in till
afterwards. If a ruler hearken to lies, all his servants are
wicked. The poor and the deceitful man meet together:
the LORD lighteneth both their eyes. The king that faith-
fully judgeth the poor, his throne shall be established for
ever. The rod and reproof give wisdom: but a child left to
himself bringeth his mother to shame. When the wicked
are multiplied, transgression increaseth: but the right-
eous shall see their fall. Correct thy son, and he shall give
thee rest; yea, he shall give delight unto thy soul. Where
there is no vision, the people perish: but he that keepeth
the law, happy is he. A servant will not be corrected by
words: for though he understand he will not answer.
Seest thou a man that is hasty in his words? there is
more hope of a fool than of him. He that delicately

*bringeth up his servant from a child shall have him
become his son at the length. An angry man stirreth up
strife, and a furious man aboundeth in transgression.
A man's pride shall bring him low: but honour shall
uphold the humble in spirit. Whoso is partner with a
thief hateth his own soul: he heareth cursing, and
bewrayeth it not. The fear of man bringeth a snare: but
whoso putteth his trust in the* LORD *shall be safe. Many
seek the ruler's favour; but every man's judgment
cometh from the* LORD. *An unjust man is an abomination to the just: and he that is upright in the way is
abomination to the wicked.*

DAY 85: ALL KINDS OF PEOPLE (PROVERBS 29:1-10)

He who hardens his neck and is often reproved
Will have sudden destruction, without a clue.

When the just rule the land, all the people are glad;
When wicked men rule, the people are sad.

A son who loves wisdom makes his father rejoice;
To spend money on harlots is not the right choice.

By justice a wise king will establish the nation,
But by bribes and deceit, there will be revolution.

He who flatters his neighbor, for his feet a net makes.
The wicked step in it, but a just man escapes.

The just man cares for the rights of the poor,
But the wicked has no interest; to him it's a bore.

Scornful men, by arrogance, set a snare for their path;
Wise men, by righteousness, can turn away wrath.

If a wise man contends with a foolish man, at best,
Whether raging or laughter, there is no peace or rest.

The bloodthirsty man hates the honest and just,
But the upright show pity for the one who's the worst.

LISTEN UP!

Proverb:
"He, that being often reproved hardeneth his neck, shall suddenly be destroyed, and that without remedy" (Proverbs 29:1).

Precept:
The willingness of an individual to accept correction is a mark of his wisdom and maturity. Who would not want to be told that he is traveling down a one-way street in the wrong direction? Why would anyone resist the advice of someone who was looking out for their well-being? Not listening to the voice of reproof is a sure recipe for disaster. If we do not heed the warning sounds in our life, destruction may be our inevitable end.

On several occasions, I have seen on the front page of our small town newspaper stories of people who have died trying to "beat the train." The names of the deceased were different, but the stories were usually similar. Even though the lights were flashing and the gates were coming down, they thought they could get across the track before the train passed. Unfortunately, they were wrong. They chose to ignore the warning signs, and they lost their life as a result. What a tragedy! A life was lost because someone refused to listen.

Those who choose to consistently ignore the voice of reason will inevitably suffer dire and irreversible consequences. How many times can the voice of the doctor, the pastor, or the friend be ignored before tragedy strikes? How many times can reason be discarded before reality deals a crushing blow? Sadly, there are many who wait too late to try to change their ways.

We must learn to heed the warning signs and sounds in our life. Rather than rejecting warnings as being invasive and restrictive, understand that they are for your protection and your preservation. Paul wrote to Timothy: "All scripture is given by inspiration of God, and is profitable for doctrine, for reproof, for correction, for instruction in righteousness: that the man of God may be perfect, throughly furnished unto all good works"

(II Timothy 3:16-17). When the Word speaks, listen up! Do not ignore the warning! Do not try to go around the gates!

Practice:

Hear the voice of God as He calls to you. Listen closely to the warnings He gives. Watch for the roadblocks that He places in your path to keep you from going the wrong direction. Listen to your pastor, whom He has placed as an overseer in your life. "Whom we preach, warning every man, and teaching every man in all wisdom; that we may present every man perfect in Christ Jesus" (Colossians 1:28).

Prayer:

Lord, I want to hear Your voice, heed Your warnings, and follow You closely. Help me not to head blindly down my own path but to listen closely to Your instructions and proceed with caution as I go forward.

DAY 86: ALL KINDS OF ATTITUDES (PROVERBS 29:11-27)

A fool, when provoked, utters all in his mind;
A wise man controls anger by biding his time.

If a ruler will hearken to the lies that men tell,
His servants are wicked and will tell lies as well.

The poor and the deceitful will come together;
The Lord gives light to their eyes—to one, then the other.

The ruler who faithfully judges the poor,
His kingdom should forever be firm and endure.

The rod and reproof give wisdom a face;
A child who is left to himself brings disgrace.

When the wicked are multiplied, transgression increases,
But the righteous will know the day when sin ceases.

Give your son correction; he'll give rest unto you.
It's delight to your soul; that's the best thing to do.

Where there is no vision, people perish away;
Keep the law and be happy from day unto day.

No servant will be trained by lessons alone;
He'll understand your words but he'll be like a stone.

Do you see a man who is hasty to speak?
There is less hope for him than a mind that is weak.

A servant who's pampered from childhood and on
Will expect you to treat him just like a son.

An angry man stirs up disputing and strife;
A furious man causes much sin in your life.

A man's pride is the cause of humiliation;
To be humble gives honor and great exaltation.

To partner with thieves means you hate your own soul,
For you swear by an oath and you know it's not so.

The fear of a man brings a snare to your life,
But whoso shall trust in the Lord shall be safe.

The favor of rulers is the place where most trust,
But justice from God is what's right for the just.

An unrighteous man is abhorred by the just;
The upright considers the wicked accursed.

THE WAY UP

Proverb:
   "A man's pride shall bring him low: but honour shall uphold
the humble in spirit" (Proverbs 29:23).

Precept:

It is paradoxical but true that the way up is down and the way down is up. Jesus said, "For whosoever exalteth himself shall be abased; and he that humbleth himself shall be exalted" (Luke 14:11). This may not always be true in the world's economy, but it is always true in God's kingdom. History gives us many examples of those who rose to high heights but ended in total disgrace. Adolph Hitler gained control of much of Europe and wanted to rule the world, but he died by his own hand in an underground bunker. Benito Mussolini, the dictator of Italy, attempted to follow him in his quest for power, but his life ended in disgrace.

King Saul, the first king of Israel, was handpicked by God Himself to lead Israel. He was a number one draft pick. No one was better suited for the job than Saul. However, despite his great qualities he had a fatal flaw. Saul's pride destroyed his position in the kingdom and prevented him from leading God's people. His pride negated every other positive characteristic and was the root cause of his bitter demise.

Once as I prayed for God to make me humble, it seemed to me that God said, "Humble yourself!" I realize now that to be humbled by God would not be a pleasant experience. God's ideal is for us to take the necessary steps to subdue our pride and be clothed with humility in God's presence. Peter said, "Humble yourselves therefore under the mighty hand of God, that he may exalt you in due time" (I Peter 5:6).

God will always have a place for you if you are humble. There was a young preacher who went to try out for a church. When he stepped into the pulpit he was filled with pride and confidence. Despite his self-confidence, he made many mistakes in the delivery of his sermon and came down from the pulpit after service, chagrined and embarrassed. An elderly lady of the church spoke to him kindly and said, "If you had gone up (to the pulpit) like you came down, you would have come down (from the pulpit) like you went up." He found out by experience that the prideful will be brought low, but God will sustain the humble.

Practice:

A person who pushes his way forward is ofttimes resented, but the humble person is respected and honored. Do not set yourself up for failure. Remember that pride goes before a fall. "Humble yourselves therefore under the mighty hand of God, that he may exalt you in due time" (I Peter 5:6). "Humble yourselves in the sight of the Lord, and he shall lift you up" (James 4:10).

Prayer:

Lord, do not let my pride get in the way. Help me to humble myself before You. "The sacrifices of God are a broken spirit: a broken and a contrite heart, O God, thou wilt not despise" (Psalm 51:17).

PROVERBS 30

The words of Agur the son of Jakeh, even the prophecy: the man spake unto Ithiel, even unto Ithiel and Ucal, Surely I am more brutish than any man, and have not the understanding of a man. I neither learned wisdom, nor have the knowledge of the holy. Who hath ascended up into heaven, or descended? who hath gathered the wind in his fists? who hath bound the waters in a garment? who hath established all the ends of the earth? what is his name, and what is his son's name, if thou canst tell? Every word of God is pure: he is a shield unto them that put their trust in him. Add thou not unto his words, lest he reprove thee, and thou be found a liar. Two things have I required of thee; deny me them not before I die: remove far from me vanity and lies: give me neither poverty nor riches; feed me with food convenient for me: lest I be full, and deny thee, and say, Who is the LORD? or lest I be poor, and steal, and take the name of my God in vain. Accuse not a servant unto his master, lest he curse thee, and thou be found guilty. There is a generation that curseth their father, and doth not bless their mother. There is a generation that are pure in their own eyes, and yet is not washed from their filthiness. There is a generation, O how lofty are their eyes! and their eyelids are lifted up. There is a generation, whose teeth are as swords, and their jaw teeth as knives, to devour the poor from off the earth, and the needy from among men. The horseleach hath two daughters, crying, Give, give. There are three things that are never satisfied, yea, four things say not, It is enough: the grave; and the barren womb; the earth that is not filled with water; and the fire that saith not, It is enough. The eye that mocketh at his father, and despiseth to obey his mother, the ravens of the valley shall pick it out, and the young eagles shall eat it. There be three things which are too wonderful for me, yea, four which I know not: the way of an eagle in the air; the way of a serpent upon a rock; the way of a ship in the midst of the sea; and the way of a man with a maid. Such is the way of an adulterous woman; she eateth, and wipeth her mouth, and saith, I have done no wickedness. For three things the earth is disquieted, and for four which it cannot bear: for a servant when he reigneth; and a fool when he is filled with meat; for an odious woman when she is married; and an handmaid that is heir to her mistress. There be four things which are little upon the earth, but they are exceeding wise: the ants are a people not strong, yet they prepare their meat in the summer; the conies are but a feeble folk, yet make they their houses in the rocks; the locusts have no king, yet go they forth all of them by bands; the spider taketh hold with her hands, and is in kings' palaces. There be three things which go well, yea, four are comely in going: a lion which is strongest among beasts, and turneth not away for any; a greyhound; an he goat also; and a king, against whom there is no rising up. If thou hast done foolishly in lifting up thyself, or if thou hast thought evil, lay thine hand upon thy mouth. Surely the churning of milk bringeth forth butter, and the wringing of the nose bringeth forth blood: so the forcing of wrath bringeth forth strife.

DAY 87: AGUR'S ADVICE (PROVERBS 30:1-10)

The prophecy of Agur, Jakeh's own son,
Spoken to Ithiel and Ucal by a man.

Surely I am more brutish than any other man,
And I don't have the capacity to understand.

I have never learned wisdom, so I do not know
Enough knowledge of the Holy, to His way clearly show.

Who ascended to heaven and descended again
With the wind in His fist, and all waters in a band?

Who hath established all the earth here below?
What's His name? And His Son's name? You, the
  secret don't know!

God's every word is pure; He's a shield unto them
Who believe every word and put complete trust in Him.

Do not add to His Word; He'll reprove if you do.
You'll be found as a liar, but His Word's still true.

Two things of you I require that will please;
Before the time that I die, don't deny me of these.

Keep me far from vanity and lies while I live;
Grant me neither poverty nor riches, just needful food give.

Lest I be full, deny God, and before Him shall say,
"What is the name of the Lord, anyway?"

Or lest I be poor and be tempted to steal,
And profane God's name or miss out on His will.

Do not a servant to his master condemn,
Lest his master blame you instead of him.

GUESS WHO?

Proverb:
  "Who hath ascended up into heaven, or descended? who hath gathered the wind in his fists? who hath bound the waters in a garment? who hath established all the ends of the earth?

what is his name, and what is his son's name, if thou canst tell?"
(Proverbs 30:4).

Precept:

In the Old Testament, God was a mystery! He was a secret.
But many of the passages of the past come alive as you read
about Jesus Christ in the New Testament. In Acts 8:30 when
Philip met the Ethiopian eunuch, he was reading the fifty-third
chapter of Isaiah's prophecy. As he read the passage, Philip
asked him, "Do you understand what you are reading?" Philip
began at the same verse of Scripture and preached Jesus to him!

In 1941, as a ten-year-old boy, I received my first Bible. A
preacher told me that if I would read it through, he would give
me a dollar. Although his offer was enticing, I was not able to
fulfill it. However, when I left home to go to college, I made up
my mind that I was going to read the Bible from cover to cover.
I told myself, Whatever you find out, you are going to believe
it. You are not going to just follow the religion of your parents;
you are going to follow what the Bible says.

I read from Genesis on through the books until I came to
Isaiah. When I read Isaiah 43:10-11, I made a wonderful discovery and a great decision. It said, "Ye are my witnesses, saith the
Lord, and my servant whom I have chosen: that ye may know
and believe me, and understand that I am he: before me there
was no God formed, neither shall there be after me. I, even I, am
the Lord; and beside me there is no saviour." I discovered that,
without question, Jesus Christ of the New Testament was
Jehovah God of the Old Testament. And I decided that I would
believe and teach that Jesus is the one true God.

I found the answer to the question the writer Agur asked in
Proverbs 30:4: "What is his name, and what is his son's name,
if thou canst tell?" Isaiah 9:6 says, "For unto us a child is born,
unto us a son is given: and the government shall be upon his
shoulder: and his name shall be called Wonderful, Counseller,
The mighty God, The everlasting Father, The Prince of Peace."
The name is Jesus Christ.

I Timothy 3:16 says, "And without controversy great is the
mystery of godliness: God was manifest in the flesh, justified in
the Spirit, seen of angels, preached unto the Gentiles, believed
on in the world, received up into glory." Jesus is our Creator,

our Savior, and our Comforter. Thank God for the wonderful revelation of the mighty God in Christ Jesus!

Practice:

Jesus was not just a man or only a prophet. He was God manifest in the flesh. Rejoice in this truth and share it with those around you who may not realize just who Jesus is. "Hear, O Israel: The LORD our God is one LORD" (Deuteronomy 6:4). "But to us there is but one God, the Father, of whom are all things, and we in him; and one Lord Jesus Christ, by whom are all things, and we by him" (I Corinthians 8:6).

Prayer:

Thank You, Lord, that You are Emmanuel, God with us. (See Matthew 1:23.) Thank You for revealing Yourself to me through Your Word. I thank You for the truth of one Lord, one faith, and one baptism (Ephesians 4:5).

DAY 88: THE LOST GENERATION (PROVERBS 30:11-14)

There is a generation, they their father will curse,
And their mother they will not bless but do something worse.

There is a generation that, in its own eyes is pure,
Yet still lives in its filthiness, which none could endure.

There is a generation that is haughty and proud;
Their eyes are lifted up and their voices are loud.

There is a generation whose teeth are as swords;
Their words are as knives which they use on the poor.

Their hatred is toward all the needy on earth,
The unborn, the old folks, the unfortunate birth.

NEVER SATISFIED (PROVERBS 30:15,16)

The horse leach has two daughters that cry continually, "Give!"
Four things never satisfied that need something to live:

The womb without children, and the fire that goes out,
The grave that wants more, and the earth in a drought.

THE CURSE (PROVERBS 30:17)

The person who will not his father give honor,
The one who will withhold respect from his mother,

The ravens of the valley shall pluck his eye out;
The young eagles shall consume his eye, without doubt.

THINGS WE CANNOT UNDERSTAND (PROVERBS 30:18-19)

There are three things too high; they're too wonderful for me.
Yes, four things I do not understand, you see:

The way of an eagle that can fly in the wind,
That can soar to the sky and come down safely again.

The way of a serpent, how it lives without feet;
It can move, it can climb, it can swim in the deep.

How does a ship stay on top of the waves?
Then the waters come back as on course it still stays.

It's the mystery of life, how that God made His plan
With a man's love for woman, and a woman's
     love for man.

BEYOND WONDERFUL

Proverb:
     "There be three things which are too wonderful for me, yea,
four which I know not: The way of an eagle in the air; the way

of a serpent upon a rock; the way of a ship in the midst of the sea; and the way of a man with a maid" (Proverbs 30:18-19).

Precept:

Solomon in all his wisdom admitted that there were four things he did not fully understand: the flight of the eagle, the movement of a snake, the buoyancy of a ship, and the development of love between a man and a woman.

I have flown on two international flights to Israel. What an awesome experience to travel in an airplane, thirty thousand feet above sea level. Even though I have experienced it, I still do not understand it. I have heard all the explanations, but I still do not know how such a large piece of steel can fly hundreds of miles through the air. However, it does not keep me from enjoying the advances of modern aviation.

What makes a ship float? It seems that the weight of it would cause it to sink. The largest ships on the ocean can be longer than fifteen hundred feet and can weigh over 550,000 tons. Several years ago, there was talk of a ship that would stretch one mile long and reach twenty-five stories high. I do not know how it works, but ships are being used daily by millions for recreation, for combat, and for commerce.

What is love? At my wedding they sang, "Love is a Many Splendored Thing." I will never forget that day. We have now been married for forty-five years, and I still cannot get over it. My grandson asked me, "Why do people want to get married, anyway?" I cannot explain love, but I know the blessings of its presence in my life.

Life is filled with many wondrous things that I cannot explain. All of these things simply point to the incredible power of the God we serve. David said, "I will praise thee; for I am fearfully and wonderfully made: marvellous are thy works; and that my soul knoweth right well" (Psalm 139:14). As we survey the greatness of our God, we must concur with the sentiments of David and give praise unto God.

Practice:

You do not have to understand everything to appreciate God and all His greatness. "Praise Him for his mighty acts: praise Him according to His excellent greatness" (Psalm 150:2).

Prayer:

Lord, I praise You for who you are and for all of the wonderful things that You have done for me. I thank You that You revealed Yourself to me, and that You chose to come and live in my heart.

DAY 89: THE UNFAITHFUL WOMAN
(PROVERBS 30:20)

This is the way of an unfaithful wife:
She eats of her pleasure, then will her mouth wipe,
And says, "I have done nothing but that which is right!"

THINGS WE CAN NEVER ACCEPT
(PROVERBS 30:21-23)

There are four things for which the whole earth is distressed.
Yes, there are inequities we can never accept:

There are princes who walk, though a servant bears rule;
Though a fool may eat well, he is still just a fool.

A woman who's hateful, is hateful, though wedded,
And inheriting your riches won't remove what's imbedded.

THINGS THAT ARE LITTLE BUT MIGHTY
(PROVERBS 30:24-28)

There are four things that on earth are quite weak,
But exceedingly wise are the lessons they speak.

The ants are a people not strong at all,
Yet in summer prepare for the winter and fall.

The conies, a feeble folk, something like rabbits,
For safety build houses in rocks; that's their habit.

The locusts, without leaders, work in cooperation,
And go forth in bands with no supervision.

The spider takes hold, won't turn loose, and is found
In the palace of kings with great people around.

BE THE BEST YOU CAN BE! (PROVERBS 30:29-33)

There are three in the number of things that go well,
And a fourth one that joins them in things that excel.

A lion is mighty among beasts of the jungle;
He'll detour for no one, none will cause him to stumble.

The greyhound is fleetest of all of his breed;
Not one of the dogs can his record exceed.

The male of the goats is fierce in a fight;
He'll back up for nothing or no one in sight.

A king is the leader of his nation and men.
He's commander-in-chief; there's no one above him.

If you have been foolish and proud in your walk
Or boasted of evil, then please stop your talk.

For the churning of milk then turns it to butter,
And twisting a nose makes it bleed with much vigor.

So do not continue stirring up trouble;
Don't let your ego make you burst your bubble.

SMALL BUT WISE

Proverb:
"There be four things which are little upon the earth, but they are exceeding wise" (Proverbs 30:24).

Precept:
In a parable of four little creatures of the earth, the proverb presents a valuable lesson of what can be done by creatures that are not considered valuable or important. They illustrate what we can do if we will try.

The ant is a small insect that works diligently through the summer to provide food when winter comes. The ant has learned to do a simple task and do it well. It is small but industrious; its strength is in the fact that it has a sense of the coming needs and takes wise precautions through a God-given instinct to store up for the future.

There is a practical lesson and a spiritual lesson. We can prepare for our future physical and financial needs, by laying aside a portion of our income for future necessities. We can prepare for our eternal future by laying up for ourselves treasures in heaven where thieves do not break through and steal and where moth and rust do not corrupt.

The locusts are praised because of their ability to work together with no apparent leader. They realize the power in numbers and work for the common good of all. How needful is this lesson! We need to learn the beauty of cooperation. "Things increase at a ten-fold rate, whenever we cooperate."

In unity there is strength. When each individual decides to work for the common cause, then something can be accomplished. Working alone will not accomplish what the synergy of working together is able to achieve. We need to learn the lesson of the locust.

The coney is an animal much like a rabbit, which makes his home in the rocks. He is defenseless and vulnerable when he is caught outside his den, but when he hides himself in a hole in the rocks, he is protected from danger. Many times we are tempted to wander outside of what is spiritually safe for our lives. We have an adversary who is waiting for us to journey outside the safe zone of our spiritual rock. "The name of the LORD is a strong tower: the righteous runneth into it, and is safe" (Proverbs 18:10).

The spider with its many legs has proven its ability to reach out, to catch hold, to hang on, and to "ride it out" until it is carried to a new destination, even a palace! Like the spider, we must be willing to reach for the opportunities that come our way. The spider is not picky about what it latches on to. Do not be selective in your opportunities. Take what comes and greater things will follow. Zechariah asked, "For who hath despised the day of small things?" (Zechariah 4:10). Never underestimate what God can do with something small! Like the ant, store up;

like the coney, hole up; like the locust, group up; and like the spider, grip up! Remember that little is much when God is in it! Small, but wise.

Practice:

Even if we are small and our talents may seem few, we can still accomplish much for God's kingdom. Use whatever you have been given, and you can be great in the kingdom of God.

Prayer:

Lord, help me to realize the opportunities that come my way and to take full advantage of them. Help me not to despise the day of small things but to seize every opportunity, even though it may be small.

PROVERBS 31

The words of king Lemuel, the prophecy that his mother taught him. What, my son? and what, the son of my womb? and what, the son of my vows? Give not thy strength unto women, nor thy ways to that which destroyeth kings. It is not for kings, O Lemuel, it is not for kings to drink wine; nor for princes strong drink: lest they drink, and forget the law, and pervert the judgment of any of the afflicted. Give strong drink unto him that is ready to perish, and wine unto those that be of heavy hearts. Let him drink, and forget his poverty, and remember his misery no more. Open thy mouth for the dumb in the cause of all such as are appointed to destruction. Open thy mouth, judge righteously, and plead the cause of the poor and needy.

Who can find a virtuous woman? for her price is far above rubies. The heart of her husband doth safely trust in her, so that he shall have no need of spoil. She will do him good and not evil all the days of her life. She seeketh wool, and flax, and worketh willingly with her hands. She is like the merchants' ships; she bringeth her food from afar. She riseth also while it is yet night, and giveth meat to her household, and a portion to her maidens. She considereth a field, and buyeth it: with the fruit of her hands she planteth a vineyard. She girdeth her loins with strength, and strengtheneth her arms. She perceiveth that her merchandise is good: her candle goeth not out by night. She layeth her hands to the spindle, and her hands hold the distaff. She stretcheth out her hand to the poor; yea, she reacheth forth her hands to the needy. She is not afraid of the snow for her household: for all her household are clothed with scarlet. She maketh herself coverings of tapestry; her clothing is silk and purple. Her husband is known in the gates, when he sitteth among the elders of the land. She maketh fine linen, and selleth it; and delivereth girdles unto the merchant. Strength and honour are her clothing; and she shall rejoice in time to come. She openeth her mouth with wisdom; and in her tongue is the law of kindness. She looketh well to the ways of her household, and eateth not the bread of idleness. Her children arise up, and call her blessed; her husband also, and he praiseth her. Many daughters have done virtuously, but thou excellest them all. Favour is deceitful, and beauty is vain: but a woman that feareth the LORD, she shall be praised. Give her of the fruit of her hands; and let her own works praise her in the gates.

DAY 90: KING LEMUEL'S LAMENT (PROVERBS 31:1-9)

These words of mine which by God were dictated,
Are the words of a king, which his mother related.

"You're the son of my womb! Heed the words that I say.
You're the son of my prayers! Listen and obey.

"Do not waste your strength in immoral ways;
Do not spend your love in unkingly plays.

"It is not for kings to be drinking wine
Or desiring strong drink when they dine,

"Lest you should drink and forget the law
Or pervert the cause of the one who has woe.

"Strong drink serves for those who hurt and grope;
Give wine to those who have no hope.

"Let them forget their misery and shame,
Remember no more their poverty and pain.

"Open your mouth with the word that God spoke;
Give justice and wisdom to those who are broke.

"Open your mouth for those with nothing to say;
Plead for your sons who are falling away."

KEEPER OF THE SPRINGS

Proverb:

"The words of king Lemuel, the prophecy that his mother taught him" (Proverbs 31:1).

Precept:

Peter Marshall, the late chaplain of the United States Senate, wrote a book in which he told of a town that had hired a man to keep watch on the springs in the mountains, which were the main source of their drinking water. Later, the town decided it was costing too much money, so they fired "the keeper of the springs." With no one there to safeguard the water, the springs became polluted. The town then decided that they did need a keeper of the springs. The author then compared mothers as "the keepers of the springs" for their children.

The leadership of King Lemuel was effective because of the influence of his mother. Lemuel's name means "dedicated to the Lord!" Like Hannah, the mother of Samuel, Lemuel's mother seemed to have made vows to the Lord before the birth of her first-born son. Lemuel's position as his mother's first-born son and the child of her dedication to God made him special in her sight. Because of his special place, she gave him special instructions.

King Lemuel's mother told him that he should not drink

wine, which would make him drunk and cause him to forget the law. She also told him that he should not weaken himself by becoming involved with promiscuous or fortune-hunting women, but that he should dedicate himself to defending justice and the rights of the poor and needy who had no one to stand up for them. She urged him to take his responsibilities seriously. (See Proverbs 31:1-9.)

Everyone needs a mother like Lemuel's who will nurture him in the fear and admonition of the Lord, teach him principles of righteousness, and be the "keeper of the springs" for her children's lives.

My own mother was one such lady. She was the great-granddaughter of a Methodist circuit-riding preacher, and she loved and lived her religion. She was a virtuous woman and had a heart for holiness. She did not allow liquor or playing cards in our home. To her, they were reminiscent of gambling, which she was strongly against. She was also a praying woman.

I can remember a time when I was holding a revival and became very ill. I thought I would not be able to go to the service that night, much less preach! However, about 2:00 PM that day I started feeling better. Not only was I able to go to church, but I was able to preach. The next day, my mother called. She said, "Son, where were you yesterday at 2:00 PM? I felt a burden to pray for you. I asked others to pray with me, and we all sought God for you." I revealed to her how sick I had been and that around 2:00 PM I began to feel better.

May God give us more mothers who will serve as the "keepers of the springs" for their children and will be responsible for encouraging them to be pure, honest, and just in their lives and leadership roles.

Practice:

If you are a caregiver of children, do not underestimate your value or influence in your children's lives. In this corrupt world, they desperately need you to keep watch and guard the things that are allowed into their lives. Do not let them be polluted by ungodly books, music, videos, Internet sites, friends, or other influences that would taint and corrupt them. Keep the stream of their lives fresh and pure.

Prayer:

Lord, I thank You for those who were "keepers of the springs" in my life. Help me to keep careful watch over those whom You have entrusted into my care. Let me diligently protect them from anything that would endanger their lives with the harmful effects of sin.

DAY 91: THE WOMAN OF WORTH
(PROVERBS 31:10-31)

Who a woman of virtue, can find on this earth?
She's more precious than rubies or jewels are worth.

The heart of her husband trusts her, so that he
Will need nothing more to feel rich as could be.

She will do him much good and nothing that's wrong,
Stand beside him for life, in the place she belongs.

She seeks woolen and flax for the goods she creates,
As she willingly works with the things that she makes.

She is like merchant ships, who travelers are,
As she seeks her provisions, brings food from afar.

She arises at dawn, her household to feed;
Gives her maidens their portion and direction they need.

She considers a field she can buy on her own;
Plants a vineyard from earnings she has prudently shown.

She is girded for toil, and her arms she makes strong
For the work that she does and enjoys, and prolongs.

Till her project is finished, her candle is bright;
Taking care of the rest, she will stay through the night.

She puts hands on the spindle and the distaff she plies.
She is generous with the needy, and she helps the despised.

The winter no fear for her family holds;
With scarlet they're all warmly dressed for the cold.

She is covered in tapestry, purple, silk, and in style,
While her household is royally dressed all the while.

Her husband sits in the town at the gates;
With the elders he of their judgment partakes.

She delivers fine linen to the merchants for trade,
Sells her sashes to buyers who find them well-made.

Her clothing is majesty and excellence and might;
She has nothing to fear, for her future is bright.

Her mouth she shall open and speak from her mind,
And the tongue of her teaching is prudent and kind.

She's concerned with the welfare of her household at heart,
And she eats not with idleness her morsels of meat.

Her children will rise and her blessings will tell,
And her husband speaks praises of her, just as well.

"Many women have done nobly but like you there are none;
You have strongly excelled and them all have outdone."

We know favor's deceitful and beauty is vain,
But a woman who fears God should rightly be praised.

We should give her the fruits of the honor she makes,
And let her own works give her praise in the gates.

PARTNERS

Proverb:

"The heart of her husband doth safely trust in her, so that he shall have no need of spoil" (Proverbs 31:11).

Precept:

Marriages were made in heaven, but they are experienced on earth. God planned Adam, the first man, and Eve, the first woman, as expressions of Himself. They were different in physical form as well as nature and temperament and with different strengths and weaknesses, yet together they completed one another perfectly and in their union reflected the image of God. Marriage is more than a contract, more than a covenant, more than a consummation, or a conception—it is a fulfillment of God's divine plan.

Proverbs 18:22 says, "Whoso findeth a wife findeth a good thing, and obtaineth favour of the LORD." When I married, I had been a licensed minister for eight years and was already pastoring a church. My wife not only became my partner in marriage, but in ministry as well.

Throughout the past forty-five years we have worked together, prayed together, played together, eaten together, and raised a family together. The houses we have lived in were not the biggest or the best, but with her ability to create a warm, cozy environment, she made each one a home. Her constant companionship has enriched my life.

As with anything in life, there have been some bumps in the road and we have been through some difficult times, but we shared them together. She has been a faithful wife, and I have always trusted in her.

My wife's care and confidence and her management and provision have made it possible for me to sit with "friends in high places." Our four children can join with me in praising the character and competence that my wife possesses. She is a perfect example of a beautiful lady who fears the Lord and is highly favored. I am thankful that she is my life partner. "Likewise, ye husbands, dwell with them according to knowledge, giving honour unto the wife, as unto the weaker vessel, and as being heirs together of the grace of life; that your prayers be not hindered" (I Peter 3:7).

Practice:

When the music fades and the lights dim, what lasting effect will you have on the lives of your family? Will you have passed the test and conducted yourself as a person who has gained their trust? Will it be said of you that you were faithful? Will the memories of your character and strength be a source of inspiration to all who knew you? Strive to excel in every area of your life so that it can be said of you that you have been worthy of the trust that has been placed in you.

Prayer:

Lord, help me to cultivate characteristics in my life of trustworthiness, dependability, and commitment to my family and to You, my God. May I always treasure Your Word and the precious truths it contains.

Notes

Preface:
[1]*Webster's Ninth New Collegiate Dictionary* (Springfield, Massachusetts: Merriam-Webster, 1988), 439.

Proverbs 1:
Day 3,
[2]Oxenham, John [quotation on-line] from "the Quote Lady," Karen L. Oberst (28 November 2005). *http://www.quotelady.com/authors/author-o.html.*

[3]Lowell, James Russell, "The Present Crisis" from *The Yale Book of American Verse*, ed. Thomas R. Loundsbury [book on-line] (New Haven: Yale University Press, 1912). *http://www.bartleby.com/102/128.html.*

Proverbs 2:
Day 6,
[4]Foss, Sam Walter, from "The Coming American," July 4, 1894, *http://en.wikipedia.org/wiki/Sam_Walter_Foss.*

Proverbs 3:
Day 7,
[5]"The Declaration of Independence" in *The Rebirth of America* (Philadelphia: The Arthur S. DeMoss Foundation, 1986), 14.

[6]"The Supreme Court Decision, 1892: Church of the Holy Trinity v. United States" in *The Rebirth of America* (Philadelphia: The Arthur S. DeMoss Foundation, 1986), 21.

[7]"Benjamin Franklin" in *The Rebirth of America* (Philadelphia: The Arthur S. DeMoss Foundation, 1986), 31.

Proverbs 6:
Day 18,
[8]Coleridge, Samuel T., "The Eolian Harp" in *Bartlett's Familiar Quotations*, ed. John Bartlett (Boston: Little, Brown and Company), 381.
Day 21,
[9]*http://en.wikipedia.org/wiki/Motel_6.*

Proverbs 8:
Day 24,
[10]Thinkexist.com Quotations 1999-2006. *http://en.thinkexist.com/quotation/all_that_is_necessary_for_the_triumph_of_evil_is/205479.html.*

[11]Nieomoeller, Martin in *Bartlett's Familiar Quotations*, ed. John Bartlett (Boston: Little, Brown and Company), 684.

[12]Andersen, Hans Christian, "The Emperor's New Clothes" in *Eventyr, Fortalte for Børn (Fairy Tales, Told for Children)*, originally known as *Keiserens Nye Klæder*, 1837. From Wikipedia.

Proverbs 9:
  Day 27,
  [13]Pilato, Donna, "The Meaning of RSVP" (About, Inc., a part of the New York Times Co., 2006). *entertaining.about.com/cs/etiquette/qt/tip122500. htm.*

Proverbs 10:
  Day 31,
  [14]Bellis, Mary, "Liquid Paper" (About, Inc., a part of the New York Times Co., 2006). *http://inventors.about.com/od/lstartinventions/a/liquid_ paper.htm.*

Proverbs 11:
  Day 34,
  [15]Ottley, Ted, "Bad Day Dawning" (Courtroom Television Networks LLC, 2005). *http://www.crimelibrary.com/serial_killers/notorious/mcveigh/ bed_10.html.*

Proverbs 14:
  Day 43,
  [16]"Fatal Accident Involving JFK Jr" at AirSafe.come, Critical Info for the Traveling Public. *http://airsafe.com/events/celebs/jfk_jr.htm – Revised: 15 January.*
  Day 44,
  [17]Tocqueville, Alexis de in *Tocqueville in Democracy in America*, 1835.

Proverbs 15:
  Day 45,
  [18]Wilcox, Ella Wheeler, "Solitude" in *The International Thesaurus of Quotations*, eds. Eugene Ehrlich and Marshall DeBruhl (Harper Perennial, 1996), 366.

Proverbs 16:
  Day 49,
  [19]Stanphill, Ira F. "Happiness is the Lord," 1968.

Proverbs 17:
  Day 51,
  [20]Wyse, Lois, in "The Quote Garden: A Harvest of Quotes for Word Lovers" (updated June 3, 2006). *http://www.quotegarden.com/grandparents.html.*

Proverbs 19:
  Day 57,
  [21]*Webster's New Twentieth Century Dictionary Unabridged*, Second Edition, 2123.
  Day 58,
  [22]Bradford, John, "The Writings of John Bradford" in *Bartlett's Familiar Quotations*, ed. John Bartlett (Boston: Little, Brown and Company), 143.

Proverbs 21:
  Day 65,
  [23]Watt, James, "Auto Math" in Web Cars (In association with Amazon.com, November 2001). *http://www.web-cars.com/math/horsepower.html.*

Proverbs 22:
　Day 67,
　[24]Hugo, Victor, *Les Miserables* (The Literature Networks, Jalic, Inc., 2005-2006); available at *http://www.online-literature.com/victor_hugo/les_miserables/*.
　Day 68,
　[25]Frost, Robert, "Good Fences Make Good Neighbors" in *The New Dictionary of Cultural Literature*, 3rd edition, ed. E. D. Hirsch Jr., et al. (Boston: Houghton Mifflin, 2002). *http://www.bartleby.com/59/3/goodfencesma.html*.

Proverbs 23:
　Day 70,
　[26]Declaration of Independence, *http://en.wikipedia.org/wiki/United_States_Declaration_of_Independence*.
　[27]Declaration of Independence, *http://en.wikipedia.org/wiki/United_States_Declaration_of_Independence*.

Proverbs 25:
　Day 75,
　[28]*http://www.quotablelincoln.com/quotedisplay.Php?LastName=Lincoln&page=6*.

Proverbs 26:
　Day 79,
　[29]*http://en.wikipedia.org/wiki/Boomerang*.

Proverbs 27:
　Day 80,
　[30]Burns, Robert, *The New Dictionary of Cultural Literacy*, 3rd ed., ed. E. D. Hirsch, Jr., et al. (Boston: Houghton Mifflin, 2002). *www.bartleby.com/59/*.

Proverbs 28:
　Day 83,
　[31]Shakespeare, William, "Julius Caesar" in *Bartlett's Familiar Quotations*, ed. John Bartlett (Little, Brown and Company), 215.

About the Author

REVEREND W. C. PARKEY received his bachelor's degree in history and English from Oklahoma University in Norman, Oklahoma, in 1954. He has been a licensed minister with the United Pentecostal Church International for fifty-three years. Throughout his tenure he has been involved in many different areas of ministry and has served in a variety of leadership roles.

He evangelized for several years and has pastored churches in Sperry, Oklahoma; Kansas City, Missouri; Independence, Kansas; and Poplar Bluff, Missouri. He worked one year in St. Louis at the World Evangelism Center as the first promotional director for the Harvestime Radio Broadcast. He was instrumental in the opening of Gateway College of Evangelism and served as president there for nine years.

The author has been actively involved in the writing ministry of the United Pentecostal Church for many years as well. He was the first editor of *The Conqueror's Tread*, which he started while serving as Youth President of the Oklahoma District. *The Conqueror's Tread* later became *The Conqueror* magazine, which is now the official magazine of the Youth Division. He served for twenty-five years on the Curriculum Committee and for twenty-three years on the Board of Publications. He is a prolific writer and has written many songs, articles, tracts, and lessons that have been published in various venues of the UPCI.

He has been married for forty-five years to his wife, Betty. They have four married children who are all actively involved in full-time ministry: Jeff and Beth Dillon, who pastor in Winchester, Virginia; Keith and Barbara Braswell, who work as the Information Technology Directors at World Evangelism Center; Bill and Stephany Parkey, who pastor in Tulare, California; and Bryan and Lisa Parkey, who pastor in Poplar Bluff, Missouri. They are the proud grandparents of ten grandchildren: Tyler, Tiffany, and Trey Braswell; Kayla Dillon; Zakery, Zarisa, Zayne, and Zyan Parkey; and Dylan and Kinsey Parkey.

W. C. Parkey currently serves as bishop at Cornerstone Tabernacle in Poplar Bluff, Missouri. This is his first book. For more information visit his Web site at *www.waysidewells.com.*